The Genius in Your Wound:

Life's Worst Can Reveal Your Best

Allan W. Dayhoff, Jr., D.Min.

First Edition.

ISBN: 978-0-359-60803-4

Evangelize Today Ministries, LLC

4206 Mellwood Lane, Fairfax, VA 22033

Other books by the author:

Church in a Blues Bar

Tattoos: Telling the Secrets of the Soul

Evangelize Today Ministries, LLC is an organized church, 501 (c)(3) non-profit, and a member of the Presbyterian Church in America.

For more information about our ministries visit
www.evangelizetoday.info.

Table of Contents

Forward 5

Acknowledgments 9

Chapter 1: Prologue 13

Chapter 2: Introduction 25

Chapter 3: The Behavior of Wounds 35

Chapter 4: The Character of Genius 57

Chapter 5: The Tell-tale Heart 71

Chapter 6: Dr. Jekyll and Mr. Hyde......................................79

Chapter 7: Ground Hog Day 97

Chapter 8: The Man Behind the Mask..................................119

Chapter 9: The Cigar..137

Chapter 10: The Rescue..151

Chapter 11: Funny 'cause its True...159

Chapter 12: The Girl Who Came in from the Cold 169

Chapter 13: The Visitation...179

Chapter 14: Rest for the Weary 191

Chapter 15: The Elephant Man...207

Chapter 16: The Afterword...233

Study Guide 243

About the Cover Artist..247

About the Editor...248

About the Author 249

Foreword

Can rare events repeat themselves? Can lightning strike the same place twice? As a resident in Florida I have no trouble believing it can, and it does. Our state is the lightning capitol of the US. But the lighting strike I'm talking about is my encounter with Allan Dayhoff. About eighteen months after my first, chance meeting with him at the Starbucks overlooking Tampa Bay, I was sitting with him in the very same place. And just as he had riveted my attention in our first conversation, now he was doing it again. Al has this friendly, disarming way about him that is inviting. Though he jokes that there are people who are on to him, I've enjoyed the kind of ease he creates. He's as comfortable to be with as sliding on your favorite pair of slippers. But you can almost count on there being a used staple, a stick, or even a bent paper clip lying hidden in the comfy fleece lining. It's bound to prick a tender spot and cause you to wince. Still, you like the slippers. Maybe that's his Genius.

The first time I met Al, I showed up as a favor to a friend whose Virginia drawl turned a simple sentence into the length of a whole paragraph, "Mike, you've got to meet this guy!" I trust Tommy's enthusiasm and confidence in people, so I did—meet Al. Three hours into our visit I hated to see it end. That's led to an unexpected collaboration on a variety of projects, including a week-long adventure to the Sturgis Motorcycle Rally where Al and his team of intrepid researchers interviewed tattoos.

Why? He had the not-so-crazy idea that out of the half million people who travel to the Black Hills of South Dakota every year for this iconic American festival, there just might be a few with tattoos that we could talk to. So, there we were in early August, at ground zero—downtown at the corner of First and Main. Our twelve-foot-long booth (two borrowed tables from a local church, covered with an attention-grabbing orange tarp) had stacks of his new book <u>Tattoos: Telling the Secrets of the Soul</u>. A 7-foot by 3-foot black banner with huge white letters stopped people in their tracks. DOES YOUR TATTOO HAVE A STORY? I'm not overstating it when I tell you that we found ourselves operating what turned out to be an open-air confessional that ran from morning till night every day, for a week. In some ways it was at the same time too easy and too overwhelming. The twin challenges our team faced was to keep hydrated in the baking sun and to risk listening to the wounds. People wanted to talk, hundreds, thousands of them. Souls that wore the marks of their lives on their skin—I mean heads, faces, necks, arms, legs, yes and all those other parts too. Sometimes there were too many people for the five of us. Sometimes their stories were too painful to take in.

Though he threatened to get me tattooed by surreptitiously sedating me, I came home to my wife, whose close inspection yielded a sigh of relief—no ink! I grew a beard instead. Tattoos aren't my thing. Maybe not yours either. But studying people is. As we talked, as I listened, I discovered there really isn't any difference between us—me and folks with tattoos. It's just that it was easier to learn about the amazing journeys they're on because they've written them on their skin. Well, their high-priced artists did. It's apparent that something—and for most tattoo wearers, lots of things—were important enough to wear the signs of them in broad daylight. Incredibly, some of the people who told us their stories were relieved to finally have someone pay attention. People who'd been tattooing their stories for 10, 20 years acted as if this was the first time they got to tell them to anyone. I was astonished. How could anyone ignore the obvious? The signs are there. Isn't anyone the least bit curious? Isn't anybody listening?

Back to my second lightning strike with Al. Before Sturgis was even a thing in his complicated mind, he was in Florida again. He invited me to coffee—his favorite ploy. As I was settling in to the comfort of this growing friendship, just as he was about half way through his cigar, he asked "So, Mike, what happened to you?" I winced. The slipper had a thumbtack in it! As quickly as I tensed, it was like I'd gotten a shot of Novocain that seconds later had moved me past the hurdle of my pain. I didn't have any tattoos pointing out the wounds in my journey; was it that evident I had some?

Even though I instinctively wanted to leave, another part of me was relieved that he asked. Like the people on the streets of Sturgis, I wanted to be asked. I wanted to be known. I decided I wanted to stay. We talked. He told me about his observation that a lot of people he'd encountered with Genius-like abilities seemed to evidence a kind of restlessness that was connected to a wound. For many, it wasn't necessarily one event, but a theme that emerged from their experiences of hurt and pain. He was working on developing these observations into a book. Would I consider writing a chapter? Over the next few months that invitation morphed into editing the work.

Over the past six months I don't think a week has gone by when we haven't been massaging this project, making discoveries about the relationship between the wound and its Genius. As we've teased out the implications of this idea there have been moments when our efforts seemed to skew away from the immediacy of individual experiences, in the direction of a more detached clinical assessment. Of course, that's always the safer approach. One time, Al said, "Michael, keep your wound close." I didn't want to do that. I wanted to finish the book. But just as he had the Genius insight that tattoos are sign posts telegraphing the secrets of the soul, he'd realized that cracking open an understanding of the Genius living inside us depends on a keen attention to the nature and behavior of our wounds. So, despite the inconvenience and counterintuitive posture of not being a dispassionate observer, I did as he suggested. I held my wound close and discovered more about the breadth and depth and expanse of my life —and more about the subtle but evident presence of Genius—than I'd even seen before.

Al has hit upon a Genius insight with enormous implications for all of us, no matter how well-adjusted or how tortured any of us might see ourselves to be. For the people whose breathtaking stories you will soon read, for his work with ministers who struggle to reconcile their humanity with the divine calling they seek to fulfill, and for you—there is buried treasure hidden within the wounds of life. If it's true that we are created in the image and likeness of God, then that amazing character resides in every one of us. The Genius hidden there, waiting to be revealed, seems to be stirred by a disturbance—sort of your own personal earthquake—that moves things around, releasing character traits coded in us by our Father. While the most apparent effects of our wounds are never erased, they are forever changed.

Nearly 40 years ago at Princeton Seminary, I sat listening to more lectures on theology, psychology, spirituality, education, history, philosophy, and the Bible than I can count. They were delivered by some of the most brilliant teachers who painted a picture of life and work that I and my classmates would take up as ministers, counselors, preachers and teachers, in realms of human experience that would turn our lives upside down. While I wouldn't trade what I learned from my elders, there's a sense in which nothing I received from them could prepare me for the difficult lessons of life until I found myself in the midst of its storms. No matter how grounded anyone of us believes ourselves to be, in the hour of greatest need, there comes a moment when we are alone and there is nothing but yourself. Me—only me.

But not only me. There's the One who made me, who called me into Being, out of whom I was created, and from whom I am. And that, as the poet once said, "has made all the difference!" And not only are you and I not alone. He in whose image and likeness we were made, is in us. Though we are not gods, little deities who strut the earth, we are God's. And, His life, His character, His creative power, His glory, His beauty, and His way all cause us to shake our heads in wonder and disbelief, though we welcome and long for the superhuman nature of His life in and all around us. "The whole creation waits in eager expectation for the revealing of the children of God." Romans 8:19. We are drawn to the experience of life which is not bound by the limits of time, space and our temporal existence. We are attracted to Genius like bears to honey. The thing is, we often do not see the character of God in our own lives because we exert so much energy trying to cope with the effects of our wounds. But there's so much more than meets the eye.

Wounds create change, generally unwanted. And yet there is no universal law which says all pain is a repudiation of life. The great 19th century English churchman, John Henry Richard Cardinal Newman wrote, "To live is to change, and to change often is to become more perfect." I'm thankful to Al Dayhoff for the opportunity to see my wounds and their accompanying changes in my life as providential gifts revealing a path to the true self, a son of God in whose image we all have been fearfully and wonderfully made. As you read this book, keep your wounds close.

Michael A. DeArruda

March 2019

Acknowledgments

I owe much to my participants in this adventure.

My current season of professional life includes coaching other ministers. These are my residents—my heroes and mentors, in many ways. Working with them is my heartbeat and daily delight. They were the first to explore this "Genius in the wound" concept with me. Together we venture into the "wild" to encounter people and the culture outside the traditional church structure. This is a sacred space of discovery. My residents often allow me to observe their experiences in the wild as well as in the scary places of their own souls. My heartfelt thanks go to first them, my brothers and sisters.

Special thanks go to Michael DeArruda, my editor. Michael has become a soul partner in this journey of research, discovery, exploration, and writing. Our storytellers speak colloquially, so much of the book is not written in standard English. This is a challenge for any editor, but by skillfully preserving their voices, Mike ushers the reader into a quiet, authentic encounter with the protagonists. This book would not be what it is without his care and insight.

I must also express my appreciation to James Pavlik, who literally rescued and restored essential files that were, for all practical purposes, lost. Without James's technical skills, there would be no book.

Many thanks are due as well to Mike Welborn. Despite daunting obstacles, Mike remains undaunted. He barely has the use of one cancerous eye, and yet he put hundreds of hours into this project. This 70-year-old man must manually lift his only good eyelid, look through a handheld magnifying glass to see the computer screen, and use a flashlight before tapping each computer key. Hard to imagine, but true. Thank you, Mike.

To my wife Deb, who continues to support the way I live, explore, travel, and relate to many of our dear friends outside the church ... your gift of hospitality, and your iron will to serve beyond what is physically reasonable never fails to challenge me deeply, and always for the better. Thank you, Deb. I love you.

The debt that I owe the storytellers in this book cannot be calculated. For many of them, the process of detailing their experience was one of anger, hurt, resentment, and tears. Emotional hurricanes happened with little warning as these brave souls dared their voyage. I suspect that all of their lives were changed by this journey.

The narrators of this book were not selected because they are Christian—even though a number of them are. They have embraced something that many in the Western Church may need ... acknowledgment of their essential brokenness and recognition of its value. Brokenness—this is the human condition. It can be inherited, self-inflicted, imposed by another, or—as is often the case—all of the above.

Perhaps not surprisingly, few of the writers were willing to use their names. I too have camouflaged myself for a variety of reasons, not all of them noble. The desire for disguise may have stemmed from my own paranoia of being found out, or perhaps the ecclesiastical system lead me in this direction. No matter. I am in this life like everyone else.

As I invite you to consider the Genius in your wound, let me leave you with a meditation, a reflection by Fr. Richard Rohr, a Franciscan priest from Albuquerque, New Mexico. Think about your life, your hopes and dreams, your nightmares and regrets, in the context of Fr. Rohr's words.

> The risen Christ is the standing icon of humanity in its full and final destiny. He is the pledge and guarantee of what God will do with all our crucifixions. At last we can meaningfully live with hope. It is no longer an absurd or tragic universe. Our hurts now become the home for our greatest hopes. Without such implanted hope, it is very hard not to be cynical, bitter, and tired by the second half of our lives.
>
> It is no accident that Luke's Resurrection account in the Gospel has Jesus saying, "I am not a ghost! I have flesh and bones, as you can see" (Luke 24:39–43). To Thomas he says, "Put your finger in the wounds!" (John 20:27). In other words, "I am human!"—which means to be wounded and resurrected at the same time. Christ returns to his physical body, and yet he is now unlimited by space or time and is without any regret or recrimination while still, ironically, carrying his wounds. "Before God, our wounds are our glory," as Lady Julian of Norwich reflected.
>
> That Jesus' physical wounds do not disappear is telling. The mystical, counterintuitive message of death and resurrection is powerfully communicated through symbol. The major point is that Jesus has not left the human sphere; he is revealing the

goal, the fullness, and the purpose of humanity itself, which is "that we are able to share in the divine nature" (2 Peter 1:4), even in this wounded and wounding world. Yes, resurrection is saying something about Jesus, but it is also saying a lot about us, which is even harder to believe. It is saying that we also are larger than life, Being Itself, and therefore made for something good, united, and beautiful. Our code word for that is heaven.*

I thank God for the gift of Jesus's resurrection. Otherwise, I would never have known the significance of my wounds.

Rev. Dr. Allan Dayhoff

March 2019

---

* Rohr, Richard. "Jesus' Bodily Resurrection." Center for Action and Contemplation. April 1, 2018, adapted from *Immortal Diamond: The Search for Our True Self,* by Richard Rohr. Jossey-Bass: 2013: 84–85, 87. https://cac.org/jesus-bodily-resurrection-2018-04-01/.

Chapter 1: Prologue

The Genius in Your Wound

If we conceal our wounds out of fear and shame, our inner darkness can neither be illuminated nor become a light for others.

— Brennan Manning
Abba's Child: The Cry of the Heart for Intimate Belonging

None of us lives without threats to our existence. Even as infants, unconscious of this truth—or much of anything for that matter—we find ourselves afflicted by one assault after another. Hunger pangs, diaper rash, colds, skinned knees, and fear of the loss of love graduate to more sophisticated versions of the same things over the span of our years. As surely as the sun rises every day, we know that there is no such thing as existence without pain. We are inevitably wounded by life.

Contemporary preoccupation with the intangible, nonmaterial effects of suffering have, I think, obscured our appreciation for the original definition of the word "wound." Before the significance of psychology emerged in the nineteenth century, a wound was understood as something purely physical: a disruption in the seamless membrane of skin, an injury to living tissue—muscle, organs, or bone—caused by a rupture, tear, or incision. Before the miracles of modern science and medicine, a wound could mean the end of life. Fortunately, between our natural healing abilities and the advances of modern medicine, our bodies usually recover from the wounds we suffer. Tissue is restored, function is regained, integrity returns, and pain subsides, even if a scar remains, reminding us of the wound.

Our bodies give us the ability to function in the world; they are the homes within which we exist. In them and through them we experience our lives and create worlds of meaning. Ask anyone about the significance and value of life and they will invariably talk about experiences—physical sensations, imagination, thought, and emotions like love, gratitude, joy, sorrow, honor, fulfillment, and wonder.

But we are not only physical beings. For most people, being human is grounded in a sense of meaning, value, and purpose, not only within ourselves, but in relationships with others. This is why couples, families, neighborhoods, and communities matter to us. It isn't only how well our bodies work that makes us appreciate life: It is what we experience with others. Relationships most often define the quality of our lives.

These nonmaterial, intangible, but very real characteristics are just as natural as the skin that holds our bodies together. Just as our physical being is regularly subject to wounds, so too are our nonmaterial parts—our thoughts, emotions, and souls. Violation of any of these essential intangibles—without which we are not human—can be more disruptive, more wounding to the core than any physical injury.

Despite the "sticks and stones" mantra we recited as children," we've learned that we are vulnerable when the integrity of body, mind, or soul is violated. What you say about me, how you treat me, the abuse you hurl so carelessly do hurt me. Our susceptibility to emotional, psychological, and spiritual injury makes us angry, and if the hurt is big enough or frequent enough, we are left with a wound that is not easily, if ever, mended.

We suffer nonphysical wounds perhaps even more often than we injure our bodies. I'm willing to bet that in the last few moments of reading, a flood of memories about your experiences have come rushing forward. You may now be remembering life-shaping events that not only hurt your body but touched your soul. Such wounds have achingly persistent effects on us.

Like you, I have experienced the same things—perhaps not the same details, but many of the same effects. The fact that we have all been deeply wounded is ground zero for insight into possibilities and promises of life you might have written off a long time ago. There just might be a Genius in your wound.

Unexpected discovery

When we grow just old enough to imagine what life might be like we often ask ourselves What do I want to be when I grow up? As time goes by the question changes to Who am I? and often morphs into Who do I want to become?

I didn't start out wanting to be a minister when I grew up, but that's what I've been doing for the last 30 years. Yet even though I founded and established a fairly successful church in the metro DC area, I began to grow restless. I was fulfilling others' expectations, not pursuing my passion for exploration and adventure. I tried to preach myself into enthusiasm for my work, but it was useless. Eventually, I did what we ministers ask our parishioners to do all the time—I took the proverbial "leap of faith" into the unknown. I left my congregation, which in the church world can be worse than divorcing your wife.

I found myself in a suburban blues bar and was strangely drawn to its patrons. Suddenly, shockingly, my passion for the adventure of life returned. I discovered my flock! So, this is who I am? A broken, disillusioned adventurer who is strangely attracted to people like me? The next question was, Who do I want to become with what I know about me? The answer is still unfolding.

In time, I was able to get far enough away from my experience to examine it. I discovered that many of the same things I had gone through—like wearing the institutional straitjacket that I'd willingly put on—were being experienced by other ministers and pastors. Like me, they were trying to help others, trying to figure out who they were and who they wanted to be. Many were searching, uncertain, angry, and frighteningly depressed.

I thought, If I've been through this and can see it happening to others, maybe I could talk to disillusioned, foundering clergy like myself. Maybe together we could get to a place of insight that just could be life changing. So, in addition to pastoring a blues bar—definitely not a career path outlined in the course catalogue at my seminary—I have added the roles of coach and mentor to my portfolio.

I now have a network of pastors all over the country who are in "residency" with me. Together we explore their unique life adventures and callings. Our goal is to become healthier, more effective ministers—people who can be present with those who are hurting and wounded. After all, what is Christian ministry if not to find the lost, restore the broken, and help the injured? That's how Jesus described the job of the Good Shepherd.

Working with these fellow travelers is exhilarating. It's my passion. I wake up every day excited about hearing their voices on the other end of the phone. I always learn something from my residents. These special relationships have been the source of surprising inspiration.

I've spent much time building these relationships, and my residents know they can trust me. I'm humbled that they have invited me into the truth of their lives, where they are painfully aware they are not who they tell others they are, and not who they want to be. This would be a nightmare for anyone. But ministers have an especially heavy burden because they are profoundly averse to disclosing their wounds and admitting their brokenness. This isn't surprising, since something that would be a "problem" for most people would become grounds for the dismissal of a minister. My clergy buddies are often stuck between the devil and the deep blue sea.

The apostle Paul, one of the most famous pastors of all time, confessed this dilemma: "I have the desire to do what is good, but I cannot carry it out. For I do not do the good I want to do, but the evil I do not want to do—this I keep on doing." (Romans 7:18–19) A few verses later, Paul writes, "What a wretched man I am!" (Romans 7:24)

This is Paul—after Jesus, the single-most-influential person in early Christianity! Paul, the planter of churches, the author of most of the New Testament, the zealot converted from pharisaical judgment to humble penitence. Like many good ministers, he saw himself as seriously and deeply conflicted. I hear this same despair and disillusionment from some of my residents.

When you work closely with someone you learn who they are; I treat the coaching relationship with each of my residents as a sacred, confidential space. As with your family doctor, to have any chance of healing you have to get at the core issue. If you aren't sure about the doctor's competence, you won't trust him, and you won't disclose what really hurts. Together we have discovered what their aches and pains are really all about. More importantly, our journey has unmasked a discovery about the effect and potential in our wounds.

Here's how it happened.

I can't hear you

Like many people, ministers live inside the echo chamber of their professional culture. Most don't intend to, but it happens. The demands of the institution slowly but surely turn us from the liberators we want to be into captives. After a while we lose contact with what I call "the wild," the outside world where life happens. If we are to live full and balanced lives, that's where all of us need to be. This is especially true for ministers.

The role of minister in our culture seems to come front-loaded with the expectation that clergy are supposed to tell you what's right and wrong. At the same time, both minister and public have adopted a distorted stereotype that the minister is a bigot in shepherd's clothing. Of all the noise bouncing around inside the echo chamber of the church, this may be the most damaging. But it doesn't have to be this way.

In my own professional journey, I came to realize that telling people what I thought they needed to hear (i.e., right and wrong) was a disastrous strategy. It kills authentic engagement faster than you can blink an eye. Why? Because everyone wants to be heard! But all too often I have seen those of us in the church poised to give answers to questions that aren't being asked, and totally missing the ones that are.

Think about how many times you wanted to pour out your heart to a friend. But because it's hard to put these important things into words, it takes you a few minutes to say what's weighing on your heart. In the meantime, while you're talking your way into what you want to disclose, your friend jumps in to "rescue" you, assuming they knew what you were going to say before you said it! This happens all the time, especially when clergy try to "help" their parishioners.

The work I do with my residents pivots off this foundational principle—shifting from the pathological behavior of listening to tell, to supportive and compassionate listening to hear. For ministers who live in church culture, this shift is next to impossible. The reason? Because they're used to the listening-to-tell dynamic. Their flock is used to it. They've been schooled to listen to the Holy Man pronounce the Truth. After all, who can argue with someone whose official role is spokesperson for God?

Couple that with the minister's psychology— I know a lot, dammit. Just ask me and, if you don't, I'll tell you! That's a toxic brew that can't do anything other than poison real dialogue and stop all disclosure. People clam up. Even if the people in the pews are sick and tired of one-way conversations (and they are) life in the echo chamber reinforces the expectation that the minister's job is to listen in order to tell you what you need to hear. For the 20% of the population that still attend church every week, that arrangement might work. But it hasn't worked for the other 80% in many decades.

If ministers are to change this dynamic, they have to change the way they engage people. They cannot remain ensconced in the womb of mother church and expect to make any real difference in the world. The antidote for this disease is to get ministers back into the wild, learning how to be true spiritual seers by listening to people's stories. In my work coaching clergy, I strategically kick these overgrown birds out of the nest so they can learn to fly. But sadly, flying is an instinct that has been conditioned out of them.

As I listen to my residents, I hear their frustrations about what is not going right in their churches, in their relationships with their parishioners, and with the denominational officials to whom they are accountable. Their pain, depression, and disappointment are palpable, and touch almost every area of their lives, including their families. During my consultations I realized I could spend a lot of useless time commiserating with them, rearranging deck chairs on the Titanic, or I could do something completely different. (Trust me, I tried the deck-chair reset multiple times, but that wasn't the answer. The ship continued to sink.)

The most dramatic changes I witnessed in the ministers I've mentored have come from getting them out of their churches, their offices, and their committee meetings and into the wild. I challenge my residents to go to coffee shops, bars, community festivals, and little league games to rub elbows with moms and dads and vendors, and yes, even barflies, to experience the real environments in which people live. In time they earn the right to strike up conversations with the sole purpose of listening to hear—AND NOTHING ELSE. Their job is to shed the internal identity of professional minister and simply be with people—watching, seeing, noticing, and listening to hear.

For most it's an excruciating assignment because they are used to deference from people around them. This isn't always conscious. It happens because they've spent most of their time cooped up in the church house with people who are used to taking direction from the cock of the flock. In the wild the minister can't assume that the people around him share the same language, assumptions, or world view. But that's a good thing, because in the absence of the familiar, the minister is forced to cultivate senses that have become dormant.

The resident must make a conscious decision if this shift into an unfamiliar environment is to do him or the people around him any good: Will I be here like a tourist, just getting by, or will I consider moving in? The answer to that question will determine whether the resident can make the transition from his ivory tower into the lives of people. His theology tells him God knows and loves these people, but he has never encountered them. What would my church say if they knew I was doing this? What would the bishop, executive, synod, consistory, vestry, or presbytery do if they found out?

Too late, you're working with me, and you signed up for this!

Despite their fears and trepidations, nine times out of ten my residents make their way into the wild, led by their hearts and souls. And when they do, they come alive; I hear it in their voices during our weekly check-ins. They sound like they've witnessed the resurrection! And they have—their dying souls have become connected to people in ways that they'd almost forgotten was possible.

But the thing about moving outside of the familiar, outside our comfort zone, is that we become, well, uncomfortable! Ministers outside their churches are often like first-time dancers, with two left feet. Over time, working with dozens of residents, I discovered something that I've come to realize is truly significant: No matter how comfortable they become in the art of listening to hear, they invariably hit a wall.

Listening to other people and really hearing them can be like open-heart surgery. Without realizing it, the stories my residents hear about the horrific and inexplicable experiences people have endured, suddenly breaks open a wound they didn't know they had. Something they hear reveals a blockage in their own lives every bit as real as a clogged artery that requires emergency intervention. This wound, suddenly exposed in a way the resident could no longer ignore, rears up so loudly that the person they are listening to begins to sound like the teacher in a Charlie Brown cartoon—a muffled and indistinct trumpet—because the cry of pain from the resident's own heart drowns out everything else.

Of course, I am conscious of the same dynamic working in me—I have wounds that distract me from being able to hear what others are saying. No one gets through life unscathed. But recognizing the presence and power of my wounds has helped me appreciate the struggle that this book is about.

The noise of my wound

I have learned not to take lightly the invitation to be inside a minister's head and heart. Ministers are, of course, as human as everyone else.

Each one is different, with unique strengths and deep, well-hidden wounds. If you want to know what a minister's challenges are, just visit the damp basement or long-ignored attic of your own heart; dare to look at what has been stored up there, forgotten, but still part of your life story.

Alcoholic parents, secret addictions, repressed rage, moral failure, violation of conscience, marital dissatisfaction, infidelity to professional standards, and many other scourges sear the souls of millions of people. Nobody sets out to suffer, but suffer we do, from incidents as old as our family tree and as fresh as this morning. What do you do with the pain, the dysfunction, and the noise of your wounds when you're trying to be a good father or mother, a good son or daughter, a responsible and dedicated professional?

Well, a lot of us just buck up and carry on, but it's like trying to drive a V6 when three cylinders are out of commission. There's an awful noise and we know something's wrong with the engine, but I don't have time for this, dammit. I have to get to work! So, we push on, believing that we can overcome the misfiring engine of our lives. The noise of our wound—and what it's about—is a disabling drag on every aspect of life. But a lot of us have become so used to it we can't imagine life any other way. And so, we Just. Keep. Going.

I've seen it in hundreds, thousands of people from every walk of life. Ministers are no exception. In fact, I've learned the most about how this drama works through my collaboration with wounded ministers. I don't think there's any other kind, actually—wounded ministers, that is. Just like everybody else who draws breath, ministers are human. But they have a unique burden—representatives of God.

I'm sure you are more familiar than you want to be with the dueling tensions between your demons and the better angels of your nature. Precious few people in this world escape the internal struggle between good and evil. But imagine the dilemma lived by those who are clergy. Not only are they expected to be living examples of godliness, they have to live with the internal moral, spiritual, and psychologic inconsistencies that plague everyone.

Except they can't. If anyone desperately needs freedom from the torment of knowing that they routinely violate their fervent commitment to righteousness, it has to be ministers. But no one can survive the conscious battles between good and evil without one or more of these things happening:

- Denying that a battle exists by shutting off awareness of life-threatening inconsistencies.
- Intermittent or chronic mental illness sometimes leading to suicidal ideation.
- Addictive or compulsive behaviors designed to compensate for the pain of internal wounds and contradictions.
- Spiritual surrender to the unmanageable inconsistency of life; turning over control of life to God. In the twelve-step tradition of Alcoholics Anonymous, this is your Higher Power. In Christianity this is the experience of being saved from the

eternal effects of our moral and spiritual brokenness by accepting the grace and mercy of God found in Jesus Christ.

As my resident ministers ventured into the wild, listening to hear, becoming students of the human experience, I discovered that, metaphorically speaking, nearly all of them hit a cast iron steeple at 90 miles an hour. No skid marks.

It saw it happen once, then again, and again. It became a pattern. What's going on here? I wondered. Why couldn't their minds be retrained to listen to hear without shutting down? No matter how willing they were to engage in this new model of ministry, my residents were becoming disabled by the exercise of listening in the wild. Why?

As I turned over report after report, listening carefully to what they told me about their experiences, I began to hear what was underneath their frustrations. I discovered that the noise of their own wounds was so loud that they could not hear what other people were saying. And there didn't seem to be any way I could help them turn down the volume.

To help the resident make any kind of progress in learning to listen, we had to first find the source of his internal noise. This is where dignity matters. I've worked diligently to cultivate safety, trust, and a nonjudgmental character—critical tools in the laboratory of human experience that can elicit truthful insight. In other words, I've had to "listen to hear" what my residents are saying.

Ministers have developed a highly specialized artform: the ability to talk about themselves in ways that are intended to obscure the truth from themselves and others. A lot of the time, maybe even most of the time, they are completely unconscious of this. But they do know that there's a chasm a million miles wide between what they preach and what they live in their souls.

Like the rest of us, ministers are protecting deeply wounded egos. They are afraid that someone will find something wanting, defective, or unorthodox about them—something wrong. They are afraid of being judged. Where would that judgment happen you ask? Why in the church, of course—the place where it seems everyone is running scared about whether they are really loved, respected, and accepted—or not.

How bizarre! The very place where people ought to be rushing to bathe in the waters of restoration turns out to be the place where people—especially the ministers—are on guard, fearing that the slightest sign of imperfection will become their downfall. So, to keep up appearances, ministers have become expert in the art of projecting personality competence, which sometimes comes off as moral superiority (that's where the bigoted shepherd stereotype arises), making sure others know that they are not at all as conflicted and human as the rest of us.

I suspect the average minister goes into the religion business to fix something—in the world, in his family of origin, and inside himself. (The latter two are often unconscious reasons, and when pointed out, are frequently denied, at least at first.) Do I dare tell you that there is a lot of spiritual BS shared between ministers? There is. But because I am one, I'm pretty good at smelling it from a long way off. Most aren't trying to misrepresent themselves. It's just that they don't know what they'd do if they really had to come to terms with their own brokenness. Sadly, most ministers know too well that their denomination publicly proclaims grace, mercy, and forgiveness, but practices just the opposite in the way clergy are treated by the people in charge. So, they've learned to play the game.

This is where our coaching relationship differs. I don't hold any power over my residents. I am tenacious in fighting with them and for them, so we can both learn what is preventing them from hearing what is shouting from inside their own soul.

Making the transition

Shifting to a listening-to-hear mode begins with understanding what noise within the minister is blocking his ability to hear and understand others. When these ministers venture into the wild, stepping out from behind the protective shield of their pulpits, titles, and clerical robes, their wounds are exacerbated. Each one's inner narrative seemed to grow louder and bolder, claiming more territory in their soul as they left the safety of church culture. Understanding this phenomenon, we look at each person's wound, and listen to the noisy inner narrative that it generates, to uncover something profound—a kind of symbiotic relationship between the wound and its Genius.

As we ventured outside the safety of professional identity and familiar religious culture, my residents often felt threatened by the noise of the unhealed wound. They would often retreat back to their base—the church building, the theological framework, their one-way, self-insulating conversations and theologically laced pronouncements. The deeper the resident's plunge into the wild—the untamed, natural, nonchurch world—the more likely he was to experience the wound that was safely hidden as long as he remained inside the church.

What narratives do these residents battle? One lives by pivoting off of his father's voice: "Shame on you." Another has listened, every hour of every day, for 60 years to the reverberating echo: "You're a useless Idiot." One resident can't stop hearing the sound of his parents who bullied him; he recoils to bullying triggers that go off every day, everywhere. Another resident bears the strain of perfectionism he feels is expected of the firstborn child, the first minister in his family, in compensation for the tortured legacy of his family's past. Unable to end the pattern set in motion by his emotionally aloof father, another resident cannot break out of the disheartening cycle of arm's-length relationships with everyone around him, both in the church and elsewhere. Another resident fat-shames himself all day long.

Then there's the resident who suffers the ongoing trauma of his parents' divorce. Unable to come to terms with the rupture of his family as a child, now he struggles as a husband, father, and minister to project the image of perfect family to the world, except that's far from what it really is. His accusing conscience violates every waking moment. He cannot rest. One resident experienced unspeakable sexual trauma that resulted in her building an entirely imaginary and safe city inside her mind and dreams.

As more and more of my residents reported what they initially thought were failed attempts to connect with people in the wild, I came to appreciate that long before they could become adept at listening to hear anyone else, they needed to listen to the very noise that was crying out to be heard from the deepest recesses of their own lives.

The other side of the coin

But I've also discovered something else, quite unexpected. Despite sustaining life-changing wounds (and often because of them), each and every one of my residents expresses real Genius! Not only that— they don't know it.

Even though most of them would deny that their lives are significantly defined by, even driven by, the wounds they have experienced, they are constantly caught up in its power, frequently tortured by it, trying to medicate, run from, and deny it. But there's a redemptive, transformative side to this dilemma that few have been able to appreciate. The very thing that threatens to devour them is, at the same time, inspiring a breathtaking creativity that I can't identify as anything other than Genius.

What is Genius? This book is my attempt to explain this often-overlooked characteristic of human experience by inviting you into the stories of people who have spent most of their lives licking the very wounds from which the characteristics of Genius have been pouring out—though they haven't always seen or known it. For more than two years I have watched and listened to them describe their arduous, convoluted lives. There have been tears, tantrums, and even some ravings as we explored places closer to the core of themselves than they'd ever seen or touched before. Given the nature of this exploration it won't surprise you to learn that I was told to go to hell more than a few times. I am humbled by their brave and persistent character.

This is not a collection of silver-lining stories designed to convince anyone that the traumas we suffer aren't as painful and disruptive as they are. No, these are first-person testimonials that reveal layers of meaning far beneath the surface of their scars and wounds.

From these brave (if reluctant) souls and countless others, I have learned that the force of life inside of us is far more creative, transformative, and miraculous than we know. The presence and effects of our wound so distracts us that we most often focus solely on its pains. Don't misunderstand me—I am convinced that life is hard, that it hurts, that it costs. But what if the wounds we sustain are not simply disabling impairments? What if our wounds are actually the incubators of gifts intended to make life better for ourselves and others?

What if there is a Genius in your wound, a Genius that can transform ashes into beauty? What if your life is not primarily, or even situationally, about the suffering you endure? What if there is a Genius already flowing out of you that is the reason, the purpose of your existence? From what I have witnessed in the lives of the people you will soon meet; I've had to ask myself if this relationship between the wound and Genius isn't a glimpse into life beyond the veil that ordinarily goes unnoticed.

Let's take a look behind the curtain together.

Chapter 2: Introduction

Wounds, Genius, and Superpowers

Trees

Those who knew Greg were concerned that he might not be safe. But their concern never resulted in what would have been a fully warranted intervention. He was the older of two young boys who lived in a violent home. A child who has no real voice, and cannot begin to imagine any alternative, learns to keep quiet. Even though he ached inside Greg hid a lot that hurt him because he wanted his home to work. What choice does a little boy have?

Early on, Greg learned how to cover for his drunken father, a skill he would hone over many tortured years. Imagine an 8-year old serving as wingman for his dad when they were in public together, even helping him find his way home when he'd had too much to drink. "Dad turn here...now!"

Greg's father was a functional alcoholic who tried to cover his tracks with humor. He lived in a sort of tripping Dean Martin skit from the 60s. Still, just about everyone loved him, even the family—and son—who were subjected to the much less than funny side. "It's always 5 o'clock some-where" was his swagger and con.

But after five, when the sun went down, Greg's father would revisit the demons of his childhood, a God-awful, constantly repeated story of broken bones, suicide, and the life-long terror of never being safe. Fueled by alcohol his yelling could last all night long. Listening, afraid in his bedroom, Greg knew the forecast—storms with flooding, lightening, and hail. He often thought, How can Dad yell all night? It would last for 3, 4, even 6 hours. Where did he get the energy? What could possibly give a mortal man, such super human power to keep on yelling?

Greg loved his father but needed the safety that eluded both of them. He couldn't find a place where he felt free, where he could escape from the soul-crushing weight of his father's stormy nights. Robbed of sleep Greg would drag himself to school, dead tired. Weakened in body and mind he felt embarrassed by the meager contents of his lunch—a few crackers and a box of raisins—whatever he could find before leaving each morning. Once he saw a girl at lunchtime with cupcakes and imagined a world where his parents were up and awake to see him off to school, handing his lunch box filled with homemade treats.

By the time he was five years old, Greg had begun to explore the forest around his country home—but always within sight of the house. He was allergic to bees. If they showed up, he had to run for his blessed life back to base. Knowing from experience that he was vulnerable to serious consequences, Greg quickly learned how nature worked. Honey bees were slow to anger; yellow jackets were just plain crazy; and wasps were the B1 Bombers with payloads he never wanted to experience.

One day the forest beckoned. Going further than ever before, he discovered a mysterious world. Picking up rocks he uncovered big black spotted salamanders and centipedes that were in constant wriggling motion. Then there was the mystery of mushrooms that brought a rush of fear and excitement. Can they be eaten, or will I die? The young boy felt invincible. Daniel Boone never died, and I am just like him!

Even though his forest was principally made up of trees, Greg hadn't really looked at them. He'd kept his attention at ground level, and within view of his house. But one day he suddenly noticed a whole world of trees, in detail. Little baby ones, ones with thorns, and ones with sticky bark. He arched his neck, looking up the vast length of the highest ones. He just stood there, staring at the green tops that pieced the bottom of the sky. The trees were steady and solid. In time Greg ascribed personality to them. They were constant, reliable, always there. And the sound of the wind catching their limbs and leaves was like a song. The forest of trees was a safe and welcoming place. Greg felt good being there.

It wasn't long before Greg was visiting the forest every chance he got. He escaped from the house mostly during the day, after school. But nobody seemed to notice when he wasn't there—at least nothing was said about it. Believing his secret departures were unknown, Greg's confidence grew, and so did the distance between his home and his place—and time—in the forest.

His discovery of the trees led, as it does for lots of children, to the inevitable quest to experience more. He began to climb. As if a new dimension of life had suddenly been discovered, now, nothing was more important to Greg than climbing. He wasn't sure if it was desire or danger that drove him. Gauging the danger, he wondered, What if I fall, will I make a sound? All of 9 years old but feeling like a giant he pushed his limits as if they didn't exist, climbing, higher, and higher. He hugged the tree, inching like a centipede, straining to grab hold of the highest branches. And once as high as he could go, precariously balancing himself in the wind, he experienced the devious delight of peeing on the world below. A young boy's ultimate expression of freedom!

One night, Greg sensed that the weather forecast inside the family house was more ominous than usual. This time it wasn't beer, it was liquor. Beer usually triggered a category 1 hurricane, but vodka could quickly mushroom into a category 5 with sustained, destructive, gale winds. It was after 8 o'clock and dark outside. When the storm started Greg pushed up his bedroom window, climbed out, and walked in the moonlight to his favorite tree. He'd memorized the arrangement of the branches. It wasn't difficult for him to quickly climb to safety. Bats would soon be out dining on their crazy flying buffet of insects. Who cares if insects get eaten, they deserve it for stinging me.

Early the next morning Greg woke up in the tree. At first, he panicked not knowing where he was. But when he got his bearings, he carefully climbed down, crept back through the bedroom window, and slipped into his bed. Had his night time escapade been discovered? Judging from the usual depressive fog that hung in the house after a stormy night, no one knew he'd gone. He felt a vague and empty sadness that no one missed him. But before the emotion could register its full meaning on his longing heart an overpowering exhilaration erupted. He was thrilled with the raw excitement that he'd escaped the house in the middle of his father's rampage and got away with it!

As Greg grew through his teens the trees became bigger, farther away, and often on his mind. He learned to weave his arms, legs, and body in the branches, so he wouldn't fall to the ground when he slept in them, which he was doing more often. It was the one place where he felt protected from the storms, he most feared, even if it was raining outside. His arms were often scraped from hugging and squirming up the trees, but it was easy to make up stories that would keep curious adults away from any discovery of his secret tree life.

Eventually he reached a stage when the necessity of survival ignited innovation. In high school the guidance counselor asked Greg what he wanted to do with his life. He said, "Live in trees." Amazingly, the counselor replied with earnest encouragement, "Then go do it!"

Greg began to design treehouses like the ones he saw posted on the internet. He developed masterful hardware designs that allowed the trees to flex while keeping the treehouse screws and bolts anchored tight. It seemed that every new life experience inspired Greg's imagination. When he saw "Lord of the Rings," "Robinson Caruso," and even old black and white Tarzan movies, he would design—and sometimes build—a new tree house. Driven to seeking relief from the never-ending storms of his father's rage, Greg had found the haven that helped him survive. In the trees he found a place of peace where he could think, grow, learn, and heal.

Greg is not the only child captured by the allure of a treehouse. Maybe the reason we are drawn to trees is that they beckon us upward, toward a private home where we can hide from the onslaughts of the world at our ground level life. Trees are majestic, wise, old, and invite us to come and live respectfully, but more importantly, freely, in their strong arms. The higher the tree the greater the risk, the more seclusion, and the opportunity to discover scenes of beauty—on the horizon, and in one's soul. Whether in a tree house or in the home we want to preserve as our castle, we have a kind of primal desire to build a special space, a sanctuary, a place others can access only when we are prepared to invite them in, but which keeps us safe from all intrusions when we are not.

A ladder ascending 30 or more feet straight up to a tree house lair is a tether between earth and sky mounted only by those most brave–or by those most desperate to escape from the things that threaten them. Whether a young child or a grown adult, sometimes we are held in suspended animation, teetering delicately between fantasy and reality about the possibility that we will never leave this refuge. The private treehouse is a place just big enough for one, out of sight from everything below. Perched up in the trees you have a vantage point from which to peer down on ground-dwellers, safe in the knowledge that you are protected from them. But safety is not enough for the soul. It needs light, hope, and vision. Aloft in the trees you can scan the horizon and see far off places that your heart longs to claim and hold as your own destiny. Whether in our dreams and imaginings, or in the coarse, twisted wood adorned with gracious green lace, we run to the trees to experience something other-worldly. There in the trees is where some of us have most effectively imagined ourselves.

Type "treehouse" into your computer's web browser and look at the images the search pulls up. Spend time with the pictures, look closely at them and let your mind wander. The images might trigger something inside leaving you to wonder if there's more to the silly idea that drives people to live in the trees.

The link between the wound and its Genius

Greg was quite obviously tormented by his father's wound. Undiagnosed, and untreated as it was, Greg inherited his father's pain. Like the unconscious reaction when you unknowingly place your hand on a hot stove, Greg instinctively withdrew from the searing source of pain. But just like the hand burned by the stove, Greg's pain went with him when he fled to the trees. Though he put himself at a safe distance from the effects of his father's stormy rage, it had already scarred his soul. But it's as if Greg's keen sensitivity to his father's wound—which Greg could not avoid—sharpened his senses, endowing him with, or opening up to him, creative, inventive, imaginative abilities that are nothing short of a Genius intuition.

One of the most amazing expressions of the Genius that fired out from Greg's wound revealed itself in his search for safe, life-nurturing refuge. Even though robbed of the reliable, nurturing guidance the young boy needed but would never receive from his father, Greg was left to imagine actually living his life on his own, and he did it in the trees. The foundational safety and trust every child needs but which was stolen from Greg, created a hole in his soul. And yet, out of that formless void a miraculous sixth sense was born. The knowledge he gained from his life in the trees gave him a rare understanding of that world and ignited an insatiable desire to learn and use the tools he needed to become a treehouse guru. The Genius that erupted out of Greg's wound inspired him to invent a way to safely sleep through the storms of his life and give many others a way to do the same too.

One of my residents once told me, "In my youth I was branded an idiot but surprisingly I've found, and, in a way, I understand other idiots. I know their body language, their defense mechanisms, their denial, and their coping skills because I've used them all. It's taken years for me to realize that the wounds sustained in childhood have given me a kind of instinctive empathy that draws me to my kind. For a long time, I wondered how and why I seemed to be able to pull another closeted soul out into the daylight, all the while respecting the idiot's dignity."

Hearing firsthand accounts like these, I began to see a relationship between a kind of unexplained insight into the experiences of others and the previously hidden, unseen effects of my own life story. Like the early morning sunrise after agonizingly long, cold, and dark wintry days, I began to arm to the idea that the chaos and cruelty that scars our lives is not the beginning nor the end of the story for any of us.

The bullied kid who became a minister lived with a hair trigger that could unleash a torrent of internal rage at the slightest hint of judgement and ridicule, even when it wasn't there at all. But that enhanced sensitivity seems to have another side to it. A kind of sixth sense ability to notice things in his environment that are different, that stand out. Remember those workbook exercises that asked you to pick out the item that didn't belong in the group? Some wounded souls seem to have the ability to see what's around them that way. Except instead of things, they are drawn to people who don't belong to the larger group.

At the same time, I noticed these dynamics with my residents, I started interviewing people with tattoos. I suspected there must be a reason for them, so I just asked, "Does your tattoo have a story?" One after another I heard such moving stories. Each one was griping. And yet, they were familiar. I'd heard them before. I'd witnessed them firsthand unfolding in the lives of the people I pastored. But none of them wore pictures on their skin. I was bowled over by the discovery that tattoos are actually portals, windows into the soul-wrenching experiences of their owners' lives. This initial fascination turned into focused research for my previous book, Tattoos...Telling the Secrets of the Soul. I discovered that for the vast majority who wear them tattoos are a manifestation of the inside writing on the outside. The soul is telling its secrets on the live canvas of the skin in permanent ink—45% of the population, at last count. And this is happening at a time when church people are scratching their heads wondering how to connect with those outside the church. They're called 'nones'—those who reject any involvement with organized religion. The more I investigated the tattoo phenomenon the more I wondered, "Why have so many of us completely missed it?"

In nearly every one of the thousands of interviews I've done, I've heard the story of a bullied, bruised, wounded life. Frankly, I've been shocked at the power of the connection I've made with the people I've interviewed. Listening to these wounded souls I was amazed to discover that I already knew what they would say. Of course, the details of each person's experiences were unique. But once their story began to unfold, I could almost instantly connect with what they felt, what they thought, why they responded to life the way they did—the way they do. Something about my own anguish, triggered by the details of another person's story, seemed to give me Genius insight into the suffering that was telegraphed by the tattoo. Friends, they are not just pictures, strange symbols etched in flesh by people on the fringes of life. They are signposts about what's going inside the soul. I began to realize that the wounds of my own life might have given birth to a Genius ability to connect with others who suffer like I have. Genius may be the other side of our wound!

People in the wild, especially those not connected to any traditional church or faith community, don't care whether the axioms, principles, or teachings of church, philosophy, or culture are true. They are not won over by academic credentials or by how slick the speaker and his presentation might be. What the people in the wild care about is whether any of that works. Folks in the wild will listen if they sense that someone is speaking out of their authentic experience of life. Is there evidence in how and what he is says that admits, "You know, I am wounded too?"

Genius Superpowers

I understand Genius to be an unusual, deeply perceptive superpower that seems to be latent in everyone. But it's most often and more easily seen in children. Here's an example of what I mean.

I was camping at the Rhythm and Roots music festival in Rhode Island. Nearby me, was a family with young kids. They were all crawling out of their tents after a stormy night of wind and rain. Mom was eye-drooping tired. Dad was not up yet. But his little 5-year-old son emerged, with his superhero cape on. His even littler 4-year-old, bed-head sister was close behind wanting to see what big brother was up to. A perfect audience for a superhero. The conversation went something like this.

"Cloe, with this cape I can fly!"

No response as Cloe was still waking up and sucking on her sippy cup.

"Watch this Cloe." He climbed onto the picnic table and jumped. But little sister was fixed on her cup with a steady sucking, loud enough for me to drop a pin on her location.

Big brother was intent on convincing his sleepy sister of his superpower, so he got back on the picnic table. Only this time, he got a running start before launching into his short-lived flight. Now he had her attention! She was glued to his every move. The almost awake, widening eyes of his sister seemed to fuel something which was latent, but already ignited, in big brother's imagination.

He began sprinting and summersaulting and leaping like 5-year-old superheroes do. At one point he crashed into the nearby portable toilet, but heroically bounced back to resume his invincible antics. I wondered what the person inside the toilet must have thought.

This little guy was demonstrating a common fascination—held by all ages—with superpowers. Our imaginations run wild with the possibilities. What if I could leap tall buildings with a single bound? What if I could see with x-ray vision? What if I could hear people's thoughts? This is imagination that envisions life with an extra something that would equip us to do, and see, and know things that would give us an advantage, making us more useful and more helpful to others.

Look at the comic strips with Spiderman, Wonder Woman, and the Hulk! Look at Peter Pan and Tinker bell whose entire relationship was characterized by the alternating presence and absence of superpowers they needed and wanted to possess. I love Tinkerbell's superpower tantrums. When my daughter Erin was three, she demonstrated that power whenever she saw candy at the grocery checkout.

Disney movies bait an easy imagination inside us with flying carpets, talking cars, half-human horses, and space ships that go to other planets with aliens who share the same human hang-ups and insecurities we do. We have an innate superpower to imagine superpowers!

There are superpowers around us every day, but we rarely see them as that. Consider the blood hound. He has 300 million scent receptors, more than any other dog—more like a nose with a dog attached. What this nose finds is trusted as irrefutable evidence in courts of law all around the world. Add the dog's 110 pounds, a wrinkly shawl of skin and ears that collects stray cells with unrelenting stamina, and you have a bona fide superpower. Bloodhounds have been known to track a man for 130 miles. One Kentucky dog led police to track and capture 600 criminals. That's better than Batman's record.

Here's another superpower which is infinitesimally small—just a millimeter long— the tardigrade. If the earth experienced an apocalyptic event, like the sun burning out, an exploding star, or an asteroid smashing into the planet, all of life would be gone except for this unique organism. It's a microscopically small, eight-legged animal. Scientists say that tardigrades have been part of the earth's ecosystem for the past 530 million years. It is the ultimate survivor. It can endure temperatures up to -458 degrees Fahrenheit, and can live dormant, without food or water, for 30 years! It can withstand radiation doses hundreds of times higher than the lethal dose for a human. The durability of tardigrades makes human endurance look like a Kleenex tissue landing in a brush fire. Tardigrades have been found everywhere, on mountain tops, in the deep sea, in rain forests, in the Antarctic, and New Jersey. Yes, they live quietly among us, fascinating scientists who religiously study them while the rest of us are out drinking, dancing, and trying to find our way home. What's the point? Superpowers exist right under our noses, in the natural realm. You might even sneeze a tardigrade out of your nose without knowing it.

And then there is Rain Man, the nickname given to the main character of the 1988 movie by the same name about two brothers, one a self-absorbed hustler who discovers that the other, his autistic Savant sibling, is the sole heir of their father's multimillion-dollar estate. Raymond is the movie's Rain Man, based on the real-life Savant, Kim Peek. Kim was diagnosed with Savant Syndrome, a rare human condition that is characterized by the incessant need to observe strict routines, the ability to know extensive orders of numbers, dates and times, and the ability to maintain a photographic knowledge of huge volumes of information he has read only one time.

In the movie, Charlie is a hustler. He tries to regain custody of his socially inept Savant brother Raymond. His goal is to get access to claim his father's money. Because Raymond will not fly, they make the trip to Los Angeles on the road. The extreme differences in the two brothers creates an enormous struggle for them to relate to each other. Not knowing anything about his brother's condition, other than that he is odd, Charlie soon discovers that Raymond has superpowers that he's never encountered, but which can change his life. Raymond is a human calculator who can count hundreds of objects at once and keep track of them all.

Charlie is desperate for cash to cover an 80-thousand-dollar debt. Having found out that his brother can do super human calculations, he takes Raymond to a casino, where he wins big by asking Raymond to count blackjack cards. It didn't make sense to Charlie that someone who couldn't button his own shirt could have such abilities. The Savant Syndrome is a rare but undeniable real-life superpower.

The list of Genius superpowers and abilities goes on and on—from the world of astronomy and the discovery of mysterious black holes in space, to brilliant inventors such as Leonardo DaVinci, to the Mantis Shrimp which has a club that moves at the rate of 335,000 feet per second, used to kill its prey for dinner. With that kind of power, the larger species that average a foot or more in length, can easily break a glass aquarium. And let's not forget about the simple bumblebee—according to urban legend they can't fly. The classic laws of physics make it clear that the bumble bee cannot fly the way birds and butterflies do. Instead their wings beat furiously, creating a resonance that lifts them. They can fly in a straight line in a 30-mph crosswind without deviating from their direction. Their body weight alone would seem to keep this from happening and yet, rare characteristics resident in the bumble bee and some other insects make them capable of doing the extraordinary. Like humming birds whose bodies can float in place while their wings beat out a figure eight motion at the rate of 70 times per second—they can fly forward, backward, and even upside down. These are just a few of the bizarre abilities that capture our attention, defying what we think is ordinarily possible. But there are even more amazing superpowers that are exercised by people whose wounds have inexplicably unleashed Genius. Let's take a closer look.

Chapter 3: The Behavior of Wounds

In order to get a sense of what I mean by the question, Is there a Genius in your wound? it is important to define our terms. This chapter reviews the discoveries I've made about wounds. In the next, we'll explore what I've discovered about the characteristics of Genius. We begin with the wound because this is ground zero where life's traumas make such an impact on us, and which, counterintuitively, seems to trigger the release of a Genius superpower from within a person. But how does this happen?

Being wounded, whether in body or soul, is a common human experience. The last time I checked it was still true that no one gets out of this life alive. Though none of us goes looking for it, being wounded is as much a part of life as eating and sleeping, except that being wounded affects who we are and who we become even more significantly.

The body is wounded from the outside, and from within. When they are wounded, our bodies suffer, but so does our mind, heart and soul. Being wounded cuts far beyond the skin, to the quick of who we are, because being wounded thrusts chaos into the order of life that we already learned. Being wounded can seriously upset the balance of life, calling into question its meaning and purpose. We all know that we will not escape this life before we are mortally wounded, be it from a traffic accident, an incurable disease, or nature simply taking its course. Whether the wounds we suffer bring on our imminent demise or not, how we feel about ourselves, how we experience and make sense of life is affected by them. All the efforts we exert to protect ourselves from being hurt will not finally keep it from happening.

But, in fact, despite creating obvious physical and psychological pain, the traumas we spend so much time reacting to are often the vehicle by which we can become more keenly aware of the value and purpose of the most precious gift we have—our very own existence.

So, what about this all too common experience of being wounded? I've discovered at least seven characteristics about wounds.

Some very present wounds originated in the past,
before you existed

85% of the Hurricanes that hit the United States start as seedlings off the west coast of Africa. Three main ingredients contribute to their formation; warm ocean temperatures, moisture, and the rotation of the planet. These powerful, often life-threatening storms come from far beyond where we live. If we are attentive to their development, we can sometimes predict where they will go and what the effects of the storm might be. Frequently the full fury of a tropical storm is not reached until it makes landfall. But the conditions that led to its destructive force were at work far from the home shores.

Not so long ago, before satellite imagery, people were subject to what seemed to be the sudden onset of bad weather, in some cases with little or no warning at all. Galveston Island, a 26 mile stretch of land two miles off the coast of Texas, was in 1900 a popular vacation spot on the Gulf of Mexico. On September 8 that year, with very little warning and none of the sophisticated meteorological tools to forecast it, a category 4 hurricane smashed the island. After it passed and the 15-foot storm surge had subsided 6,000 of the 37,000 residents were dead and nearly 4,000 buildings had been destroyed.

They may take us by surprise and dramatically upset our lives, but storms never just appear. They take quite a while to form. In the case of many of the profound wounds that people sustain, particularly those that are psychological in nature, the conditions that gave rise to them have been brewing and strengthening for generations. Many of the people I've interviewed tell stories that reveal the brewing of wounding storms long before their victims even existed.

Think of some of the effects of the Galveston Hurricane: whole families were wiped out—the end of that line of descent; spouses and children were literally ripped out of each other's arms—grief stricken, some survivors were driven to crippling depression, loss of work, years of soulless, purposeless wandering. That heritage became part of the legacy inherited by the next generation.

A wound sustained in one life often becomes a seed planted in the next generation that matures into an even larger, more imposing force decades hence. What about the abuse, abandonment and neglect experienced by a child who struggles to survive? One day he becomes a parent who now has to be father to a child never having received the requisite nurture that would have equipped him to succeed in his adult role. What about the genetic effect of generational alcoholism and drug abuse that is carried in the lineage of a child who appears on the scene 20, 50 or a hundred years later?

I've often heard words like these, "I don't know what went on with my people, so I have no idea what happened to me. But whatever it was must have something to do with my wound, my hurt, my challenge. How I wish I could break the cycle." As I watch the explosion of interest in ancestor research through services like Ancestry.com and 23andme, I sense a loud universal driving motivation, Who am I? If I can find out who my people were, and what happened to them it might help me understand myself better.

I paid a visit to a 45-year-old man in his hospital bed as he waited for surgery to receive a new heart valve. His heart was straining mightily with this defect. Without this intervention his life would be severely curtailed. He'd die way too young. His 75-year-old mother was ever present and hovering over her grown son. I commended her for being there for her him, and the care she showered on him. She broke into a slow and careful statement, "You see, I gave him that defective heart. This is all because of me." An instinctive reaction almost prompted me to console her by telling her it wasn't her fault. But I caught myself and just listened. She got more comfort from confessing her role in her son's health than I could have offered by trying to talk her out of it. I'm not being cruel when I say that she wasn't completely wrong. We have all inherited hearts that were formed by the experiences of our ancestors. Often the wounds we experience have come from people, places, and times far removed from the here and now.

We fire where we are wired, and we wire where we are fired

This is big. We drive on roads made long before we get to use them; and those unknown and unseen pathways determine the course of our journey. Our entire nervous system is a wonder, coordinating an impressive constellation of activities that give us the abilities we have to function. Examined under the microscope, most people's nervous systems might look nearly identical. But each of us has an invisible wiring—a messaging mechanism—from previous generations and from our own repeated thoughts and behaviors. This invisible system encoded in the brain causes us to engage life and react to it based on our inherited physiology and psychology.

Whenever we try to initiate something new, that deviates from the thinking and behaviors that were pre-wired in the nervous system, it can be extremely difficult. Like trying to teach an old dog new tricks, most of us find it nearly impossible to take the new path we can imagine because we do not have the pre-wiring that would enable us to easily, and certainly not naturally, go that way.

If a child has a mother who has always seen herself as a victim, and who therefore thinks, speaks, and acts out of that frame of reference throughout the child's developmental years, the child's brain will likely be wired the way mom has taught her—whether the mom consciously intends this or not. I've actually seen a mother who lived this way criticize her child's behavior as if she was scolding herself for not being able to overcome the challenges she faces in the depths of her own life. So, the child will respond to life's challenges and opportunities—she'll fire—out of the way she has been wired by her mother's disposition. This makes the child predisposed to think and live in some ways and not in others. The child fires through life based on the pre-wiring she received, both genetically and experientially. She will move into adulthood with this pre-wiring, which will be reinforced by all of her successive experiences of life. She will actually be laying down new versions of the old wiring that will continue the patterns inherited and learned. Ever ask yourself why you can't stop reliving your wounds or the wounds of your parents? This is the reason. But the story doesn't need to end there.

If we become conscious of how we were hard-wired, appreciating that our habitual thinking and behavior has been influenced by how we were pre-wired, and we want to change, we might have the opportunity to do something about it. Some people take on the Herculean task of coming to terms with things they don't like about themselves—things that cause them to be less than they have an intuitive sense they could be—with various kinds of therapies—talk, tactile, writing, meditation, yoga, gardening, spiritual practices, smoking cigars. The people who contributed to this book all reported that the exercise of writing about themselves opened their eyes to things they never saw before. When the brain and pen work together something is unleashed, there is a flash of insight, something new is born. Re-wiring begins.

Neuroscientist, Dr. Thomas Sudhof won a Nobel Prize in Physiology for his discovery of synaptic transmission, how brain cells communicate via chemicals. Neurons that fire together wire together. "Neuronal firing" is the term used to describe this phenomenon. When the same pathway is used to transmit information the wiring adapts, speeding up the rate of transmission. Over time the wiring becomes thicker and more permanent, as if the internal wiring of the brain actually learns that it needs to increase its strength in order to support the volume of information that will pass through it.

A dancer may start off her career with two left feet. Those feet are placed in a classroom where 45-minute dance lessons take place over the course of 10 weeks. At the end of that period it is no longer two left feet, but muscle memory that dances. The dancer notices that her legs and feet have memory. A re-wiring, a retraining has taken place. Her dance classes lead to attending a dance so she can socialize, which leads to a date, that leads to marriage, and children, and grandchildren. You get the point. We fire where we are wired, and we wire where we are fired.

Psychologists have long known that negative thoughts and traumatic events can cause us to behave like we're in a NASCAR competition. Just as the cars go around and around the track, never finding an off-ramp, traumatic events cause many of us to continue to circle the original event, even repeating its ugly characteristics over and over, though we wish we could escape the effects of the endless cycle. For some people years of talk therapy will help, but the impact of the wound often dominates their lives, keeping them spinning in an endless loop from which they cannot be freed.

Some of the people who've contributed to this book have allowed me into their lives at a level that's permitted me to see their deepest wounds without knowing that they also display amazing characteristics of a Genius super power. A super power that might not have ever been experienced except for the trauma they've lived through. No, this doesn't remove the effects of the wound or its ongoing pain. But it does make a difference in how the person experiences their pain.

Perhaps you've had a taste of this from time to time. Ever feel sick when you got up in the morning only to realize that you had an important meeting or presentation that day? I have. And when I've forced myself to fulfill the obligation, even though I didn't stop feeling sick, the creative exercise I was committed to somehow changed my perspective about how I was feeling. In fact, sometimes, when I've felt miserable, sure that I could not mask my discomfort, afterward, people commended me on the excellent work I'd done. And even I, in the moment of being invested in the thing I had to do, was not aware that I was actually ill. How do I know this? Because all of a sudden on the ride home, I became aware that I felt awful again, like I did when the day started. It seems that when there is an opportunity to act, even when we feel least equipped to do so, some other power resident within us expresses itself. This is Genius. As you read the first-person accounts in the chapters ahead, see if you can detect this.

Milton Suavely Hershey founded the Hershey Chocolate Company and the town of Hershey, PA. He was a Genius who was driven to invent and build infrastructure to see his Chocolate bar empire grow. Candy needed a factory, a factory needed workers, and workers needed homes and a town to live in. Who doesn't know his name and candy bar? I'll bet your brain is giving you the sensation of tasting his life's work right now.

Milton grew up as a farm boy who had to cope with a repeatedly absent father. In order to compensate for a father who was AWOL, Milton quit school in the fourth grade. As a teen he worked for a printer. When his hat accidentally fell into the press, the ill-tempered boss fired him. Milton's aunt came up with the idea that perhaps he could apprentice with a candy maker, and so he did. There were many other small steps that would be taken. One day as he delivered an order of caramel candies to a store in New York he met his future wife, Kitty.

Years later, when traveling in France in 1912, Milton and Kitty Hershey had planned to return to home, sailing out of Cherbourg. However, urgent business matters came to Milton's attention and so they departed earlier on another ship. Among the artifacts, visitors will see at the Hershey museum is a $300 canceled check written as a deposit for the Hershey's stateroom—the one they were supposed to occupy on the maiden voyage of the ill-fated luxury liner, Titanic! Imagine, Hershey bars were almost sunken by an iceberg.

Though Milton and Kitty had been married for 17 years the Hersey's never had children. When Kitty died of an unknown disease in 1915 Milton did not remarry. It seemed that family life eluded him, both by the absence of his father in his childhood and now as an adult with his marriage cut short.

But this wounded widower with no children was not undone by the suffering and loss he experienced. No, his imagination invented with super power capacity. Hershey was known to put the wellbeing of his workers and their town far above company profits. Building a community became the passion of his life. He established the Hershey Industrial School for young people to earn skills and income, so they could build families and participate in the larger community. He endowed a medical center, hospital and the Elizabethtown Colleges honors program.

Deep inside Milton's wound which he did not speak about, was a special place of love for orphans. That love poured out in the founding of a private boarding school. Today 2000 students live and learn there.

130 faculty attend to their needs. The school sits on 2600 pastoral acres in southeastern Pennsylvania. It has an endowment of 12.5 billion dollars. The school's current challenge is that they have more money than they know what to do with.

Milton died of pneumonia at Hershey Hospital on October 13, 1945 at the age of 88. Commemorating the life work of this wounded Genius is a bronze statue of Milton Hershey holding an orphan boy in his arms. Below the statue the inscription reads, "His deeds are his monument. His life is our inspiration." I suspect the wounds that came from a life that was denied family and community created Hershey's Genius response. What about the stories ahead? What about the Genius in your wound?

Those who are wounded wound others
AKA, hurt people hurt people

It is well documented that abused children often grow up to become abusive parents. Sadly, the victims of domestic violence turn out to be abusers-in-training. A little boy who is the target of a father's wrath can become a grown man who does the same to his daughter. Those whose life work is devoted to intervening in this vicious cycle frequently reach a maddening place—they must take a break. The enormous burden of sustained emotional caring, witnessing broken bones, bruised eye sockets and scared faces, all inflicted not by strangers, but by blood relatives, is too much to bear.

Wounds threaten to impale the very person who does the wounding. The unrelieved pain experienced at the hands of the very last people on earth who should ever wrongly touch a member of their own family, holds the wounded party in a death grip. Wounds which have not been accounted for, that violate a person's conscience, have a greedy nature. They steal space in the mind, heart and soul in order to live and breathe and multiply. They self-justify because the original injury was so abhorrent. They demand satisfaction but rarely receive it. They self-generate, incident after incident; victim after victim, their chronic pain becomes the filter through which the wounded person experiences all of life, ensuring that the cycle will never end.

I do not pretend to have stumbled upon any easy answers here. But I watch, I observe, I see the patterns that play out over time, mutating in successive generations and relationships. And what I see indicates that our wounds have a gargantuan energy, with the force of a steaming hot geyser, and a destructive power like the unstoppable lava flow from an explosive volcano, consuming every living thing in its path.

The wounds that we experience are not just incidents of being or feeling wronged. When we are wounded, we experience the most painful hurt of all. You might have told yourself or someone else at times, not to be so sensitive. That begs the question of the involuntary response that has already registered in the soul. The soul cries out in hurt—hurt comes from the violation of integrity, relationship, and personhood. And precisely because this kind of violation challenges the goodness, the rightness of our being, the hurt we feel never lies dormant. Invariably it is transformed into white hot anger. Whether it is expressed subtly, or it is unmistakably volatile, hurt will have its retribution in an angry cancer that seems at times to defy even the medicine of love. Being wounded by those closest to us has an exponentially greater significance. It is not something easily, if ever, dismissed.

Wounds create a spiritual space

The force of life changes things. The great Chesapeake-Potomac Hurricane of 1933 transformed much of the mid-Atlantic, especially Ocean City Maryland. Miles of boardwalk were torn up; beachfront homes were moved off their foundations. Beach sand buried lawns, cars, streets and memories.

The unrelenting rain just kept coming; and then something completely unexpected happened. The water that piled up behind the long barrier island had risen to unsustainable levels. Together with the pounding force of the roaring swells from the ocean side, a breech erupted carving a raging, sandy river flowing from behind the popular ocean front beach community out to the Atlantic. It washed away streets, cars, houses, and even the railroad bridge. Now the land had been cut into two pieces. Ocean City inlet was created as if a planned excavation had completed a huge remodeling project. Commercial fishing changed, the railroad was no more, and from 1933 onward the tides have changed the waters in the inter-coastal waterway every day. Oysters became salty, new fish appeared, and brackish water became salt water.

An entirely new ecosystem replaced what was there before, triggered by a new space created out of the pummeling force of that historic hurricane. Often wounds do that too. The structure of our life is dramatically reshaped, a new space is created where other, fixed characteristics were before. A whole new ecosystem emerges almost spontaneously.

I see this to be a spiritual space, a place where new ideas are born, new people are encountered, people we've known are now experienced differently, perhaps holding changed value and meaning for us, and the eyes of our soul see things that were never seen before. Wounds cry out, they demand explanation, they seek dramatic recompense for the injury, violence and upset we have sustained. To be wounded is to have the coherence of life severed, pierced, halved; but life requires a viable logic, a rationale, that will permit it to go on. And so being wounded triggers the search for pain relief. Sometimes that is gotten from a drug, or enough alcohol to deaden the sensations, or some other self-distracting behavior. But that instinctive quest for wholeness—after a breech has been forced upon us—may be the most significant device that life has given to us for plumbing the depths of what it means to be. If, despite all the clever calculations and accommodations we devise, we cannot dodge the bullets of life, perhaps we can experience our wounds as an initiation into a deeper realm of experience—one that is designed to reveal more to us about who and why we are. Though few people, if any, begin the journey with their wound as the dark portal through which they will pass into enlightened insight, our wounds—like the force of the Chesapeake-Potomac hurricane, open new space, spiritual space, within us, into which we can enter to touch and be touched by something which far surpasses the pain our wounds are clothed in.

Wounds can inspire therapeutic self-talk

For multiple reasons, many of us never speak about what happened to us. This is especially true of war veterans. Fear, embarrassment, shame, horror and guilt are just some of the culprits that easily convince us to keep quiet. As Mark Twain said, "It is better to keep your mouth shut and let people think you are a fool, than to open it and remove all doubt." Undisclosed, our life-changing traumas live hidden within the secret chambers of our own soul. So, afraid of how others will see us we often choose to keep our own counsel, as if to preserve some shred of dignity. Besides, the wound was so great, so perverse, to speak of it we fear is to give it more life, more power.

But that misses what may be an even more critical function of the gift of speech—talking is how we do some of our best thinking. If you are attentive, when you speak, you can hear underneath the words, from the place where the words are formed within you. When you listen to hear your own voice, you are both speaker and audience. If you do not talk, either to yourself or to someone dedicated to listening to you, it's as if time stops. The wound will continue to determine the direction of your life like a ship's rudder frozen in one position. For a brief moment that trajectory may be appropriate. But in order to navigate the course of our lives we need to be free to make necessary adjustments. Untreated, undisclosed, misdiagnosed, and underestimated wounds have shipwrecked many who thought they were preserving their public image.

Talking to ourselves about what has happened—especially when there is no one else around—gives us the ability to do extraordinary critical thinking. This truth is experienced by people who keep a journal. Consider this profound insight, "Paper has more patience than people." So wrote Anne Frank who kept what has become the world's most famous diary. In it she detailed the harrowing two years of her family's hiding in a secret annex of her father's warehouse in Amsterdam, during the Nazi occupation of Holland. Not knowing that her family would be forced into hiding, to escape the concentration camps that were designed to destroy all of Europe's Jews, Anne began writing on June 14, 1942, just two days after receiving the diary as a gift on her thirteenth birthday. Her wound? To be forced to witness the ugliest betrayal of human existence in the systematic efforts of one people to exterminate another. Using her diary, Anne listened to the voice of her own soul from which a wisdom far beyond her years has spoken to the world. "What is done cannot be undone, but one can prevent it happening again."

Then there's the art of letter writing, hardly known today other than for business purposes. Before the era of instant communications—email, texts, social media posts, and God help us, emojis—personal letters were received as sacred gifts, for in them the essence of the writer's life—their heart, their mind, their concerns, their intentions, and desires—were revealed. "A letter always seemed to me like immortality because it is the mind alone without corporeal friend" said Emily Dickinson.

Writing a letter is obviously for the purpose of communicating something of ourselves to someone else. It's not an email blast to the world but an individual message. Sure, I could pick up the phone and speak to the person, but it wouldn't be the same. I wouldn't go to the deeper place in myself to find that part of me that most wants to be known. When I write a letter there's something of me, that feels more real, more authentic, that goes out. And long before you ever receive and read what I have to tell you, I discover that I have actually written to myself. I have taken the time to explore the vast universe that lives inside the fairly limited body in which it dwells.

Letter writing is not an art because anyone has perfected it. It is an art because, unlike the email, text or even the hastily scribbled note, you are delving into the truth of what you think and feel; you are working at carefully putting into choice, selected words, the thoughts and feelings that breathe your life into the life of the person for whom your letter is intended. Our word, not just the sound of our voice, is so very powerful. It can create and it can destroy.

I think of the opening line of the gospel of John. "In the beginning was the Word... and the Word was God." Whatever there is about us that is divine it must be our capacity for communicating what and who we are by our word. Our word is not only the calling card by which we are known to others. In this terribly instant, faster than the speed of light world, our word is the voice we need to be still enough to hear and listen to, so we can hear what is going on in the most profound places in our soul.

So, let's talk about the soul—the non-material essence of who we are. That which makes you you is designed with three-dimensional sight: observation, introspection and circumspection. Being human comes with the capacity to see what has happened, reflect upon it, and process a measured appreciation of ourselves. Now, of course, this doesn't mean everyone exercises these abilities to the same degree, or that everyone is necessarily conscious of being in one of these frames of reference as we experience life. Nevertheless, the soul watches what it experiences, reflects on what it experiences and exercises evaluation about the meaning of ourselves in relation to what we experience. It's as if we are first, second, and third person observers of our own life all in one. With this sort of three-dimensional lens, the soul observes everything it experiences. When it is wounded the soul must speak, in fact, cry out, which is why we have the need to talk and act in response to the wound.

The soul needs to speak, not just because it has been wounded, but because this is how the soul expresses itself. Whether in speech, art, music, poetry, or any other medium, the soul must speak. The healing value of talking about our wounds has been known and practiced throughout history. In fact, the ancient Greek word therapeuo meaning to heal is the foundation for the contemporary practice of therapy. One of the earliest forms of what became known in the early 20th century as psychotherapy, the healing of the mind, was good old-fashioned advice-seeking, and example-setting from parents, grandparents, tribal, community and religious elders.

Before the rise of the science-based field of psychology, the wounds of the soul were talked out in the context of the family. Children sought answers to coping with life's hurts by the counsel received from their parents, and especially from their more seasoned and wizened grandparents. Even within the last 100 years this was common. The members of a person's nuclear and highly treasured family included the elders, aunts and uncles. It used to be that extended family was intact. Grandparents were around to talk to teens on the fly or in-between meals as they often lived near or in the same house. An auntie, uncle or even cousins had just enough emotional distance to hear about their clan's younger member's drama and give it perspective. But not anymore.

The physical and emotional connectedness of contemporary families is incredibly thin compared to what it used to be. Our families are spread out, angry with each other, and broken. Many are rarely together in the day in, day out details of ordinary life. Many of us are known better by our friends than by our blood relatives. That fact that you are not likely to be surprised by what I' writing underscores how much we have lost—and gotten used to—from the deterioration of the fabric of family life.

Think about all the changes that have occurred. The global divorce rate is increasing. In 1960, 1 out of 8 marriages ended in divorce. In 2017 that rate had changed to 2 out of 5 (Unified Lawyers-Sydney, Australia) In the United States the rate of marriage has declined. While that helps lower the divorce rate it tells us that marriage is less desirable for many contemporary couples. The way families are formed, not to mention how they hold together, is quite different, and more tenuous, than was common for most of our history.

In a word, families are fragmented. Their reliability as a school for life, including how we handle the struggles we encounter, has dramatically changed. The wisdom of our elders is no longer immediately available. And this family fragmentation may be why we suffer as much as we do. Add to that the deterioration of community and the general social fabric along with an erosion of trust in and reliance upon the institutions of religion and government, and you can understand the great need for guidance, for anchoring, and direction experienced by so many people.

And let's not forget another canary in the mind shaft, suicide. According to the Suicide Prevention Resource Center, among the top ten causes of death, suicide is the second most common among youth aged 10-34, and the fourth most common among those aged 35-54. Death is of course inevitable, but death at one's own hand is not. These statistics are alarming because they tell us the souls of our people are in deep pain.

The rise in popularity of all sorts of therapies is a direct response to the vacuum created by the gutting of the family. Whether it's based on talk, drugs, behavior or any other modality, the need for therapy, to be healed, is greater now than ever. Just like a plant needs air, water and nutritious soil to thrive, the absence of any one of them fatal to its flourishing, so do people have fundamental needs. One of them is to be heard. I have an essential, primal need to be known, and so does everyone. Whether its cry is muffled by my self-consciousness or not, my soul's experience demands to be reckoned with. What happens to us matters.

Some observers who ask what the world needs now tell us that the soul's experience of trauma is the new mission field. I agree. I'm always amazed by the power that gets unleashed in a simple little conversation with someone over a beer in a bar. The happenstance of a throw-away, inconsequential encounter with a fellow life traveler seems to invariably draw empathy out of me. The poor soul who's crying in his beer while pouring his heart out, smiles at me, sometimes gives me a high five, or a hug. There's a tension that visibly leaves. He looks different than when he started talking.

But talk therapy isn't enough, or even the right thing, for some. Instead, they do yoga, or exercise or dance. Others drink, do drugs, seek repeated sexual encounters in order to feel value, safety, belonging and warmth. Have you ever sensed that a caring hug just might be the best gift a suffering soul could receive in the moment? I have. But even so, the gushing thank you has sometimes overwhelmed me. I mean, after all… it was just a hug, right? No, it was an acknowledgement that you heard the cry of a hurting soul. That's what so many want. Sure, we all cry out for relief. But what's almost always better than a quick fix is knowing that someone heard me, somebody cared.

I was with a buddy in Florida. He was going through the divorce from hell. Aren't they all? The bar I took him to was moving to the rhythms of both sad and happy blues music. To his utter dismay a woman came up and asked him to dance. I swear to you I didn't put her up to it, really, I didn't, nada, nope…. umm, oh wait.

"I don't dance," he said with the plaintive voice of a whipped pup. Fortunately for him, I was there. So, with the authority of God and wisdom of the ages, I chimed in, "Oh, he would love to!" With that my friend was whisked out of his slump and onto the dance floor.

As they danced, sharing quiet conversation with the partner he wasn't sure he should be with, he told her about his recent bout with cancer. It just came up, from out of nowhere. But it needed to. His soul had been invited to speak by a kind woman and the smooth sound that wrapped them in a dance that let him sing his own blues. When she heard his tune, she hugged him tight and long and said, "I'm so sorry."

I don't think he ever saw her again, but that experience was the beginning of a new life for my friend. Over the next three years he must have mentioned that moment to me at least forty times. Why? Because something profound was released and sincerely acknowledged in the miraculous, therapeutic stew comprised of the sound and beat of slow blues, the physical experience of holding a woman in a dance after having lost one, in the surprising disclosure of a truth he needed to tell, and in the sacred cradling of his body, mind and soul. My friend was heard, and in that hearing he was held. Oh, the wound was still there, but its raw pain had been transcended, because he was embraced with healing.

I suspect many cannot find this therapy for any number of reasons. Too risky, potentially sexual or something for women and not men. I will tell you this; in my bar (see Church in a Blues Bar-Rethinking Evangelism in a Post Christian Culture) I see souls wash up on shore from a distant life voyage and shipwreck every night. They open their blinking eyes, walk into the bar, try to hide and then someone asks them to dance. That dance creates breathing. I can't explain it... but it does.

This book is not an effort to provide clinical therapeutic analysis. But we cannot adequately address the question about whether there is a Genius in your wound without talking about the soul's need for therapy, for healing. I suspect that the deeper the wound, the more primitive, the more grounding the therapy needs to be. One dear soul who experienced a father wound told me, "It's the earth, when I gather dirt in my hands, play with it and dig in it… something begins to quiet my soul… I get better." Our wounds need to speak and be heard. They have the capacity to inspire a healing self-talk of discovery that can lead us to unexpected new insight.

Wounds hunt for relief and birth Genius insight

through forgiveness

The list of injuries and the nuances of them that we suffer could fill the pages of this book. Listen to anyone, let alone your own soul for a few minutes. and there's bound to be something that crops up as a source of pain. The older I get the more I'm aware that my body isn't as flexible and resilient as it once was. But far beyond the customary physical aches and pains associated with aging that are sedated with over the counter meds are those wounds to our souls that seem to never disappear no matter what we do. They may be as fresh as what happened this morning or as old as our great grandparents. As predictable as the sun's rising every day is the fact that living means suffering from a wound.

Human suffering is so much a part of life that you'd think we'd spend more time trying to understand it than we do. The experience of pain is so unpleasant that most of us will do anything to escape it. Preventative measures will keep us from unnecessary suffering. And if we can't avoid it, we'll find remedies to alleviate it. Millions of people have been spared the agony of uninterrupted pain with the use of morphine. And then there are those unregulated substances—alcohol, illicit drugs, food, sex, shopping, obsessive compulsive behaviors and more that we find ourselves using to deaden pain. Whether we're successful or not, we all know that sooner or later there will be another round of pain.

But what if there is something more than pain that comes from the wounds we sustain? What if there is more to the balance of our life than whether we are suffering or pain free? What if the wounds you and I experience have something transformative embedded in them?

Some sort of hurt comes from every injury but not every injury is a life-altering wound. It strikes me that the most devastating wounds we suffer are those that leave their marks on our soul, whether our body was violated or not, changing us in profound ways. The wounds that cause us the most trouble in life are the ones that torment us psychologically, emotionally and spiritually—the ones where we have knowingly violated ourselves or someone else has violated the sanctity of our person with words and deeds of the basest kinds of betrayal.

When we experience these kinds of wounds a primal cry erupts in the soul that mourns its own violation; it is fueled by a demand for justice, the longing for wrong to be made right. I have seen so many people, some in my own family, driven by the pain of their wound, believing that true justice which their violation demands would be the satisfaction of getting an eye for an eye; hunting down the perpetrator and destroying him; getting even by doing to the other what she has done to me. Perhaps you've seen it—or even been consumed by it. It's a tragic outcome, witnessing a wounded soul drinking the very poison that a perpetrator inflicted on them.

Soon you will find yourself in other chapters. There you will meet people like Mike who railed against the unfairness of his deformities, Elizabeth who bore a dead child, Joanna whose mother's pain broke her daughter's skull, and Janet whose parents were jailed for neglect. Every one of these were so sorely wounded that to say their lives were irrevocably altered is an understatement. Their wounds broke them, vaporizing the very foundations they counted on to make sense out of life. I don't have to guess, I know that many people are left there, washed up, destroyed, numbed by the shocking power of life's misfortunes. What's different about these people? It's as if the fire of life within them is so great that it could not be quenched. Something drove them beyond the boundaries of their suffering to find new meaning and new purpose. As I have heard and watched and tracked these intrepid souls, instead of succumbing to the weight of their wounds, each one has been on a mission to discover what their lives are now that the dreams and structures they held sacred have collapsed.

It's common for us to react to hurt by lashing out. Watch kids on a playground. Even if the child who is hit by another doesn't instinctively retaliate, his friends will band together to take matters into their own hands. When life delivers us a knockout punch, we either lay down in our suffering or we punch back. Either way we're still suffering. But what I've seen in the people whose stories you will soon read is a response that is far from instinctive. Instead of allowing themselves to be held captive by the twin shackles of the fight or flight behaviors that ordinarily result from being wounded, these heroes pushed forward as if there was another, an unseen realm, where a greater meaning and purpose could be seized, and known and lived. Even though many of them began their tortured comeback locked in mortal combat with the effects of their wounds they haven't remained there. Somehow, they intuited that there is another plane of existence that is not won by out smarting life's persistent afflictions. They chose to forgive.

To forgive is to give up and let go of a claim to a debt that was created by something or someone who has taken something away from you. When we are wronged, when we are wounded, whether physically or psychologically, something is taken from us—maybe our health, our integrity, or our peace of mind. Look at how many lawsuits include damages for emotional distress. Is there a rightful place in our society for restitution? Of course. But no matter how much money you might be awarded in a legal settlement, the loss sustained in an accidental death, a workplace injury, or a violent assault can never restore you to the wholeness you had before you were wounded. What I have witnessed in those who have miraculously risen above the crippling power of their wounds was the choice to let go of the "gotta get even" frame of mind. Those who have done this have experienced a freedom that helped them transcend the defining power of their wound. Doing unto others as you would have them do unto you is a way of living that sets a standard that can free you from the death spiral that getting even often ends in. The logic of forgiveness cannot run on the legs of revenge.

How did they do it? I suspect that when something is taken from us an emptiness, a void is created. Most of us are very uneasy when a new space is created because we feel a keen absence. In the counties immediately surrounding Tampa, Florida there has been exponential residential and commercial development in the last few years. Every time I'm there the landscape has changed. Huge swaths of the countryside have been bulldozed leaving large tracts of empty space. I'm quite sure that locals who've lived there a long time, who've gotten used to the way life was, hate it. Some of them protest against the development. It makes sense. They feel threatened by the loss and cannot begin to embrace the idea that there could be anything good that will come from what they haven't seen yet. In a few months, in a few years, it all changes. New neighborhoods spring up. New schools and hospitals and stores are built. New roads connect people to opportunities and experiences that couldn't have happened before. Change is very, very hard for all of us, especially when the things we hold most dear are ripped away.

But I suspect that those who are able to rise above the immediacy of the pain of violation and loss are those who have somehow transitioned from seeing the empty space in their lives to a place where something new might happen. They have allowed their soul to do some spiritual contemplation, some reflection on the landscape of their lives. The past is gone, they don't yet know what can or will happen as a result of the trauma that has bulldozed what they held dear. But maybe there is something that will spring up out of that suddenly barren, empty space. In my journey with some of the people you'll meet soon, I have been struck by their openness to other chapters which have not yet been written on the pages of their souls. For these folks it's not that the instinct for justice has disappeared. But they have come to believe and accept that what their definition of justice calls for is woefully small compared to the enormity of their need. I sense it is the willingness to forgive in these veterans of life's skirmishes which has spawned a Genius that breathes deep and free, opening them to see things they'd never seen before.

Melt down precipitates the release of a Genius power
AKA, Death gives birth to life

When my son was born, he had a daily cry time. He couldn't have planned it—or could he? It was like clockwork, from 4pm to 6pm. Every day! Because we'd never had kids before, my wife and I were hyper vigilant about everything he did. Neither the stork, nor God saw fit to include a manual of operations, so we had to figure out how he worked on our own.

So, there we were, helplessly watching this daily ritual. Our little bundle of joy transformed before our eyes into a quivering, red-faced, inconsolable, wailing new born whose cry could have broken the sound barrier. I was sure that if the neighbors heard, it would only be a matter of time before the authorities showed up asking questions about what was going on inside our paradise that was rending the neighborhood's domestic tranquility.

The fact is, this fragile baby boy was in the custody of two terrified parents who feared for his life. Of course, in such a moment, you don't tell people that you don't know what you're doing. You fake it hoping you'll get a clue, and quickly. Okay, maybe we weren't exactly terrified, but we were more than casually concerned. I mean have you ever heard the shriek of a baby whose only means of expressing his discomfort is more ear-piercing and soul-shattering than a smoke alarm going off in the middle of the night?

After we finally realized that both we and he would survive these daily outbursts I noticed how, just as instantly as it had begun, the crying ceased. It was as if his little body had to convulse that violently in order to wear itself out so he could sleep. I'm no pediatrician, but I could only surmise there must have been something much bigger than I knew going on inside him that needed to be released before every last ounce of energy was spent and he could, well, sleep like a baby.

Recently, my breath was taken away by the story of another father-son relationship. In 2005 David Sheff wrote an article published in the New York Times Magazine, My Addicted Son. Nic Sheff's raging methamphetamine addiction tore his family apart. It was a living hell with no escape. And it nearly cost Nic his life. I watched the movie Beautiful Boy, based on the memoirs of both father and son and I couldn't help thinking about the fragility of life, about my son, and how, like David, there have been times I feared for his life. Nothing new there. Every parent prays for wisdom in the face of endless moments of concern for their children. But the Scheff's story brings it all home. No matter what they tried over countless years, the effects of addiction were relentless—secrecy, betrayal, theft, estrangement, depression, guilt, helplessness, rehab, relapse, love tested beyond endurance, and yet remaining. Beautiful Boy is every parent's worst nightmare. And yet, in some ways—maybe not as life-threatening as the Scheff's—it is also everyone's experience. Like the little child who convinces himself that you can't see him when he closes his eyes, the fact that we cleverly find ways to close our eyes to the truth our souls know about the fragility of life doesn't change it.

It's amazing when you think about it. The whole world is sitting on the edge of its seat waiting for the birth of a new life. And here it comes in the breathtaking miracle of a few pounds of wriggling flesh that you can cradle in one hand. And just as the chorus of angels cues up to sing their halleluiahs, a banshee cry splits the heavens! Wait a minute. Isn't this supposed to be all sweetness and life? But before you can count to ten the very life that has rekindled your faltering belief in the order, meaning and purpose of existence, breaks out in a cry of pain. Though we want them to be "nothing but blue skies from now on" right out of the womb, our lives arc back and forth between transcendent wholeness to soul-wrenching brokenness. A lot of us have learned that. But to have to watch it play out in the first moments of a baby's life is just too much to take. We look at the child and coo-coo and sh-sh, as if to quiet the ragging cry of our own soul. Sometimes it works. A lot of the time it doesn't. This is life friends. It is fragile. It is full of fearful challenges. It drives us to our knees. It lifts us to the heavens. It is neither one nor the other. In the words of David Sheff to his son, "It is everything."

The impact of our wounds is not static. It's doesn't begin and end with the event itself, any more than the rain that soaks the ground stops having an effect when the surface dries out. No, the rain water which has seeped into the ground, well below the surface, changes the soil and hydrates the roots of everything buried in it. The rain is an amazingly powerful influence that changes everything it touches. Too much will erode the earth, cause mudslides and decimate the landscape with floods. And that's just water.

Our wounds have profound effects. Everything that touches me changes me, not only in the moment, but over time, in ways that are often unseen but very real. The impact of our wounds has a life cycle. No matter how practiced we become at containing and controlling the chaos that has ruptured us, it's an effort that will become exhausted. It's not that our wounds are more powerful than we are. It's that the story of the wound has more chapters than we are ready to read. Inevitably the effect of the wound resists being tamed, because the wound is wild. And wildness means we will be taken to places and dimensions we do not want to go and did not know existed, beyond the borders of safety. This is why, in the face of how truly awesome life is, no one of us ought to risk the self-delusion that we could never say, or do, or believe things that we find abhorrent and repulsive in others. The range of depravity recorded in humanity's story has been lived out by people whose adoring parents bent over their baby's cribs anticipating a storybook life where everyone lives happily ever after.

No, when we sustain a wound that pits us in a contest between life and death, or let's just say, the daily garden variety choices between good and evil, layers of practiced behavior build up. Not all, but many people reach a threshold of effort that leaves them exhausted, and sometimes outraged by the seemingly endless pain. Though it may not be experienced as an ultimate catastrophe, the impact of what has wounded us will eventually contribute to some kind of meltdown. Often this is intensified by an amazing array of coping strategies we have put into place in order to soothe ourselves from the pain of the original wound. Though quite unintended, a lot of the choices we make to compensate for the things which have hurt us turn out to provide only temporary relief from the minor (and major) aches and pains of life, and actually compound our problems. The name calling, bullying, incest, neglect, malnourishment, withholding of affection, and violence that cut us to the quick in places no one else ever saw, triggered the need for some kind of healing salve. Desperate to ease the pain we sometimes latch on to remedies that are about as effective as a topical spray. Not only do they not really cure what ails us. It's worse. They actually introduce a whole new cycle of self-wounding.

I've watched people live this way for years. It's tragic. But there may be some good news too. Because despite the depths to which anyone of us can sink, there's only so much trauma a person can sustain. The cumulative effect of the wounds we bear can bring us to the brink of ultimate despair. For many, this is the threshold that needs to be crossed in order for the release to finally come. Like my son's tremoring body, wracked with the violence of a primal scream, so it seems, many people find themselves on a dangerous precipice. One wrong step and they would tumble into oblivion. And yet, standing on the threshold between life and death may be the only place they can be in order to fall into life again.

Whether it's a dangerously high and crumbling peak or the proverbial rock bottom, having arrived at a place in life where you are out of options is not necessarily the end, but the beginning. A place where something new, something more real than the chaos which has substituted for real life, can be received. Ever watch someone grow old? You ought to since this is the continuum, we are all marching. No matter how a person gets there, and whether they accept it or not, the loss of ability is as reliable as the sun's rising every day. As the muscle power fades, the mind slows, and the sight dims, I have seen some who, quiet counterintuitively, have let their losses happen without a fuss. It's as if they have some kind of instinctive knowing that fighting to hold on is futile when the course of life leads to death. But those who do this don't seem to fear it. They welcome it as the ultimate meltdown, the final and compete release into a realm, a state of being, that they— and we all—are inexorably drawn to and intended for.

Having nowhere to run, nowhere to hide, all out of love, is not a dead end. It's a bridge to something new. For many it's a bridge to a Genius life. The pain may not subside, but the wound has become a device for transformation totally unexpected. To this day I still marvel at the man who told me over and over again, "I thank God for my cancer." After years of railing against it and it not going away, he came to see everything differently. I don't know why something so foul could become so cherished. But it did. "I'm a changed man because of it." Is there a window in your wound that is waiting to be looked through?

The Genius in our wound often lives near a meltdown. Yes, we need safety, yes, we need a bank account of relationships we tap into (how's your bank account of relationships), and yes, the meltdown often involves the storm of tears, mental instability, red faced anger and hopelessness. But a Genius is often born and breathes because of such storms. In the pages ahead you will see pictures of brokenness that resulted in tears that cried tears. Look as closely as you can, and as you dare, to see and sense the pathos in their journeys. You might find yourself feeling the edges of your own.

Chapter 4: The Character of Genius

The word genius conjures up a host of impressions about extraordinary ability and intelligence as we've already seen. I don't want you to be confused about what I mean when I use this term, so let's take a look at two other words that are closely associated with genius.

Prodigy

A prodigy is a child who demonstrates the uncanny ability to do things that nearly all children cannot, and which, if ever accomplished, are only done by adults, and that only after much training and experience. Wolfgang Amadeus Mozart (1756-1791) is the most famous of all child prodigies. When he was only four years old, he was already expert at playing the harpsichord. He grew to the ripe old age of 5 before he began composing music!

One striking example of his amazing musical ability occurred when he was fourteen. Visiting the Vatican in Rome during Holy Week in 1770 with his father, young Wolfgang heard a treasured choral setting of Psalm 50 entitled Misère. Only three authorized copies of the score were in existence at the time, and it was forbidden to be performed anywhere outside the Vatican. Unable to sleep the night he heard the piece, Mozart amused himself by writing the score of what he heard from memory. Incredibly, he was able to reconstruct the piece which was written not for one, but two choirs—one with five parts, and the other with four, culminating in a dramatic counterpoint with nine different parts! Later on, this display of prodigious genius infuriated the much older Austrian court composer Antonio Salieri, whom Mozart eclipsed as Vienna's most celebrated musician. Mozart is the quintessential example of a prodigy. We call him a musical genius.

Savant

Then there's the savant. A savant is someone with extraordinary, superhuman, computer-like ability that comes from a defect in the brain already in place at the time of birth or from serious trauma to the brain sustained later in life. Regardless of how the impairment is acquired it seems to unlock genius-like knowledge. In fact, the stunning characteristic of a savant is the extent of the profound functional inability, for instance, in speech, motor coordination, vision or social skills, while at the same time, possessing knowledge and information the source of which cannot be explained. The term derives from the

French word savoir which means knowing. The first case of savant appeared in German scientific literature 200 years ago. In an 1887 lecture Dr. J Langdon Down reported 10 cases of savant syndrome including one boy who had memorized The Rise and Fall of the Roman Empire, a six-volume work spanning the years 98 to 1590. The boy could recite the work verbatim, from memory—backward and forward!

For many people, the most immediately recognizable savant is The Rain Man depiction of Kim Peek by actor Dustin Hoffman in the 1998 movie. Kim's brain damage at birth was so severe that his childhood doctor instructed Kim's father to institutionalize the boy and simply forget about him. But he didn't. Kim is still alive. His disabilities are so severe he cannot button his own shirt and scores well below average on a general IQ test. Despite this Kim has read 12,000 books and remembers everything about them. He reads two pages at the same time, one page with his left eye and the other, simultaneously with his right eye. He has encyclopedic knowledge of fifteen different disciplines including history, geography and sports. He can instantly tell you the date on a calendar simply by knowing the day of the week and does complex mathematical calculations just as quickly.

There's no doubt that the prodigy and the savant demonstrate genius qualities. I wanted to put these two categories in front of you before talking further about genius so that you would not conclude that I am claiming that there is a prodigy or savant that emanates from all of our wounds. I'm using the term genius in a slightly different sense.

Genius

In ancient Rome it was believed that every person was born with a spirit that provided knowledge and moral guidance for life. The word genius comes from the root gene meaning "to give birth, beget, begin, generate". The spirit of a person is there from birth. Later on, in human history the word genius came to mean the inherent, unique talents and character traits of a person who was spoken of as having a particular genius, a natural endowment–their natural endowment– which gave one person the ability to do one set of things, and the next person different abilities. So, it was said that a person had a particular genius.

As the idea of spirits began to fade away the unique gifts of each person were understood as their personal traits. By the mid-1600s the term genius took on the meaning of enhanced mental ability. Today most people understand the term this way. We all know what we mean when we say that Einstein was a genius, someone with exalted or superior mental ability compared to ordinary levels of intelligence. But

Einstein was simply using what he was born with–and what he cultivated.

What links all three terms – prodigy, savant and genius – is this sense that there are extraordinary abilities which include knowledge, perception, and talent that inexplicably flow out of a person. So, when I speak about Genius, I am trying to put my finger on a rare, extra ordinary characteristic that seems to be latent in everyone, but which is not always known to us because it has not been expressed–yet. That's what makes it rare. Even those who have explored neuropsychology, brain structure and chemistry cannot fully explain how it is that these superhuman abilities are unleashed in certain people and not others. Still, I'm drawn to the idea that it's possible we all have undiscovered and unleashed Genius insight, ability, power and knowledge.

Dr. Darold A. Treffert is a psychiatrist and leading researcher of the savant syndrome. He has written and lectured extensively on this subject. One insight he has about how the brain works in a savant is intriguing. He suggests that there is a dormant capacity in the parts of the brain, not damaged at birth or at the time of a head trauma, that actually transfer knowledge and skills. So, while one part of the brain which controls motor function is defective, other parts of the brain are recruited to carry genetic memory through a process of the brain rewiring itself. And from that process there is a release of knowledge, ability and skill that literally baffles us. Is this how computational genius can flow from the mind of someone who can't figure out how to button his own shirt?

Treffert says this is a plausible explanation for the genius savant because there are many who are so severely impaired and yet know things they never learned, things they never studied or were exposed to. He says there's only one way this can happen–if the knowledge, ability, and skill were factory installed at the first moment of a human egg's fertilization. Friends, I'm no scientist, but from what I have seen among so many who have been psychologically, physically, and emotionally wounded, it's precisely as if the factory installed genius characteristics latent in us are somehow unleashed as a consequence of the very real traumas we have experienced.

I'm convinced there is a Genius superpower in our wounds. In the deepest, darkest parts of our hurting soul, the most unusual powers exist. There is something we instinctively know, something that we instinctively have the capacity to do. As I have researched the real-life case studies you are about to read, I have discovered at least five observable behaviors, expressions and liabilities related to Genius which emanates from the wound.

Genius is unleashed when a spiritual space is created by a wound

Though usually small at first, a spiritual space often grows incrementally larger over time. But such a space can also seem to appear overnight like some bamboo plants that grow 35 inches in a day.

Conscious awareness of a spiritual dimension appears to be absent in many people. But I've observed that when something happens—and most often that something is deemed not good— the person is moved, even forced into an entirely new frame of reference. Without the familiar hand rails of life to hold onto, a spiritual space—perhaps it's more of an awareness—appears. Where before something happened life made sense, afterward its order and predictability seems to have disappeared. But the something that is not good becomes the harbinger of something completely new, never seen or experienced before, something that opens a person to an entirely new dimension of existence and experience that changes your perception of yourself and the world. We began to explore this in the previous chapter.

Have you ever seen those grainy, black and white video cam recordings of a car crashing into a convenience store with people, cigarettes and lottery tickets flying everywhere? The sudden and unexpected disruption of everything we expect to see—patrons entering the store, walking to the cooler to retrieve a jug of milk or can of beer, stepping to the counter to pay for what they expected to find in the store—is an apt metaphor to demonstrate the effects of the wounds that pierce the assumed predictability of our lives. How and why a five-thousand-pound car came crashing through a concrete, steel and glass storefront cannot be answered from the vantage point of the camera. Nor can any explanation return the scene to life as it was before the crash.

When something bad happens, something that breaks through the structure of our ordered life, it not only feels like the chaos captured by the video cam; it is chaos. Chaos wounds us by penetrating our experience of well-being. Trying to find the answers to how and why chaos happened in the immediacy of the event is impossible. But insight about life after chaos can be found, in a dimension I am calling a spiritual space.

Let's go back to the video recording of the car crashing into the convenience store—a place that cars are not expected or supposed to be. Even though chaos has been triggered, inflicting all kinds of loss, property damage, bodily injury, perhaps permanent disability or even death, it's not as if the laws of the universe have been broken. No, the laws of physics, gravity, and biology have remained fully intact. But objects with their own inherent structural integrity have collided, being forced into the same space at the same time. In the moment when these objects meet all of them are transformed. They can't avoid transformation because they cannot occupy the same space at the same time. Thus, the wreckage, and sometimes carnage.

Now imagine that you are working the graveyard shift behind the counter at this store. You punched in at 10 pm intending to put in your eight hours, serving a few customers, stocking the fridge and maybe catching up on your social media posts. The statistical likelihood that you'll spend your evening the way you imagine is quite high. And in fact, your graveyard shift unfolds as you had imagined. You greet the morning crew as they come in the next day, and you clock out. For the past eight hours your life experience demonstrates the order and predictability that you live by. You conclude life is good. Things are working the way they should.

But now imagine another scenario. The next time you punch in at 10pm, intending to put in a typical eight hours. But at precisely 1:27am you look up from the counter because you hear the unmistakable squeal of tires outside. Less than a second later, your brain whirs into faster processing of the multiple sensory stimuli clamoring for attention. A twinkling blast of light explodes in front of you, glass flying in all directions, your body is suddenly heavy and buckled from the ramming force of what you think is a car but can't be sure because your brain reminds you cars and stores don't occupy the same space. In the same instant you feel heat, smell gasoline and smoke. Your eyes tear up from a stinging sensation. Looking upward from your position on your back, you can just make out a twirling florescent light fixture floating overhead. Then, nothing.

You wake up to searing pain throughout your body. Your head is throbbing as if it would explode. You're moving. There are indistinct voices spewing insistent commands. You can hear your breath loud in your head. Then, nothing.

When you awaken again it feels like you have fallen from the sky as the earth has rushed up to catch you. Your fingertips feel texture; your eyes open and you see a hill of white, inches from your face, a blanket. Your ears detect a beeping tone that tenses your body in fear. Where am I? What's happening? I didn't clock out. The store? What? Oh, my back, I can't lift myself. You close your eyes and sigh. Your ribs and chest torture your muscles. I was hit. Oh my God, I was hit!

Days of confusion blend together as images of people come into your mind but everything you see, and think is out of focus. You're not sure if you are dreaming or seeing. A few weeks into your hospitalization you regain full consciousness and learn the details of the last night you showed up for work. A 1978 Pontiac Trans Am driven by a 19-year-old kid, high on meth, careened out of control, bounded over the curb, banked off the gas pump and flew through the front of your store. When it came to rest you were pinned under the engine block, up against a wall. Your spine has been severed. Two surgeries to restore the function of your legs have not produced the results hoped for. You have been recommended for further recuperation and rehabilitation. It is doubtful you will walk without assistance. You have been transformed.

You conclude life is a damn crapshoot. Nothing is working as it should. What the hell am I going to do now? Whether thought or voiced, that is the question our soul screams when anything violates the foundations that support being alive. What the hell am I going to do now is akin to How do I get out of this? Why did this happen to me? Where did my life go? These questions may not seem to be particularly spiritual to you, but they are. They go to the heart of our identity and what our existence means as a result of everything having gone to hell. Isn't it amazing that when life is intact, when our bodies, and families and routines are working the way we want them to we almost never allow space for considering the big questions of life. But let something like death, divorce, a car accident, incurable disease, physical assault, sexual violation or a bankruptcy happen, and we suddenly tumble out of control, terrified and fearful.

The chaotic effect of the wounds we sustain is so great that the assumed order of life has collapsed, and we are in free fall. An almost universal response to this autonomic reflex is to grab hold of something, anything that can save us from the terror of our own annihilation—not simply physical death itself, but the disappearance of everything that gave meaning to our life.

What is alarming about this reflex is how quickly it activates even when things happen that are not a fundamental threat to our existence. Watching a near miss car crash from a distance can trigger in me the same feeling of terror as if I was the person in the car. Being late for an important appointment can upset me as if my life will be ruined. When I find out that one of my children is struggling with an important life challenge there's a part of me that becomes them. We are all that precariously close to being in free fall because life is always at risk. Even though the things that trigger awareness of your vulnerability may be different from the things that trigger mine, all of us know what it means to be wounded. All of us have an internal radar working in the background that keeps us informed about the potential for disaster. But of course, it's not foolproof and only sometimes keeps us from to get out of the way of the oncoming assault.

Admitting that we are this close to life suddenly having no meaning when bad things happen is the beginning of seeing more deeply into the nature of our own Being, why we exist and the depth of value there is in human life. In my personal experience I have stumbled upon a deepened spiritual capacity. I think you'll detect that too in the lives and stories you are about to read. I hope you will let life's inevitable crises take you deeper into your own spiritual space-a place where you see, hear, feel, understand or know something you hadn't before. I believe it is in this space that Genius can be discovered and released. You can't make it happen, but you can allow it to happen.

Genius superpowers are often thrown away

When we detect something wrong, something uncomfortable, something out of kilter, many of us want to rid ourselves of it. If the board is rotten, let's throw the whole damn thing into the fire and be done with it. If the superpower of Genius stimulates or sustains the pain of a wound why wouldn't you throw it away? Many do and stay chained to the power of the wound rather than use the power of the genius which has the capacity to transform how a person continues to enter into life.

John Walsh's son Adam was murdered in 1981. At the time of Adam's murder Walsh was an executive at Paradise Island Hotel and Casino in the Bahamas. When Adam was 6 years old, he was abducted at a Sears department store across the street from the Hollywood, California police station. Adam was alone in the toy department at a video game console. Sixteen days later his severed head was found in a drainage canal 120 miles away, the rest of him was never recovered.

Can you for a second imagine the anguish of this dear family, John and his wife Revé? They sustained a wound that will always be there. Their Paradise turned into an ever-living hell. Tears, guilt, and sleepless years followed. What good could come out of this? A Genius good, a superpower good.

The Walsh family founded the Adam Walsh Child Resource Center, a nonprofit organization dedicated to legislative reform to help improve the ability of law enforcement to find and save missing children. The Missing Children Act of 1982 was passed. Many malls, supermarkets and retailers have adopted what is known as code Adam, and first implemented by Walmart. But what John Walsh is best known for is his unrelenting new superpower in the TV show Americas Most Wanted. Beginning in 1988 it ran for 25 seasons and contributed to the capture of more than 1000 dangerous fugitives from the law. It took 27 years for Adam's killer to be found and named, but he was.

John and Revé experienced the unlocking of a genius superpower in their wound. They could have simply ignored the impulse that drove them to get answers to the most god-awful questions any parent could experience and let the wound created by the abduction of their son destroy them. But they didn't. I've witnessed so many people over the years who have been struck by all kinds of unimaginable tragedy. The vast majority of them focus on the suffering they've endured from their wound. It's quite natural and completely understandable. But when we focus solely on the hurt of the wound, life stops at that point. For most it didn't come to a physical end in death. But they did die emotionally and psychologically. Only a few people pushed through to continue to live, rather than just survive. Not that their wounds cease afflicting them, but they don't remain fixed only on what happened. The difference between those who evidence the eruption of genius from their experience and those who don't seems to me to come from the belief that because the wound has occurred the possibilities of life are effectively over. But there's another side to our wounds. And so, the genius that could be unlocked from the tragedy stays locked inside, unknown and undiscovered, effectively thrown away.

Geniuses frequently don't benefit from their own gift

They bestow the utility of the newly released superpower upon others, relating to them in amazingly caring, uplifting, and life-changing ways. An energy is released from the heated furnace of the heart that expresses itself outwardly. The wounded genius struggles with conflicting internal tensions. A superpower is birthed out of suffering, touching other people's lives. Instead of recycling the drama of the original wound, the genius seems to recreate itself in expressions of insight, knowledge and care that opens up blocked development in others, inspiring innovation.

I met Greta at a tattoo convention in Pittsburgh. She's an expert inker. I watched her from a distance but inched closer over the course of four hours of observing. She welcomed her tattoo clients with ease, like an Airbnb super host. Her smile was kind and ready. She would ask odd questions. Why are you here? What do you feel? Who do you think about? Do you want me to write what I hear?

The tattoo client seemed to me to morph into a patient on a psychologist's couch. And Greta became a trusted therapist who had the ways and entree of an uncle, aunt or grandparent. Greta's way of tattooing, how she engages her clients, is inspired by the characteristics of a genius superpower that I suspect she has little conscious awareness of. As they considered the options Greta laid out for them, her clients almost always chose option c, "Write what you hear Greta, and I'll wear it for the next 60 years." She had a line of people waiting for her ministrations; many had traveled over six hours to get her ink on their skin.

After watching her and discerning what she was doing, I approached her directly, "Excuse me, I'm researching tattoos for a book I'm writing. May I ask you questions while you work?" For some reason both Greta and the girl getting a whole sleeve of tattoos agreed. "I've been watching you." Not taking her eyes off her work she replied, "That's a little creepy "Mr.?"

"You can call me Al." Greta was more curious than put off. She asked what I observed. "You can hear what people say; you hear and imagine. They trust you to know what to put on their skin. You seem to hear something even your clients don't know they're saying."

Greta spoke "So?"

The young women getting the ink broke in, "Greta is an empath. She hears what we feel, what we can't put into words—she imagines colors, designs and abstract pictures."

There was a line of ten people listening in on the conversation and several chimed in. One man said, "If Greta hears it, that's the right thing to put on my skin." All the others nodded their agreement.

Not taking her trained eye off what she as doing, Greta leaned in with intensity as she continued her masterful interpretation of the young girl's life at the tip of the tattoo needle, and blurted out with pinpoint intensity, "Then why Mr. Al, am I such a goddamn, F---ing, messed up, emotional basket case?"

I stood quiet. I didn't feel any obligation to answer. I've come to appreciate that such moments are filled with insight that might be stunted if I say anything. This awkward moment didn't disappoint.

The young woman whose life story was unfolding on her arm broke the silence with this piercing insight, "Greta you hear so many voices... ours, yours, other times, and past generations like my grandmother's voice. You can't distinguish your own thoughts from others. You're an empath; you can't fix yourself." Nothing more was said.

I stayed silent, watching for the next thirty minutes. So, did everyone else. The only thing moving was Greta's ink gun. When the tattoo was complete, the young girl looked at it, turned to Greta and said, "It's perfect as usual. Thank you so much." She had been inked by Greta various times over the past ten years. Greta reloaded her ink as she got ready for the next patient-client. Without looking at me Greta spoke once more. "You happy now Mr. Al?"

"Yep, thanks Greta." She nodded, letting her hair fall, covering one eye. I could see she was crying as she bent down to lean into her next client's soul.

Genius superpowers are often mocked by their owner and others

Genius doesn't easily fit in the normal spaces of life. Think of a piece of furniture that is too big for the room. We spend all our time walking around it rather than using it's simple utility and pleasure. If a large man shoehorns himself into an economy airplane seat, we try not to look. Bet that's not comfortable... wouldn't want to be him, we think to ourselves.

Robert Pershing Wallow was born on February 22, 1918 and on his way to a normal middle-class life, just like his family. When he entered kindergarten, Robert was the size and weight of a 15-year-old boy. By the time he was 8 years old he had outgrown his father by an inch; Robert was now six feet and 169 pounds. In elementary school he couldn't fit behind the desk. Eventually he reached the astounding height of 8 feet, 11 inches. An abnormally high rate of HGH human growth hormone propelled Robert's extraordinary size. Though he died at age 22 there was no sign that his body would have stopped growing. This 9-foot giant wore a size 37AA shoe and larger ones were on order at the time of his death. He toured with the Ringling Brothers Circus in 1936. The international Shoe Company made him their trademark traveling spokesman. Despite this fame his ears would still turn red whenever he felt embarrassed. Sometimes people who couldn't believe that Robert was a great giant would actually get close enough to kick his shins certain that he'd fall off the stilts they were sure he must have been standing on.

Robert never took on the identity of freak that most people attached to him. He reasoned that his unusual size gave him the opportunity to be employed in advertising. When the circus asked him to wear tails and a top hat, which would have accentuated his pronounced body size, he refused.

Robert was a quiet, respectful, educated man who came to be known as the Gentle Giant.

Genius superpowers don't easily live in normal spaces, so their owners often hide their awkward characteristics. As you read the stories in the chapters ahead notice how these wounded geniuses have trouble identifying, admitting and living with their unusual characteristics.

A Genius can lift two thousand pounds with just a finger

We call some powers super because they dramatically surpass ordinary, natural abilities. That's what makes them super. They are able to accomplish what most of us can only dream about. And some even break the boundaries of all dreams. Superpowers accomplish something spectacular.

The famous Taj Mahal, literally the Crown of the Palaces, is a tombstone of sorts. Commissioned in 1632 by the Mughal emperor, Shah Jahan, it was built in memory of his wife Mumtaz Mahal. It sits on a 42-acre complex that in today's money would cost about a billion dollars. The construction included 20 thousand artisans. Nobel Laureate Rabindranath Tagore described the Taj as the tear-drop on the cheek of time. In 2007 it was voted one of the New Seven Wonders of the World and attracts eight million visitors a year.

Where did the drive and persistence come to create such an oversized, time-tested monument? It came from the Shah's grief over his wife Mumtaz's death. The Persian Princess died giving birth to the couple's 14th child.

The superpower in the Shah's wound raged until it erupted in the inspired monument we know today. Beginning in 1631 the Shah spent the next 13 years supervising the construction of this genius structure. A vast army of people were employed do their life's work that was birthed out of the heart of a love story cut short.

Designs for the Taj Mahal were inspired by other tombs and buildings. A vast intellectual energy was released at the place of a broken heart. In its time, the Taj was a ground-breaking architectural feat that students have studied ever since. The central dome is 115 feet high surrounded by minarets that soar to 130 feet.

Wounds have Genius hidden in them. Some wounds destroy life. Other wounds ignite an effort that cannot be explained in mere human terms. You and I live in the same skin, mind, soul and devastating stories of loss like the one that drove the Shah. The grief of lost love unleashed the creation of a world wonder of enormous magnitude. We simply stand in awe and amazement. Love is life. Loss of love does not always end in death. Sometimes it ignites genius. And when it does, monumental feats are accomplished with breathtaking simplicity, as if they were meant to be.

Does the physical world answer the questions of your soul? If so, that's fine... you will find dignity and welcome in this book and from this author. If you're wondering, leaning or even now falling into the exploration of a spiritual space, I wish you safe, though not unscathed travels to you friend. Those of us who go only so far as we feel safe often hold at arm's length a depth and quality of life we could know. Like the bold and adventurous children in C.S. Lewis's Chronicles of Narnia I invite you to push through the ordinary routines which have been carefully sorted and stored. Allow them to become as the fearless children did, the start of an adventure which will likely scratch your face and arms as you brave through the darkened woods just beyond the boundary of your safe life.

Warning

Most summers, my wife and I took our two children to camp grounds all over the country. Four people and a dog in a towed camper over lots of roads to explore new adventures. One of our favorite destinations was Acadia National Park in Maine. There you can hike the glorious Cadillac Mountain and, between October and March, witness the "nation's first Sunrise." It is a wondrous place, the jagged terrain, the wind carrying the scent of the salty sea, and the clear cold water that invites a fast swim. Snorkeling to see the brilliant rocks was worth the time, money, and freezing skin.

The park tumbles down from Cadillac's 1530-foot peak to the ancient granite rocks of Maine's famed coastline. The views are spectacular. One spot in particular is the place to witness the most indescribable power of the sea. Thunder Hole is an inlet formed by a break in the rocks. Rising up from the sea's floor is a smooth shelf of rock that suddenly collides with a craggy rock face which has been split by the ravages of time and the power of the ocean. That split quickly narrows into the shape of a sharp knife. When the sea slams into the shore there, it makes the deafening sound of soul-shaking thunder. Its power is mesmerizing. There's a sign on the pathway that reads, "WARNING, THREAT OF DEATH!"

In August 2009 as many as 10,000 tourists had gathered along Arcadia's shore. They'd come from all over the country to see the 16-foot storm surge created by Hurricane Bill which had passed 350 miles off the coast of New England, eventually making landfall as a category 2 storm all the way up into Newfoundland, Canada. It was a beautiful, sunny, late-summer day. Though some of the more adventurous sightseers were perched high enough for the normal volume of surf to crash and launch its spray on them, sometimes as high as 40 feet, there was a monster wave that suddenly hit the hole like a locomotive. As the onlookers scurried to retreat to higher ground, a second more ferocious swell, fueled by the distant hurricane's fury, smashed against the rocks where a group of about 30 spectators were doused from head to foot. When the wave receded, it swept seven people into the sea with it, ripped from where they stood just seconds before. Unbelievably, four of them clawed their way back to shore, but three were lost in the foaming deep.

A mother badly beaten to the ground by the wave cried out. Her husband and daughter were gone. Rescuers arrived; super-human efforts recovered two men near fatal exhaustion. After hours of desperate searching, the lifeless body of seven-year-old Clio was retrieved from the sea.

Sadly, the same story has played out at Thunder Hole from the earliest times. The raw power and beauty of the place calls the visitor to play on the edge of disaster. How many people have stood on that spot and said, "I don't see any waves, do you?" Like moths to a flame, the attraction to the wonder is too great to stay away.

So, let me advise you now. Beware, the decision to read on is a venture into a kind of Thunder Hole. You will witness rogue waves that crashed over good souls just trying to find their way in this world. You'll have to take care where to plant your feet, stepping watchfully around the wounds exposed by these brave storytellers. And beware too of the sometimes-hidden dark side of their wounds. But do press on to see and behold the awesome beauty of the hidden Genius which is sometimes revealed when the monster swells recede.

Words of warning are not always designed to drive you away. On the outside chance that these opening chapters have left you with the impression that by analyzing the phenomena of a Genius in the wound I will be protecting you from the grizzly, raw drama of life, take heed. It would be irresponsible of me not to advise you that what you are about to read may be difficult to take in. After all, life is messy. And that's the problem for us all, isn't it? When chaos erupts, we instinctively want to confine it, control it, subdue and eradicate it-or RUN from it. But chaos

invariably rears its ugly head, defying all our efforts. I suspect it is the case that the monstrous threats we encounter are there to lead us beyond a fixation with them toward something we are destined to discover but might not, without them. No, this book is not about trying to make the chaos of life more fit for our consumption by somehow minimizing its significance, or, as I said before, trying to tame it. Nor, is this some cheap, sordid attempt to capitalize on the trials of others by sensationalizing their stories. In fact, I stand in awe of those who have made this book what it is by disclosing the most inexplicable parts of their lives. Without their willingness to tell their stories you'd simply have my poor, second-hand efforts at trying to describe a country I heard about once upon a time, but which neither you or I had actually been to.

No, my words of warning are not intended to leave you standing outside, peering over the fence, for fear of trespassing. Rather, I want to advise you to be a cautious visitor into the places where each storyteller takes you. Make no mistake about my intent. I sincerely extend an honest invitation to you to come and see the fragile beauty and dangerous mystery exposed in the pages that follow. Just know that entering into these places might ignite awareness and even insight into your life. It's possible that you will hear your own story well up along the way. And that is always a precarious trek at best. Be careful, but do not shrink back. Life is fraught with danger and opportunity, wounds and Genius discoveries that change the journey by revealing more contour than we saw at first. Robert Frost famously wrote, "two roads diverged in a yellow wood. I chose the one less traveled by, and that has made all the difference." We do not know what he witnessed on that road but impact him it did. I challenge you to take the road less travelled. There are always new things to behold.

So, if you're willing, join me as we watch what is happening to these life-travelers who went down to the water's edges and stood at their Thunder Hole. Some have been hit by rogue waves, some swept out to sea, nearly perishing. It is not their sheer survival alone that inspires me, but how they have been changed that is the real spectacle worth gawking at. And not as if we're watching a house burn down. No, it's more like Moses watching the burning bush that was not consumed. Impossible you say? Trust me, it's possible. Every one of these people have stood on the threshold between the ordinary suffering and struggles of life—none of their details will surprise you, though you may be shocked—and an extraordinary transformation into a quality of life few of us ever consciously perceive. I hope you'll ask yourself Is there a Genius in my wound? Ready? Let's go.

Chapter 5: The Tell-Tale Heart

American author Edgar Allen Poe, who wrote The Fall of the house of Usher, The Raven, and The Tell-Tale Heart, is often credited with being the father of the modern-day murder mystery. His short stories captured the imagination and captivated audiences with their tension and mystery. The Tell-Tale Heart, for example, which was written in 1843, is narrated by an anonymous character who tries to convince the reader of his mental stability while at the same time planning–and committing–a murder. The victim was an old man with what Poe called an "evil," "eye of a vulture." Though he confesses that he likes— actually loves—the old man, something about his piercing eye incites a blood chilling terror that he could only avoid by killing the old man. His deed is so carefully, meticulously planned. Once the fateful hour arrives in the dead of night, the murderer hides his gruesome, yet strangely satisfying act, by dismembering the dead body and hiding it in the floor boards of his own home where the old man lived with his killer. Having received word of a suspicious shriek in the night, the police show up to conduct an inquiry. All is going well—the murderous conscience gloats in "the wild audacity" of its "perfect triumph." Gloats until the irrepressible sound of a beating heart begins to thump ever so loudly that it cannot be silenced. So deafeningly loud, he is sure the police can hear it, so loud that the man leaps to his feet and confesses his crime.

We are left to imagine the police watching as he lifts the floor boards and reveals the evidence of his dark deed. Instead of finding "that which is of God" in his wound and discovering a genius that works for good, the narrator committed a crime conceived out of a madness he cannot admit, but whose characteristics he expertly describes. The story of the Tell-Tale Heart describes the anguish of a wounded soul that creates a deformed frame of mind which then tries to resolve the soul's suffering but succeeds only in making the suffering worse.

Joanna has experienced so much in her life, yet she still musters the courage to meet each new day to try, again, and again, to make things right out of so much that was so wrong. Listen carefully. Perhaps you will hear the persistent beating of the tell-tale heart as Joanna makes the journey from her unspeakable pain into the spotlight, she now commands.

Joanna's mother was mentally tormented. She witnessed this struggle for sanity which seemed always to be slipping from her, like sand disappearing between fingers no matter how tightly squeezed. This profound drama might have easily ignited the wrath of her daughter to leave home, never to return, and never to love again. Untold events that flowed from the tortured relationship between mother and daughter might have led Joanna to harm her mother. But Joanna's wound, instead of turning gangrenous and violent, sings its story and brings her from darkness into more light. Joanna's tell-tale heart beats in the lyrics of her songs. She is a soul and blues singer.

Her beautiful voice could have easily been silenced by the choking chaos of life with mother, but instead she sings of pain, of struggle, and of her "baby coming back one day." But I'll let her tell the story.

I was born in Chicago, in 1965, into a family where only three of my eight siblings shared the same father. I'm the youngest of nine, much younger than my siblings who had all reached legal age by the time I was born. Since most of them were already out of the house, it was pretty much my mom and me alone together.

My mom was no joke. She raised nine kids in the projects on welfare, with the occasional side job cleaning toilets or watching an elderly neighbor for cash. She was also an alcoholic; not a sit-at-home, drink on the couch all day alcoholic. She was a hell-raising, humbugging, angry, and often promiscuous alcoholic. Her drinking left a huge imprint on my life and opened the door to what would become my escape, maybe even my salvation—soul and blues music.

Growing up poor in Chicago was cool. I didn't realize what we didn't have until so called "kind" people would point it out—like a well-off relative for instance. When times were good, I remember BBQs, snow, great music when I visited my favorite Aunt, and cheerleading practice after school. Hanging with my cheer-buddies was my escape from home. Mom was either sleeping off a binge, or drinking herself into another, either alone or with some drinking buddies she dragged in from the bar.

As I got older, my patience for my passed-out mom wore incredibly thin. Pulling her off the toilet so I could get ready for school or waking her from a snoring rage on the couch in order to get bus fare were routine.

Don't get me wrong. I loved Mom with all my heart. When she was sober, she was the sweetest, most generous person I knew. But when she drank, she was a vicious hell-raiser and would find a reason to curse anyone out—the mailman, my teachers–it didn't matter. I dreaded those days when she'd find her way to my school, raging up and down the halls, telling everyone I was her baby.

I used to hide in the bathroom or leave the building if I could. The teasing and whispers were too much to bear. I dealt with this all through elementary and high school. But it all came to a head when she started physically and verbally attacking me. One time she put me and the dog out–yep, locked us both out of the house for hours until a neighbor convinced her to let us in.

Our last fight resulted in me having stitches in my head. Mom had been drinking heavily. I must have irritated her or something, and she hurled an iron at me. I tried to dodge, but it crashed into my head. At first, I thought I was okay–then I started bleeding. There was so much blood and it mixed with my tears; my heart was broken. How could my own mother hurt me like this?

The neighbors cursed her–again–and took me to the hospital where my head was sewn up. My older brother got word of what happened. He made a deal with my older sister who lived in Atlanta. Before I knew it, I was on a plane headed to my sister's with just the bloody clothes on my back. She became my legal guardian and so began my life in the South.

Georgia Peach

I thought I was fancy! My sister was awesome! She not only was kind and loving, but she encouraged my creative side. My mom used to say all my poems were so sad. Duh, I wonder why.

Agony of a Black Girl

Agony of a black girl living in pain
Every day to come is filled with shame

Screaming and crying out the Lord's name
That's the agony of a black girl
living in pain

I wrote this in high school. When Mom found it, she cried, said my poems were dark. It was discouraging, but little did either of us know, I was on a path. I'd stumbled on a way I could tell what was deep, so deep inside. It didn't stop the pain, but it did give me a way to say it that somehow soothed my soul.

With the support and encouragement of my sister, I began to pursue dance, music, and pretty much anything that allowed me to be me. She picked up where Mom left off. Back home, when my mom had good days, and could afford it, she would enroll me in gymnastics, swim, and modeling at the local YWCA. Most times though, when there was no money, the modeling teacher would let me hang out in her class if I helped her clean afterwards. So now, with the consistency, safety, and love of my sister, it was nice to pursue these passions and concentrate on just that.

Adulting

After high school, I pursued a degree in Fashion Merchandising, but I soon learned this was a mistake. During the period I was a fashionista-party-girl-extraordinaire, I started attracting the wrong type of men…or should I say my body started attracting the wrong type of men. I took to the attention like a horse to sugar. I had more friends than I could count and soon I was partying every weekend, snorting cocaine, and being out of control.

But growing up with Mom my life was almost always out of control. I couldn't continue to live what I'd tried so hard to escape. I knew I had to get my shit together. So, I joined the military; the best four years of my life. It was such a relief to leave the chaotic days behind. That decision saved my life. My travels began to quench a thirst for life that I'd discovered. New food and music from other cultures touched something deep inside that convinced me life is good. I had even healed my relationship with Mom, because I finally realized that her alcoholism was a disease. She'd been told by her doctors to stop drinking or die. She stopped and got sober. Her decision—and mine— opened the door to a better relationship right up until her death. I didn't attend her funeral, and I have no regrets for not going. I never wanted to say good-bye, and I still haven't. Maybe because there is so much we should have had and didn't. I just can't close the door on everything that was unfinished.

Mom

Two failed marriages and another disastrous relationship still gifted me with a beautiful daughter and a handsome son. They were the lights in my life and the reason I veered off my creative path. As a single mom, with shared custody, I had bills to pay and there was no time for music, writing, and creating. I was too busy climbing the corporate ladder. And my efforts didn't go unnoticed. I was a shining star.

As he was growing up, my relationship with my son was normal, good, and loving. But not so much with my daughter and her father, whom I'd left because he beat me. His abuse resulted in me having surgery to remove a subdural hematoma. Hospitalized for 45 days, I learned to walk and talk again, but I was plagued for years by horrible migraines and shaking fits. Things got better, but I cringe when I see someone get hit or even bump their head.

During my children's adolescent years, my relationship with my daughter took a horrible turn. She was 12 the first time she hit me. She didn't just smack me on the arm; it was a full-blown fist punch to the face. My reaction was immediate and visceral. My boyfriend had to pull me off her. I was stunned and confused and angry. Who did she think she was that she could raise her hand to her mother? I thought, "How dare you!" In that moment I saw my own childhood flash before my eyes, and it made me sick. As bad as it was, I thought it was a one-time incident. I was wrong. Unfortunately, her behavior only got worse. By the time she was 20 I decided that she could never live with me again because I truly feared for my life.

Throughout those horrible years that began with the first punch, my daughter went into my closet, ripped up my clothes, and lied to her friends and anyone who would listen, telling them that I was a drunk or dead. I found out that she would often tell stories of woe to elicit pity from her friends; she painted herself as a good person. She was so good her stories landed me in jail.

During the last time my daughter lived with me, I took an overnight trip, only to be contacted by my landlord that someone had reported a wild party at my home. When I called my daughter, she denied everything—and I heard nothing in the background—but it was true, and the cops were called to break it up. When I arrived home the next day, my house was trashed and reeked of booze. Someone had tossed my bedroom and stolen all my jewelry, and there was vomit in my daughter's bedroom. She had two of her friends still there, helping her clean, but it wasn't enough. I was upset, but I was calm. While talking to my daughter, she continued to mouth off to me, and her friends told her to be quiet. From that point, she was always snarly and even more disrespectful.

One evening during a phone call with her boyfriend, talking loudly, and calling me "bitch this," and "bitch that," I'd had enough. So, I slapped her! We tussled, and she wound up on top of me with her hands around my throat—smiling. I managed to get her off of me and she called the police. Before they got there, she told me I was going to jail. Her logic? Because I'd been drinking—wine—I would surely be arrested. When the police arrived, she faked crying and distress. I was arrested not because I slapped her, but because when she tried to call 911, I unplugged the phone. I did it because I thought she was calling her boyfriend back to continue disrespecting me. Not in my house, on my phone!

I was booked and released. With the help of a social worker, and friends, I sent my daughter back to Canada to live with her dad. He worked hard to turn her against me, and it worked.

I've tried to have a good relationship with my daughter. She's been in and out of mental hospitals and has continued to be physically and verbally abusive to me over the past ten years. Still I continue to show her the unconditional love that only a mother can understand. Trying to save my daughter from herself is hard work. She knows she's her own worst enemy, but she won't open up. Maybe she can't. It seems like she enjoys the daily drama she creates through her lies, betrayals, and the manipulation of the people around her. But I see her pain.

Every time she's in crisis, I put on my supermom cape and rush to her rescue. My efforts are met with a hollow thank you, an equally fake hug, and a faint smile. I never hear from her until the next crisis. My family says I need to practice saying "No!" in the mirror. I agree, but how do you say no to your child when there are no other super-heroes out there to save them from themselves? Each time, I'll say to myself, "I'm not doing this again!" And yet, time after time, I'm there picking up the pieces.

It's not natural for a child NOT to love their parent. Of course, there are times when neither likes the other very much, but NOT love your parent? This has been the hardest truth to swallow. I think to myself, "I gave you my heart in whole; you gave it back in pieces."

These days, I'm an empty-nester, so my life is filled with close friends, family, and my music. I started a band and we're pretty good. We've made leaps and bounds locally and hope to see more success with our debut album. When everything else has failed—broken and twisted connections between mother and daughter, husband and wife, and daughter, and mother again—the heartbreak and betrayal I've lived comes singing out from somewhere down deep inside. What my soul knows so well comes flowing out in a song. Maybe the reason the music has taken off so well, when other things in my life haven't, is because it's the truest, realest thing I know. Yeah, it hurts, but it'd hurt a whole lot more not to sing it. Maybe that's why people listen. Maybe I'm singing their song too and they feel at home when they hear me.

I'm still a mom and I'll never give up my supermom cape. But now, it just hangs at the back of the closet instead of being worn beneath my clothes every day. A mother's love—my love for my mother, my daughter, and myself—is a mixed bag, but the foundation is love. I long for it, and I long from not getting it, at least the way I thought and believed I should.

I know that even while fighting her demons, Mom loved me. She loved me the best her demons would allow because they did not win, they did not fully claim her. I really do think my daughter loves me too, as best she can. I was abused, I was victimized, but I don't see myself that way anymore. I'm a contented survivor with scars on a heart that keeps thumping out its irrepressible longing to receive and give love. Even with such an ugly history, I continue to find peace in the music I write and in each performance I give.

Reflections

Joanna's tormented life has not gotten the best of her. In fact, when the hot iron cracked her head open—really bad—it was then that the heart's long season of lament finally came gushing out. A soul singer was born who could sing it the way it has to be sung, because it's her life's melody.

I hate what killed so much life in her. Still, Joanna's telltale heart beat out a truth that could not be muffled—her soulful blue songs sing about her love for her mother even while suffering under the weight of Mom's wounded life. Who knows what gave birth to her deep hurts. Joanna sang the blues for her mom, for herself, and for her own future family—a family formed out of the pain that longs for love that can't seem to materialize, but which sings its unquenchable agony from one generation to the next. Blues music says, "my baby left me." Soul music says, "My baby left me but, she's comin' back one day."

I don't know what's worse, head injury or soul trauma. I wouldn't wish either one on my enemies, especially not the lifelong yearning for love that every heart craves, and the more so when it's denied. Still, unpredictably and somewhat illogically, Joanna found solace in the sounds of her own heart's cries, that claim, "despite everything, I am soulfully alive!" Not everyone reaches this threshold and those who do often retreat, and fast. But Joanna didn't. Her wound hurt so bad life had to change. And while she continues to carry unknown generations of grief and disappointment that came long before the details of her story, she's miraculously pushed through to another dimension that lets her soul sooth itself by singing what it knows. Keep wailing dear heart, keep wailing.

Joanna's epilogue

To read this back brought tears and silence. A warmth spread over me and I held my head up, knowing... accepting that I am a survivor. Thank you for allowing me to share my life.

Chapter 6: Dr. Jekyll and Mr. Hyde

Robert Louis Stevenson, a Scottish novelist, poet, essayist, musician, and travel writer, authored the famous Gothic novel The Strange Case of Dr. Jekyll and Mr. Hyde. Though written in 1886 on another continent, perhaps the reason this story has so profoundly impacted our collective conscience is because the two warring personalities of Jekyll and Hyde resonate with an internal conflict many of us live with. Everyone immediately knows that to be tagged with the epithet "Jekyll and Hyde" means that a person has two distinctly separate and opposing personalities, one good, and the other evil, and you never quite know who it is you'll meet in the one person from this moment to the next.

The story is quite fascinating. Dr. Jekyll is actually a well-respected physician who has committed secret acts in his private life that he is ashamed of in his public life. As he thinks about this contradiction in his character, he decides they must be two different entities. Or does he secretly just want to be able to live out his private life without consequence? In any case, he experiments to separate these two components of his humanity. He makes a potion that transforms his body into the "pure evil" that is in him. This evil self, Mr. Hyde, a common sort of fellow, not distinguished, can do any evil thing that he imagines with no shame that would affect Jekyll, and he does. But the supply of his potion begins to run out, and the ingredients can no longer be found. In horror, Hyde realizes he will no longer be able to change back and forth between the two persons and personalities. Knowing that he is doomed to permanently be Mr. Hyde, he realizes that his evil deeds will expose him. He will be caught and have to face the consequences of his crimes. With no hope of escaping this unforeseen and dreaded result of his experimentation, Hyde kills himself.

What would you do if you could drink a potion and transform into someone else who could not be recognized as you? What would you do if there were no consequences to your present life? This is the question posed by the novel. Who are we really? Are we living out of our true self or do we masquerade the real person because we fear being found out?

Live long enough and you'll discover there is a bit of Jekyll and Hyde in everyone. Most of us are deeply invested in having a public face that is clean and respectable in the eyes of the watching world—our Dr.

Jekyll side (the well-respected physician). For some—perhaps all—underneath the public face, lives another person who conceives of and longs to do evil but who will go to desperate lengths to conceal the person who would like—dare I say, love—to act without fear of consequence or reprisal—our Mr. Hyde underbelly. Here's how the Jekyll-Hyde dual personality dilemma lives in James.

The first James, the public James, the Dr. Jekyll James, holds things together well. He does his job well. He communicates clearly without excessive passion, but with publicly appropriate strong enthusiasm. He articulates a well-reasoned argument. This James has been honed to perfection over many years, crafted through careful trial and error. He has done very well at being in control of his faculties and presents himself exceedingly well.

The other James, the social misfit, outlaw, angry, devil—may—care—James, the Mr. Hyde James, can't hold things together that well at all. He is empathetic, caring, gentle, some would say excessively emotional, who processes life out-loud. He often becomes overwhelmed with empathy and strong emotion. When he does, he breaks down into a stream of consciousness, say-the-first-thing-that-comes-into-your-head, almost unreasonable character. This Mr. Hyde side of James came natural to him. It seems to have been effectively wired by key women in his life. Living out of this unpolished self has never been rewarded, respected or honored by his peers, and certainly not by public or professional authorities in his life. But I suspect it is in the personality of this second James, The Mr. Hyde James, that the truer, more authentic-self resides. That may sound counterintuitive. But read on. And despite the misfortune he has consistently experienced whenever he has engaged life out of this part of himself, it is as this person James has actually expressed the gifted Genius he is.

James's gift is most evident in situations that elicit empathy, concern, and compassion for others. This second James, the Mr. Hyde James who risks self-loathing alongside public derision, has the uncanny ability to interact with many different people who are hurting and in pain within the same time frame. He is able to empathize, care, and engage with them without personally imploding. Frankly his capacity and ability to stay in the tornado of others' unpredictable emotion is beyond impressive. His Genius allows him to be able to care for a lot of people and care a lot for each one. The Genius James evidences seems to have equipped him with a sort of radar that spots people who are wounded, who have been bullied, who have had their hurts minimized, or who are living in a broken shell of life, crying out for compassion and care. When James is not in his exceedingly competent Dr. Jekyll persona, he administers healing compassion and empathy that those who are suffering know is absolutely genuine.

But this Genius has a dark side as well. When James is in touch with his wounded self and sees others who cannot empathize, but who offer only cold, calculated reason, watch out! He cannot tolerate the measured, respectable, Dr. Jekyll-like types around him, who make black-and-white pronouncements about other peoples' experiences and sometimes about James' own pain. This ignites a rage within him with a force larger than life. He's like a caged raccoon, who becomes viciously defensive, verbally aggressive, turning-over-table mad! He's always hated physical violence and aggression, and nobody thinks he would go there, but when he comes at them with the passion and intensity of his fury of words, people proverbially hide in the corner by shutting down their ears and wanting him to stop speaking."

His extraordinary sensitivity to those who are weak, and suffering does not extend to those who present themselves to him intact. This second James, the Mr. Hyde James, has very little compassion for those who have very little compassion. It's ironic, really. For this quintessential caring man who can sense and respond to wounds like a bloodhound, there's a limit. He does not understand that most everyone, including those who would deny it, suffer from life's wounds. What other people experience as James's saint-like ability to bless people by seeing and receiving them as they are, is the very thing that blinds him to seeing others whose wounds may hide behind a veil of self-protection.

Perhaps an analogy from the Avenger movies and the greater Marvel universe created by the Genius Stan Lee will help. Each member of the Avengers is a superhero. They each have a superpower, a Genius. But everyone of their superpowers caused great destruction as they were learning to control them. Special devices were used, and precautions had to be taken to keep these adolescent superheroes from harming themselves and others. The Hulk needed to be kept from being provoked by his friends. Wolverine had to learn to not hurt himself and others. Each superhero had to learn when and why their special superpower should be used, and how it could be used in combination with one another's superpower—Genius gift—for the most effective results.

So, who wins out, Jekyll or Hyde? Who should win? Which personality acts as a safe a retreat from your Genius gift because of its latent power that puts you at odds with others? And, even if you know what your Genius personality is, can you control and use it for the greatest good? Can you use it wisely and not be destroyed by it?

James' Story

If you asked me to say in one word what my wound is, I probably couldn't. So, I'll give you two: cruel people! Or said with more care, UNAWARE PEOPLE. These people didn't physically abuse me. Instead, they spoke and did unkind things that hurt me deeper than I wish was true. And I see it repeated over and over again in how others are treated. This is my wound.

Even now I'm asking myself, how I can say cruel or unaware people are the source of my wound when I had such wonderful experiences throughout my life. How did I come to see myself as Nothing Wonderful, yet still be able to see the beauty in others? These questions are difficult to answer, but I'll try. There are four especially painful memories from my childhood.

Get shorty

In my younger years, I was actually a pretty short kid, at least that's what I thought anyway. I was constantly ridiculed by the other kids at school. It bothered me a whole lot, and the irony is that I viewed much of my childhood through this lens, even into adult years. It's odd that I had this self-consciousness about being short. Recently I had a conversation with someone who knew me growing up, and someone who knows me now. The person who knows me now looked at the other person and straight up said, "Was he actually short?" The person who knew me back then responded by saying, "I don't know, not super short, he was probably average height for his age." Wow, I didn't remember it that way. I felt myself become defensive and upset when the person who knows me now tried to substantiate my claim about being short. But why? Perhaps you and I will find out as my story progresses.

Two front Teeth

Another very clear memory, is getting my front two teeth knocked out while riding a metal runner sled down my driveway. The sled's runners hit gravel, I went lurching forward, and smashed my mouth against the wintry cold ground. Bang, the teeth were gone! Here was another physical anomaly that would draw unwanted attention. I was a kid who was missing his two front teeth before they should have been gone. I don't remember being made fun of for that, but I was painfully aware that I felt different from the other kids because of it.

No big deal

For reasons I still don't fully understand, I was consistently mocked and mistreated by my peers from first grade up to about seventh—from about 7 years old to 14. That was bad enough. Deeper than this though, and perhaps at the core of my wound was never feeling like my parents understood, no matter what I told them. I remember getting hurt and crying from the pain, and of course, the inevitable mocking from my class mates that followed. Even though I was shunned by my peers—who really weren't—at least I could rely on the fairness and care that my teachers and parents would express. And there's perhaps the deepest disappointment, and frankly, the greatest source of panic, because instead of acknowledging what happened, instead of sharing my outrage and pain, I was told, "Oh don't you worry about them; they're just being cruel." Yes, I already knew that. I wanted you to tell me that it mattered to you that I was hurt. I wanted to hear you say, "What happened? Where are those boys? We'll see about this." But no, you simply told me to buck up, be a big boy, and not to let my tears show them my weakness. This feeling of being alone, misunderstood, different—and aching inside from it—triggered even more despair. I really don't know what I thought was worse—being made fun of by my peers, or not receiving empathy from the adults in my life who should have given it.

Getting hammered

Like a lot of boys, I suppose, from time to time I was commandeered by my father to serve as his helper on some work project. I was not interested in this sort of thing but it's what was expected of me. One time I hit my thumb with a hammer. It hurt like mad, throbbing so that I thought I'd be sick to my stomach or faint. I instinctively knew that my dad should stop what he was doing and come to my aid. But he didn't. In fact, he brushed it off as just part of learning how to handle tools. I wanted his empathy. "Hey, Dad, look at me, your son. I'm hurting dammit!" Well, that's what I might say now. Then, I was just a kid, always on the verge of knowing I was going to be disappointed by the people who should have looked out for me, but who assumed I should just suck it up and be a big boy. Why couldn't you see the hurt that was building on the inside. Was I supposed to sooth myself! What's the point of being an adult if you can't provide solace, comfort, and care for your kids? What's the point? Don't you care? You don't care? Am I not worth caring for?

Whenever I hear the horrific stories of what so many others have been through— tragedy, heartache, pain, suffering, and death—and then think about myself, I feel like I have no right to talk about my wounds. Compared to them, I have nothing to complain about. Shouldn't these people be the ones to speak? Don't they have more of a right than I to talk about wounds?

People with real wounds are like Joni Erickson Tada whose spine was severed in a diving accident and who has lived as a quadriplegic ever since; like Syrian refugees whose lives are on the verge of extinction every day; like children who have lost their parents in tragic accidents, and countless others with horrible physical maladies. The things these people have experienced are unimaginable compared with my relatively calm and un-tragic life. But I still hurt. I was wounded, and I continue to feel it even though the circumstances pale in comparison to lots of others.

Many of us have experienced illnesses, chronic pain, depression, divorce, difficult pregnancies, miscarriages, infertility, less than loving parents, the loss of a loved one way too early, a demanding boss, various addictions, hospitalization, surgeries, being bullied or made fun of as a child or an adult, and the list of insults to life, internal and external, goes on. These things are real struggles for us. Through them we feel real pain, and they leave real scars. We don't feel heroic or especially significant by having suffered. Instead, we simply feel the effects of them, and because many people experience the same things, we understand that these kinds of wounds are common. But common wounds are devastating. Their pains are excruciating. The circumstances of my wounds will never make headlines, but I hurt— not only from the original injury but from being overlooked, unnoticed, minimized, and even ignored. If I can't talk about what I've experienced how can I process it? What am I supposed to do with it?

Well, one thing I've done is to compensate for the pains. Like a turtle, I protect myself by tucking in my exposed parts to avoid danger. So, I talk a certain way, walk a certain way, relate to others a certain way. I hold things loosely that should be held tightly. I love things little that I should love much. I live this way in order to keep myself from experiencing the pain all over again. In a word, I live a guarded life, always on alert because I'm afraid it will happen. What's "it?" It's not being ignored; no that would be difficult, but not impossible to take. "It" is my person being trivialized, diminished, considered worthless. "It" is what happens when I see you, but you see me to be less than you. Not tall enough, not strong enough, not man enough, not clever enough, not savvy enough, not resilient enough, not stable enough—not enough. And when I feel not enough to you, you are telling me—or at least I hear you saying it—"Who you are is insignificant." "What you are doesn't matter." "There is a 'you,' but 'you' don't count." And when I feel like this, which is most of the time, I am in a constant state of hurting. Not a way of living I want.

As I look at myself, I don't see the possibility of any purpose, efficacy, or beauty in my wounds, because even though I hurt, I don't think I have real wounds, or at least not ones that are significant enough to share. I tell myself that I don't believe this, but I must since this is what I feel. I believe I'm Nothing Wonderful, nothing even to glance at, nothing to notice, nothing, and no one to see here. But if I can't account for what happened to me then it's as if I'm telling myself I don't matter. It's one thing for me to get that message from others who I thought were supposed to care and didn't. But when I have no place, no voice to raise about what happened to me, that I hurt, that I ache deep inside my heart and mind, well then, it's as if I'm recycling the original wound over and over again. Just like others told me when I was young, I'm inadvertently telling myself that I'm no one special, Nothing Wonderful, while something deep inside is crying out to be appreciated as being precisely that, infinitely special, and completely wonderful. Talk about a psychic dilemma!

If I could title the story of my life, I'd call it, Nothing Wonderful: Seeing the beauty in others but not in me. Why? Because for the longest time I didn't believe that I really had a wound and if I did, I thought it was just your average, every day, run-of-the-mill wound, stuff that happens to everyone. But recently with the help of others I've discovered that my wound is real, its fact, its presence, is justified. My wound is just that, mine. It is unique, because I am unique, but it is also common, because many of us have these same types of experiences. If my wound is real and matters, maybe I do too.

Growing up in my skin

If you had the ability to choose the idyllic circumstances of your birth you just might choose a five-acre piece of land in a rural town in Ohio with my parents and siblings. As I write this, I am sitting in a small room above the General Store that I would ride my bike to throughout the summer months in order to get penny candy and a pop after playing a game of pickup tackle football at the park.

I grew up in a small town where one set of grandparents and a bunch of their kids—aunts, uncles, and cousins-lived nearby. They were originally from the city but moved out and settled in a rural town on a small 20-acre farm. They had nine children. My father was the oldest. The other set of grandparents lived nearby as well. They moved to Florida for a while but then came back. They had three children. Their youngest is my mom.

My mom's father was a shop teacher in school, and a golf pro. When he was younger, before my time, he was signed to the MLB majors, Chicago Cubs I believe, as a pitcher. But in an unfortunate accident in the shower (but fortunate for my existence) his professional career was cut short. Right after that, he met, and in the course of a day or two, married my grandmother. They had three children.

Grandpa loved westerns, ginger snap cookies, and milk. He'd get irritated when us kids got loud (not in a bad way, he just couldn't take too much noise). He taught me how to golf and throw a football and baseball well. He died of cancer when I was around 17. Grandma was sincere love, gentleness, kindness, and compassion. She died of cancer when I was around 21. I could always count on my grandpa to tell it to me straight up, and my grandma to care about me as a person.

My dad's father repaired heavy machinery at a company up in one of the larger cities about an hour away from where we lived. He liked to laugh and be around his children and grandchildren. He worked his machinery job, his farm—equipped with dairy cows, took care of his house and his family, and never had any problem with us noisy children. He was incredibly dependable. I loved the way he would smile and laugh. He was the last grandparent to die; I was in my early 30s then.

My father's mom had the most significant impact of anyone in my life. She died when I was in my early 20s. She was always at home, and always there for us kids. She wasn't afraid to correct us but was never shy about loving us. Grandma always told us about how Jesus loved us. Whenever I walked through the door to her house, she hugged me, asked how I was doing, and made sure I was treated to her fresh baked cookies and bread. I was sure it was prepared with love, just for me.

With this storybook backdrop you might conclude that I had a near perfect life, but still be waiting for the proverbial other shoe to drop when it comes to my immediate family. But that was pretty awesome as well.

I had a good spiritual influence. My dad's mother led almost all my family to faith in Jesus as Lord and Savior. My dad got a job in a local factory, bought a five-acre property about two miles down the road from his parents, and built a basement home there. Shortly thereafter, my older brother was born. It was a rough delivery. He was born breach—they tell me he was blue. My Grandma knew what to do. They dunked him in warm then cold water, and he survived with no side effects. He is almost three years older than me. He gave my mom a run for her money during his birth and growing up too. About two years later I came into the world. I'm told that her pregnancy with me was easy, and the delivery was even easier.

We loved to play outside whether it was or wasn't snowing. My brother was a great pal most of the time. He played with me and let me join him on many outside adventures that we had together. He was a pretty awesome older brother.

When I was nine or so, my mom got pregnant once again with my little brother. He was also born at home and it was a rough delivery. As I remember, it was pretty scary. I think my dad asked us boys to pray, because they were concerned about possibly losing him. God was good and he was born. He was full of life and energy. Mom and Dad loved him, and he was spoiled, like almost every last child born late in the game.

Mom and dad were friends with another couple who had two boys that were the same age as my older brother and me. We spent a lot of time with them, that included as many weekends and summers together as possible.

When I was a bit older and we weren't hanging out with our best friends or one of our cousins, we would ride our bikes about three miles to the center of our town. Here we would get candy and pop at the General Store—where I'm writing this—or we'd find some neighborhood kids to play a game of pickup football in the park. When none of these kids were around, we would go to the baseball diamond, hit balls around, throw, and catch.

My brothers and I did not attend the local public schools. We went to a private Christian school in a nearby town up until I was about 14. This school was connected to the church where we worshipped. My mom taught there for quite some time until my younger brother was born. So, she'd drive us to school, teach all day, and then we'd all come back home together.

I wish I could tell you that I had a perfect life in these pretty wonderful circumstances, but that wouldn't be true. Others didn't treat me the way they should have, and I didn't use all the opportunities and wisdom that I was afforded. The blame goes all around.

Things were pretty great for me until I got to elementary school age. I was surrounded by people who loved God, loved me, and loved others. They taught me all about the bible, all about God, and all about the work of Jesus Christ. The one thing I was missing, however, was being taught about me, who I was.

Now, to be fair, they probably did, but it wasn't in a way that I could understand. Sure, I knew that humans were created in God's image, but I didn't understand what that meant, how valuable they are. So, that meant I didn't understand how valuable I was, or even who I was. And this is where the trouble erupted in my life.

How I expressed the me I knew, didn't fit with the "you" others thought I should be. I was just a kid. I didn't have the ability to respond to the weight of social convention about what a young boy should look and act like. Heck, all I knew was what I thought and felt, and I certainly couldn't express that in the context of what I might one day come to know as being made in the image and likeness of God. I was struggling to claim my own sense of being while a lot of other people around me, and I mean a lot, were giving me the unmistakable message that my being did not conform with proper being. How could I claim myself, my own worth, my dignity, my beauty in the face of everyone telling me I didn't measure up to the norm? I say this, and yet, even at the time, I knew deep down inside, the me I was is good, a gift. But I was too young to process it. This is where my wound is found—being hurt and not receiving the empathy I craved. And, like every two-edged sword, this is my Genius—being able to see pain and respond to it by giving empathy and compassion to others.

But as significant as the characteristics of my wound is my gift. And the two seem to be inextricably tied to each other. The gift, my weird Genius if you will, emanates from my being, from the depth of who I am. I am, and have always been by nature, a gentle and empathetic soul. I hurt when others hurt, I sense their pain, I feel their wound. I can feel when people are hurt, even to the point of crying. My heart aches and breaks at the aching and breaking of others. When my natural bent was combined with the hurt I experienced from being this person and exercising this innate quality, a Genius gift was born.

I believe all gifts come from God, even the ones that cost us a lot of trouble. Often, they are embedded in our nature. Our gifts are the way we emulate the character of God. But at least in my case, the gift had been cultivated by life experiences—both good and bad. I am a gentle and concerned soul. I seem to naturally take the side of people who are unfairly treated, especially when that treatment cuts to the quick of who they are as a person. I hate to see people suffer needlessly, whether self-inflicted, other-inflicted, or simply see bad things that happen to them.

By heredity and example, I think I learned about this gift of compassion from my mom. For example, I had a gag reflex when I ate food that didn't have the right texture or taste. My dad would always make me at least try it. But when I fought against him mom would look over at my dad with these eyes of hurt, compassion toward me, and a bit of sternness, which in some sense was asking my dad to take my pain into consideration. This was my mom. And it's how I am too. Ironically, later in life, with my own son, when he was picky like me, and my wife was making him try the distasteful food—like my father did—my mom would sit next to him and eat some of the food off of my son's plate. This was the kind of woman she was, and it was wonderful.

So, the empathy and compassion that I have is a gift, but it's not easy to carry. My bent is contrary to many of the stereotypical male tendencies. Being this way I felt like someone on the island of misfit toys, like a train with square wheels on his caboose, a water pistol that shoots jelly, a Charlie-in-the-box instead of a Jack-in-the-box, a spotted elephant, a bird that swims, a cowboy that rides an ostrich, or an airplane that can't fly. In many ways, my Genius gift landed me in a place of misunderstanding. I was seen as, and I experienced being a misfit. So, it is a place of weakness, but it is also a place of strength.

Recently I've begun to see my Genius and claim it. This is quite a change for me because these characteristics have always been the cause of so much unsolicited demeaning from others. So, I've been able to take a certain kind of delight in the who that I am. I am able to look at another person and see that who they are really matters, that their hurt matters, and their pain does too. I can look at a person in a room who is lonely and hurt. I can feel their pain; I can sense their deep wounds. When I do this, I can become hot with anger toward those around who can't see what I see. Or, I can stay in the authentic Genius gift which feels the pain of others and turn toward them with empathy. I have a choice.

The dark side

Let me tell you about Earl. He was an annoying little kid, always making fun of me. He mocked me incessantly (can't remember about what, but it went on for months). Then, one day on the basketball court, I snapped. I grabbed him by his shirt and threw him to the ground. It wasn't premeditated, it just happened, but it felt right. It felt good, after all he deserved it. But I was the one who got in trouble. Yah, after months of the endless tormenting that no one else saw or cared to see, I acted out. And I was the one who was punished for it. Yup, right there in the Christian school—swatted five times with a wooden paddle that had holes in it.

The physical, social, and personal humiliation I experienced when I let my rage respond to being mocked taught me this is not a good strategy. Though my explosive antics on the basketball court weren't planned, I did make a conscious decision that day. I would never again let someone goad me to the point that I would fly off the handle like that. Whatever sensitive caring I might have toward others, or toward myself, I wouldn't let that innate temperament mutate into violence. It was one thing to be ridiculed. It was quite another to add insult to injury by letting myself be tricked into additional public shame and humiliation. From then on, I adopted a public persona that was carefully scripted, calm, cool, and collected. I thought I had this figured out. Made good sense. I had control of the situation.

The only problem is that I come unglued when I see some other poor soul, wounded and vulnerable, who is simply trying to hold onto some semblance of sanity in the face of mocking and mistreatment. I feel like I am sitting in the stands at the basketball court all over again, but this time as a spectator watching myself, young Jamie, provoked to the point of tears. The rage builds up in me and I want to grab the perpetrator by the throat and throw him across the floor.

I know someone who is by some many counts a dear, wonderful person. She's had a rough past, lots of issues, and was written off as unstable by her spouse and her local church leadership. I was asked to help mediate the situation. I thought I had everything under control. But when I heard the judgements and accusations, the wholesale dismissal of who this person is, I almost blew up. What I heard took me right back to the place of being the little child who was ridiculed just for being who I was. Fortunately, I was able to keep my cool. I was able to advocate for this woman. The long knives had to be withdrawn and some headway was made for her cause—her cause? Her person! But this happens to me all the time. Maybe my thoughtful strategy for coping with the inevitable insults I would witness wasn't as effective as I'd hoped.

For decades I thought that I had effectively developed a set of competencies and social skills for the purpose of covering my deep wounds I suffered as a child—being made fun of for being short, being mocked and mistreated, and many other circumstances where I needed comfort and empathy but was never given it in the way I needed. But I'm coming to realize that this has been a myopic understanding. Instead of seeing myself as a whole person who is responsible for his actions—not the respectable Dr. Jekyll divorced from the separate persona of the evil Mr. Hyde—I saw myself as a victim who was acted upon. I have sustained the belief that what was acted upon me produced within me a personality trait that was not my fault. I wouldn't have become mad as a wet hornet if others had not disrespected me. But alas, people disrespect each other all the time. What do I do with the wound that oozes with compassion for others in my condition, and simultaneously oozes with infectious, putrid anger?

Why can't I see my own beauty? Why didn't others help me see it? Why couldn't the children, and especially the adults in my life, hear the cries of my soul that asked, "Why don't you understand me? Why don't you value me? Why can't you see what I see?" When I ask these of myself, I'm crying out my hurt, crying out the repeated experiences of being dismissed for who I am. I try to make sense of it but there is no sense to be made. Why rarely ever has a satisfactory answer.

No, I don't think the answer to why will get me anywhere. So, I am beginning to ask how. How can I see my own beauty? How can others help me see myself? How can my soul's cries be heard in a way that brings insight, even if suffering persists?" The only way I know is not by expecting that the scales of life's injuries will ever be balanced in the way I want. Instead I must discern and use the gifts that have been given to me, the gifts of compassion which have been awakened by the very traumas that have been carelessly inflicted. It's as if I'm coming to see that my healing is actually inside my wound. If, instead of viscerally responding to the gaping violation of self that has severed me in the deepest places—something I do without thinking—I sought to offer compassion to myself, I just might find and cherish who I am.

Children are so vulnerable, but so are we all. They naturally seek affirmation, and rarely receive enough of it—I didn't. Out of their deep hurt, which is a longing to be cherished, they sometimes retaliate by putting another person down so they can experience themselves as lifted up. But it's a futile effort because the outcome is never realized. We simply remain wounded people who wound other people.

It happened to me—this almost instinctive retaliatory behavior born out of my wound—and it was so bad when it combined with my more naturally delicate temperament. I felt weak, I felt like a misfit, and others saw it. When my weakness was exploited, I became hurt, I wept, I looked for someone to hear and validate my suffering. My mom was the only one. Most others told me that this was life, that I must "suck it up!" They simply couldn't understand my sensitivity to what was wrong. I thought that what I saw that was wrong was evidence of my strength, but to them it was the opposite. Their prescription for my soul sickness was for me to "suck it up." But sucking it up would be to deny the way I am, the who I am, the very core of myself. This is how I was made, fearfully and wonderfully, in my mother's womb. This is the gift of my being which I understood as being created in the image and likeness of God. Could I really "suck it up" and deny myself to become not myself? They might as well have asked me to become a tree or a weed. It would have made as much sense.

When we expect someone to change, suppress, or deny their very own image we are essentially telling them to erase themselves from the picture of life, to vanish, to return to a state of non-existence. At the very same time that I sensed and took delight in the uniqueness of my own existence, my own being, I was being systematically schooled to reject myself by becoming someone I was not. I'm not a physicist so I don't fully understand the concept of anti-matter. But if there is a human equivalent, I was being told to become anti-James—not simply against myself, but worse, to become not myself. Impossible! At the very same time I was learning this revulsion of myself by others who would not or could not take me as I am, I was also being taught in the classroom and the church house that I am to "love my neighbor as myself." If this was how I was supposed to love myself, God help anyone around me. I'd have to reject them just as I was being rejected. No, not rejected—repudiated, nullified, made void!

My weakness, my Achilles heel? I care too much about what people think about me. A frighteningly dark Mr. Hyde rage, nearly unbounded by conscience, rears its ugly head whenever the sensitive, intuitive, overly compassionate capacity I can't shut off is challenged by others. It's as if I'm continuing a fight that was initiated in childhood and never won. But it has to be won. In the same way, whenever I see the need of others to be protected, heard, defended-loved, yes, that's it, loved—whenever I see them mocked and bullied, I think I use their cause to vicariously continue fighting for my younger self who had no champion. Could it be that like Dr. Jekyll, I don't believe that this part of me will ever be acceptable? Am I using the misfortune of others as my secret potion that gives me guilt free, consequence denying permission to go back into fighting the unwinnable fight which has dogged me my whole life so that I can express the full force of rage that flows from my wound?

When I feel dismissed, misunderstood, and overlooked I turn into a caged animal, like a porcupine ready to shoot his quills. I defend myself at all cost through intellectual and logical persuasion. I engage every ounce of my ability to convince people that I have a reason for being the way I am. I argue and repeat the same thing in as many ways as I can. I wear people down. I even try to convince myself that I am justified in my weakness. The alternative? I could simply say, "This is who I am." But I don't.

Perhaps I have exhausted you with my mental machinations which alternately seek to figure out why I am the way I am, but which more often slip into overdrive, a frame of reference that pretends to want insight but is driven instead by the desperate need to subdue whatever and whoever threatens my existence. Of course, the full darkness of this proclivity I will not let anyone else see. Maybe I haven't let myself see it all. I'm afraid Mr. Hyde has nothing on me when it comes to the capacity for self-destructive malevolence.

Reflections

Yes, the compassion James feels for others is a gift. But it's a two-edged sword which may have more significant, and currently, adverse implications for him than he realizes. His righteous indignation is invariably triggered. He knows this will happen despite any insight about this dynamic that he has. The fierce rage that inevitably erupts inside him is both the result of an insatiable desire for acceptance as he is for who he is, and a vehicle to express care—but only if he will allow himself to embrace his own unfortunate experiences, rather than to constantly feel trapped and stifled by them. The fact that he keeps repeating episodes of rage at the mistreatment of others suggests he has not accepted himself. At a profound level he still experiences himself to be the little boy who doesn't fit in.

James's emphasis on the perceived injustice done by "cruel people" is a repeated projection of his wound into every situation in life. It's as if he can't get out of his own way, that he is doomed to recycle this hurt, even though he knows much of what is going on. This driven-ness to do battle with everyone and everything he perceives as judging and rejecting him is a profoundly powerful characteristic of his wound.

Despite the Genius gift of superhuman sensitivity to the brokenness in others that James possesses—and I have seen with my own eyes and heart its awesome ability to bring a depth of care that has changed people in the very ways James himself wants to—that Genius has not become a source of comfort for the injury he's felt in the depth of his own soul. Like many who possess Genius characteristics, the goodness of James's gift is dangerously overshadowed by this gaping wound that he cannot or will not allow to heal. It is dangerous not only because he is prone to see all of life through this painful lens. There are many whose wounds have become the filter through which monumental acts of courage, bravery, and human triumph have been achieved despite their chronic presence. No, it is not the presence of the wound which is dangerous for James. The greatest danger is in his inability to reconcile the wounded boy who continues to long for love with the socially adept, bright, functioning, capable man.

This was Dr. Jekyll's downfall. He treated what he found abhorrent in himself as if it was another self. Because he could not reconcile who he was—good and bad in the same person—he took the risk, and was eventually overcome by entertaining the violent, evil character of his personality. This could happen to James. Though he says his chief complaint is that others cannot and don't accept him as he is, I wonder if it is more that he finds the very part of his personality which was wounded and gave birth to a heightened awareness of brokenness in others, the thing about himself he most abhors. Like Dr. Jekyll he cannot shake this part of himself, but neither does he easily live with it. James uses the plight of the wounded souls around him as a seductive potion that permits him to rail time and again against those who do the wounding. This ritual cycle sustains a dualism in James that keeps him from reconciling his innate character's Genius with the wound it helped to set the stage for. Despite the obvious good which has come to countless people James has encountered, the gift seems to be possessing its owner rather than the other way around.

His Genius sensitivities are so greatly overshadowed by the pain of his wound that he seems to insist on reenacting the dynamics of the original events that afflicted him. His Genius could very well be his downfall because the very things that evoke his compassion are what invariably drag him into the experience of others. And it does so with such laser-like precision that it's as if he does not simply seek to champion those who are like him. He has taken up their cause and become them! By delving once more into mortal combat for the sake of his own soul he holds out hope that his hurt will be vindicated. The internal torture he endures is excruciating. He tells himself he just needs to accept God's acceptance of him, and love like Jesus does in the meantime. Knowing that he does not feel the reality of what he wants to believe, it's reasonable to wonder if this is just one more layer of self-condemnation that reinforces a lifelong pattern of pain.

James's story may be closer to yours then some others you'll read. Have you told yourself that your suffering doesn't compare to others, so you should just suck it up? James is speaking to you here and asking you to understand that you do matter. Let James's anguished story speak into the depths of yours. Perhaps you can hear the very words he wanted to from the people he was certain he needed to hear them from "I'm sorry. I know that must have hurt. Tell me more about what happened. You matter. You are a treasure."

We're all torn on the inside, to one degree or another. It's, well, in James's own words, it's pretty common. But not so common as to be overlooked. These ancient words say it about as well as I know how:

The good I want to do, I don't do.
Instead, I do the evil I do not want—
and I seem to keep on doing it.
Who can save me from this certain death?

Romans 7:15

I'm convinced that every soul is created in the image and likeness of God, no matter how profound, or common, the torments of this life might be. All of us are struggling to reconcile the contradictions that plague us. Don't bury your head in the sand, trying to hide from them. Instead, work to discover the Genius gift that is yours. It will be your life line to coping with and understanding your essential struggle. We all have one. In fact, it might be that at the core, it the same struggle, just expressed in different ways in everyone's life. But the struggle must be met if you are going to live the heroic existence you were created to live. Yes, there is a foundational internal conflict. Your gift is God's Genius in you that will draw you to himself in whom, as it turns out, we all live and move and have our Being.

Maybe, just maybe, James can learn that each person has a hidden gift of Genius, and that not all people can see as he does. Maybe, just maybe, James can develop his gift of empathy for those who cannot see the pain of others. Maybe, just maybe, James can use his Genius to help others understand what he sees and show them how to care and love them. Maybe, just maybe, James could permit another person's gift to touch him and he would discover that there are many different gifts apportioned to many people, his being just one, which taken with all the others can strengthen everyone in his community. I believe it's possible. I'm dubious about whether it is probable. But I've been wrong before. I hope I am again.

Chapter 7: Ground Hog Day

If you were forced to repeat the same day over and over again, what day would you want it to be? The day you fell in love for the first time? The day you went to your favorite vacation spot? The day you drove for the very first time without your parents in the car?

What about the day you were wounded in your child's forming soul when no one was around to protect you?

The 1993 movie Ground Hog Day is an iconic story that finds a man trapped in a repetitive cycle of the same day—but not by choice. Phil Connors is an arrogant Pittsburgh weatherman who is forced to take what he considered to be the polar opposite of a hard news assignment in the small town of Punxsutawney, Pennsylvania to cover Groundhog Day. But there's a strange twist. Every day Phil Connors wakes up in Punxsutawney, it's the same day. Phil is forced to engage life, and himself in slow motion. But though he initially feels trapped in this déjà vu, he discovers that he does have choices. The film is ambiguous about the duration of the time loop. One film critic placed it at 10 years. The story you will soon read is a true–to–life time loop played out over 50 years!

But before we get there, let's return to Punxsutawney Phil.

Resentful about the assignment, and condescending toward the town, its residents, and its only claim to fame, Phil makes the obligatory, bored–to–tears report during the annual Groundhog Day parade. Hoping to quickly wrap up his duties to return to the big city where he is sure he belongs, Phil's unexpected stay in the last place he wants to be exposes his sarcastic, petulant, and self–absorbed personality to everyone. Eventually, even he sees it.

A blizzard that the smug weatherman predicted would miss Punxsutawney strikes full force leaving the news team stranded in the little town. Connors wakes up the next morning, and to his utter confusion it's the second of February—again! At first Phil toys with the day, testing it to see if it really is a repeat. So, he changes his behavior while everyone else says and does exactly the same thing they did the previous day. But this time loop repeats, over and over. Every day starts the same—the alarm clock goes off at 7:00 am, playing Sonny and Cher's "I Got you Babe."

Connors wonders if he is insane but finally decides he's not. Once he's resolved that he's stuck in this repetitive story, and that there seems no way out, a devilish, cynical side of him takes over. He tries to seduce pretty women, incites a police chase, and even steals, knowing the day will unfold exactly the same no matter what he does. When he tries to win over Rita, the beautiful news caster, he is met with maddening failure.

Eventually, his frustration builds to a crescendo. He smashes the alarm clock, kidnaps the world–famous groundhog whose winter shadow is legend, and dies in a fiery crash off a cliff... only to wake up, once more, to the same 7:00 am alarm and, "I got you Babe."

Connors tries in vain to stop this vicious cycle. He tries suicide. He electrocutes himself; a truck runs over him; and he jumps from a tall building, each time waking up the next morning to the maddening repeat of the morning before.

As a way to channel his growing desperation he delves into a conversation with Rita the pretty newscaster. Because the day repeats again and again, he is afforded the chance to perfect his approaches to her. Rita becomes convinced of Connor's story after his arrogance and egotism have finally melted away. He finally begins to speak out of the depth of his heart with no hidden agenda. She encourages him to view his gift—this newfound authentic self— as something to benefit others.

Stripped of his self–serving, public façade, Phil begins to focus outward, spending days and weeks learning about people, really seeing them, and strategically intervening to help them. He does the Heimlich maneuver on a choking man; he saves a boy who falls from a tree. He even attempts to rescue a homeless man who, in the end is unable to be saved. As a result, Phil makes many profound discoveries and is surprised by the skills he's developed to make a positive difference in the lives of others, all because the endless day—what he first considered to be a nightmare—became the healing balm of deliverance from his own wounded life to a life of authentic presence. Now Phil is open to himself and the world around him. Almost miraculously, he has become beloved by the community he despised because he has finally yielded to the something more resident inside him.

Near the end of the story, the day begins the same as every other before it. But there's something different. Phil realizes he loves Rita. He reports on Ground Hog Day with so much genuine enthusiasm that the excitement of the event is palpable. Everyone is fixed on what Phil is saying. That night Rita accompanies him to the room where Phil's alarm clock has marked the endless progression. When they awaken the next day, the spell of the never–ending day has been broken. The alarm clock goes off at seven, but this time it plays "Almost like being in Love" from the musical Brigadoon, the story of another little town whose characters were stuck in time.

You are about to read Dave's story. It's hard because his soul cries out for both time and suffering to stop. He's a minister. You'll watch him struggle to believe what he preaches. Sometimes it works. But living in what he experiences as a never–ending time loop, Dave is continually reminded of his wounds. His pain does not subside with time, or perspective, or theological insight—it persists, growing even more difficult with each passing year, leaving him worse off.

But there's something more to the story. Though Dave feels trapped by time and suffering, frequently un–consoled by the grace and mercy he preaches to lift others, there's another side to him. A rare, Genius gift that empowers him to break out of the chains of a time loop to a time before time. On many days he's like Phil Connors, flailing in the midst of a life that feels like a cruel straitjacket. Occasionally though, he's able to accept his lot and use his circumstances to do good.

Dave's story

"Before she was your mother, she was my daughter." The sentence stopped me in my tracks. It stunned me into silence–and keeps me there still. Up to that point, I'd been very vocal with God–and not in a particularly pious or respectful way, especially as I got older. With the passing of time, my tone with God became progressively more confrontational. I was weary of the waiting, pleading, cajoling; He'd promised that if I cried out for understanding, He would grant it. At least that was my takeaway after reading Proverbs 2:1–11 at age 15. My son, if you accept my words and store up my commands within you... wisdom will enter your heart, and knowledge will be pleasant to your soul. Discretion will protect you, and understanding will guard you.

He promised wisdom, insight, and understanding if I pursued it more zealously than wealth, so I did. I took Him at His word and began a life of crying out for wisdom, for understanding. I did what the Good Book said.

To be sure, in tidbits here and there, I did gain wisdom. God was good to His word... except in response to the deepest, most anguished cry of my heart, a cry that gradually became, not just a cry for wisdom, but a demand for an explanation. Hence, I developed an increasingly angry, confrontational disposition toward God. He owed me!

This lifetime of pleading, which morphed into my demands of Him, came with a toll. I finally came to my wit's end. My cries were pointedly NOT answered. Now it was a wrestling match. If you know the story of Jacob wrestling with the Angel of the Lord; that's how I felt. A pitched, winner–take–all bout: "WHY DIDN'T YOU HEAL MY MOTHER?!" This was my first acknowledgement of my real wound.

The fury that was finally breaking the surface of my soul was scalding to anyone unlucky enough to be touched by it. It was molten, and I was beyond caring. Nothing else mattered now. And ironically, it was because I had finally burned out in all my efforts to remain patient, waiting for God to address this heart aching question, that I finally sought counsel. I needed help. If I didn't get it, I feared for my mental and emotional stability.

And, so I did. It came in a few different forms. The first was when the leaders of the church where I serve as pastor, graciously agreed to grant me an extended sabbatical. They might not have known the details of my inner turmoil, but they witnessed its effects on me. Let's just say I was more than prickly. And I couldn't hide it even if I tried. Their concern was genuine, but it wasn't for me alone. They were concerned for the welfare of my wife. They intuitively recognized the danger to her if my situation was not effectively and immediately addressed.

The second party to intervene was my wife herself. She is second only in sequence. She is first by a wide margin with regard to her love, patience, and devotion. To say that I could not have endured without her would be an extraordinary and inexcusable understatement, to the point of insult. I can only guess at the source of her capacity for perseverance without resentment toward me for the years of the metastasizing anger that came out of me sideways.

The third party was my counselor. He has proven to be an amazing source of wisdom and encouragement. He is quietly supportive, yet willing to lead me through the emotional minefields which dot the landscape of my personal history. It was in the counseling setting that the statement, Before she was your mother, was made. It was in conversation (That term conversation is euphemistic: so calm, so rational. I was anything but calm or rational when the moment came. Yet, when it did, I was stopped – mid–sentence if memory serves–and stunned into silence.) While the counselor looked on, I melted down.

An unholy trinity

The process that led to this moment had begun more than 15 years earlier. I had experienced a breakthrough in understanding my past and its impact on my life. My wife and I had just begun a relationship with a mentor. His favorite word was, and still is, disruption. He provided that disruption by recommending a book for me to read, The Wounded Heart, by Dan Allender.

In one of our early sessions, I had casually mentioned that I had been molested as a 10–year–old camper by a counselor at a church camp; that it had happened only once (which upon further recollection was incorrect), and was no big deal, a thing of the past. I later learned that nothing could be further from the truth. This thing of the past was infecting and informing every aspect of my life. Our mentor nearly got whiplash from hitting the brakes when he heard this statement. Wisely, he insisted that I read Allender's book, so I did.

As I read, the volcano of my molten anger had its first major eruption. What flowed out of me took me completely by surprise. This was the biggest initial insight into my own soul. Before that moment, I used to think that my core problem was with lust and dabbling in pornography– a holdover from adolescent curiosity. My frustration with this cyclical experience of lust made me very angry. But this was just the surface view of what was hidden much deeper. The more I read the more my wound's fissure opened wide, exposing the throbbing anger at the heart of my pain.

I was astonished to realize that my dilemma was exactly opposite what I thought it was. I wasn't angry about lust. It was my anger that expressed itself in lust, the drug that sedated my seething anger! Sexual preoccupation and release gave me temporary relief from recurring anger (which has protected a bottomless well of pain), in a way similar to what alcohol does for the alcoholic, or drugs do for the addict. Only in my case, I didn't need a bottle or a syringe. The drugs I used were prepositioned for easy launch by the design of God.

That realization–that God's own design was being used against me– only magnified and intensified my anger. What do I mean by God's own design? That sexual attraction and experience are part of what it means to be human; we are created to enjoy sex in mind and body, just like we are created to enjoy food because we need it to be healthy. So, you can understand why I felt trapped, and the One who was supposed to rescue me didn't.

He was permitting his own bio–chemical architecture to be hijacked and used against me... just as He had allowed my mother to be afflicted with a long–term, systemic, debilitating disease; and just as He had allowed my capacity for joy to be used against me by my abuser.

What to do? I doubled–down on trying to resolve my existential nightmare. But frankly, now knowing what I did, threw me into a state of panic.

The linkage began these three dilemmas was clear, and as the fog lifted, showing me their connection, my anger seemed to take on mythic proportions. I couldn't admit this was happening however, because I had committed myself to eliminating anger [read subduing, ignoring and denying it]. After all, anger is bad, right? Especially if you're a minister. But my efforts weren't working. The truth was staring me in the face and the immediacy of the anger I felt was inescapable.

The molestation I experienced at age 10 was arguably—if not a direct result, at the very least—a predictable byproduct of my mother's disease. What had been, in my brief five–year existence, a cheerful, secure, and loving family environment, was suddenly hijacked by her disease. At five, I was incapable of understanding the radical implications her struggle had on my sense of stability and wellbeing. The games, the play, the laughter, the happiness, the carefree joys I had tasted in those early years of idyllic family life were gradually, definitively, and irrevocably displaced by uncertainty and mistrust of my own emotions. In the wake of her illness and increasing pain came my heartache at losing the life and mother I had known. Watching my father's efforts to find a solution repeatedly come to nothing planted a seed of deep frustration. By the time I was 15 I gave up on believing there were any solutions at all.

But before I reached that wizened age, I had to pass through age 10, the time when I experienced a crucial betrayal of whatever vestiges of childlike joy still remained possible in me. It was a mortal blow. I would never again be able to experience, in the core of my being, childlike delight, or confident hope or trust. Why? Because the core of my being was adulterated.

My camp counselor–turned–predator–abuser was a lively, buoyant, life–of–the–party kind of guy. Whenever the whole camp gathered for large group activities, he was consistently at the center of the fun. He awakened something in me that had been dormant, or nearly so, for a long time–half my life, as a ten–year–old.

His love–of–life personality invited me to risk playing again. He welcomed me in a way I hadn't known in a long time. There was something I sensed in him that promised the possibility of returning to a time of joyful innocence.

Even though I was not one of his assigned campers he got permission from my counselor for me to spend the night with his group. I liked being taken under his wing. But once there, the promise of a special friendship turned into a nightmare. He invited me into "special time" with him in his sleeping bag, a kind of closeness reserved for his special boys. It was the promise of his attention that drew me in. Nothing I'd experienced in my tender years could have prepared me to know that my hero was a homosexual pedophile.

Bastard. Son–of–a–bitch, bastard! Every time I recall those moments of innocent trust betrayed, the volcano within me stirs. Its seismic rumbles of rage reverberate through my soul–over and over again. And yet, I rehearse it again, not imagining that this time it won't happen–like reading the account of JFK's assassination or the crucifixion of Jesus– as though this time the assassination or crucifixion won't happen. No, it isn't that expectation at work.

Instead, I rehearse these events now hoping that by coming to terms with them, I might be able help someone else to keep on struggling through their own pain; that somehow, I might help them move through their own story to find some peace. For, as I have been learning of late, there is hope. It may be hard won, but it is there. But I'm getting ahead of myself. I will revisit the gift of hope in a moment. For now, I'll resume my story.

As bizarre as it now seems, after that session of camp was over, the so– called counselor actually sought me out for a visit in my home. Until I was talking with my mentor, I'd forgotten this. Evidently, I must have responded to the counselor because he showed up. While my parents were in another part of the house, he molested me again. I'm not sure exactly what it was that told me this was not right, but I knew for sure when it happened in my home. I had the presence of mind to tell him to stop; that I wanted no further contact with him. Thankfully, it ended there—IT being his contact with me. But the effects of IT didn't end.

I don't hold my parents accountable for what happened to me. It is tempting to lay blame at their feet. They were so absorbed in their own struggle—with mom's health—that they were not alert to mine. My adult logic tries to tell my child logic that to hold them responsible would be completely unfair. But the child knows his parents are supposed to provide safety. Do you hear my conflict?

They were attentive to me in every conventional sense. But these events were anything but conventional. They occurred at a time when people sincerely trusted leaders—in the Church and everywhere else. It may have been naïve to do so, but we did, everyone did. Neither my parents nor any other adult had given me cause to doubt the absolute uprightness of their intentions. I had friends who couldn't trust their parents. But mine were worthy of my trust. In fact, I view them as much victims of my abuser as I was. We were all attacked by his betrayal; we were all violated.

Oddly, when I finally realized that my mother's disability and my innate desire for parental affection made me vulnerable to abuse by an opportunistic adult, I began to see that God's grace had been at work in her life. I know, it sounds strange, but follow me. When she was diagnosed with the disease, mom's prayer had been that God would give her the ability to raise her children. I was the youngest when all of this happened. Looking back, she did remarkably well, in view of the amazing, overwhelming challenges she faced from her disease.

In the course of my formal studies in preparation for ministry I discovered that in the times when the Bible was written a man was not considered to have attained the status of "elder" until he was 40. Until then, he was still viewed as a "young man." My mother died almost two months to the day after my fortieth birthday. Her prayer was answered with almost mathematical precision. Her task was completed. She had raised her youngest child into his seniority. It was, I am convinced, God's grace toward her that prevented her bearing the additional burden of having to face what happened to me as a boy. She had had enough to face, and He spared her that heartache. She never knew.

Within two years of her death, God began to answer my own longstanding prayer—for wisdom and insight in light of the life–long anguish I had carried. Beginning with the mentor and then discovering and reading the book he recommended, I began to realize the significance of the dimensions of my own story for the first time. As the implications of my molestation began to sink in, there was a period of rapid increase in awareness, insight, and understanding. But after that initial burst, things seemed to plateau.

My struggle with anger continued; it didn't subside. Greater awareness, yes; change, not so much. The harder I worked at removing and repressing this nagging shadow that haunted me, the more emotionally drained I became. At the point of near complete emotional depletion, I was burned out.

Burnout is not merely physical and emotional fatigue—it is an existential inability to carry on. When I was 15, I was confronted with the suicides of kids my age. Could there be a more tragic end to a life hardly begun? We've all learned that for some the prospect of living a meaningless life, rooted in despair and futility, can be unbearable. Only death can end the pain.

Now, in my fifties, I have discovered why older people can reach the same desperate conclusion as my once teenaged counterparts. To look back over your life, having done your best to live with purpose and virtue, but to face the wounds of insurmountable pain, misfortune, chronic affliction of mind, body, or conscience, you decide death is the only way out. I'm not talking about the insights I've read in Psychology Today. I was on that threshold. I thought about this route of escape. I didn't think I could go on another minute. It was the most frightening moment of my life because I could see my life turning into death by my own hand.

It was in this emotional state that I turned to the counselor I mentioned before. And with him, I discovered a fourth, as yet unrecognized driver of my anger—my father.

The father wound

One of four heroes in my life—alongside both of my grandfathers and Martin Luther King, Jr.—my father had been a World War II Marine. Two Purple Hearts, a Bronze Star for valor on Iwo Jima, my father brought strength and determination to all he did, at home, at work, in our church, and in our community. He embodies all the aspirations that I could ever have, both as his son and as follower of Jesus.

He was a warrior in the best and noblest sense of the word. He fought to defeat fascism. He fought to build a business on honorable and just principles, from which not only he and his family could benefit, but from which both his employees and their families could, as well. He demonstrated that he judged men by the content of their character, not by the color of their skin, long before Dr. King articulated his dream. He followed Jesus, trusted Him, and sought to inspire others to do the same.

He didn't "push his religion." He simply lived it with integrity, and happily credited God with any blessings that came his way. And he loved us, his family. He loved my mom faithfully and well. He smiled easily, listened carefully, disciplined with tempering mercy, and kindness, loved beauty, gave generously of all the resources God had given him. My father loved me. How, then, could he possibly be a factor that contributed to my anger?

As with my mother's health, his contribution was unintentional. It was a byproduct of his virtues which were applied to the mission of fixing my mother's disease. He was a Marine, after all; and a Christian. Marines win; Christians love. Marines complete their missions; Christians alleviate human suffering. Marines achieve objectives; Christians build loving relationships. Marines do not retreat; they simply attack in another direction. And Christians do not give up; they persevere, because God is the one who gives them strength.

This man imprinted his spirit on me. No, I never became a Marine. I did not aspire to share in my father's business. I inherited my mother's love of literature, and my grandfathers' love of the law, equity, and justice.

What I inherited from my father was his desire to make a difference, and specifically to overcome my mother's disease. I would join him in the mission of fixing Mom's health. I would pray, and study, and be involved in her care whenever and however I could.

But from the age of 10, when I was violated by the camp counselor, my battle became—for the balance of my life—a two–front war. I would continue to pray for my mother to be fixed, and labor to that end; but now, I would also forever fight a defensive action against mistrust, against the insecurity born of betrayal, and the accompanying confusion of my experience of sexuality. In other words, I was trying to help take care of my mother who could not take care of me, support my father who was distracted from taking care of me, and take care of myself, still too young to possibly accomplish any of these!

In the course of my education, I would shift from the pursuit of law to the ministry. It was not a calling I preferred, but when confronted with the ways the practice of law was evolving from a pursuit of justice to a pursuit of "winning," I preferred ministry after all. As a minister, I could pursue "fixing" on a grand scale. What better way to fix lives than through the proclamation of the gospel!

So, in response to God, the One who loves me and whom I love... the One who permitted my mother to become diseased and progressively an invalid; the One who permitted me to be molested; the One who permitted my father to engage in an ultimately futile quest to heal my mother—I became one of His ministers. I would contribute, in His name and on His behalf, to fixing the world by proclaiming a gospel that carried a vision of righteousness and justice based on faith in Christ. I would aim at helping people to fix their lives, which (I assumed) they would be only too eager to do, once they understood the great benefits that came to them when they believed in Jesus.

I would contribute to fixing the Church, to address the ways in which it had drifted so imperceptibly from its first love—of Christ. I would do all of this—and I would fail, miserably. I would come to the end of myself. I would burn out. I would ultimately balance on the precipice of life and consider whether I should jump off.

I was spent, exhausted. I couldn't fight any fight—good, bad, or indifferent—any longer. I could no longer wear the warrior mantle of my father which I had presumed to shoulder. I could not fix my mother, I could not fix the world, I could not fix anyone. I had utterly failed even to fix the one person within my universe who I ought to have— me! All of my efforts left me frustrated, angry, and sickened with the bitter taste of impotence when all I wanted was to make things right. I was done in.

The work I was doing with my counselor peeled back layers of resistance and scales of blindness that finally allowed me to see what I had not known was there all along. And my new sight revealed powerful forces that hit me like the mightiest oceans swells, sucking me under. I could not find the surface. I could not breathe. When I finally bobbed to the surface through the aid of my "lifejacket" counselor, gasping for air, sputtering, and choking, I saw the waves, the incessant billows which had been beating against me all my life—the root of my anger, my lust, my failure. It was God Himself! I had spent my life shifting my anger from one object to another, from one failed mission to another. But the shadow over each of these failed efforts was God Himself.

I wept.

Uncontrollably, as the realization broke over me, I sobbed and raged against Him.

Why?!

Why did You rob me of my mother?!

Why did You permit the last vestiges of my joy in childhood to be robbed from me by a pervert?!

Why did You subject both my father and me to lives of frustration at not being able to fix the one we loved?!

WHY?!?

A pause, and then...

"Before she was your mother, . . . she was my daughter."

Silence. I stopped. The sobbing stopped. The rage, mysteriously, stopped. I listened attentively as my counselor spoke again, like an oracle of God.

"Before she was your mother, she was my daughter."

I – what?

"Before she was your mother, she was my daughter. And –"

And?

"And before you were his victim, you were my son. And –"

There was more?

"And before he was your father, he was my son."

Silence. I sat in a state I don't quite know how to describe.

A scene emerged in my mind's eye. The prairie. Nothing on the horizon for as far as the eye could see. A steady wind, neither warm nor chill. The prairie grasses waved like the sea. The sky a piercing, brilliant, cloudless blue. And me, sitting cross–legged in the grass. Neither young nor old. No compass. No pathways. No landmarks. Nowhere to go, only this space to stay. Lost in this space. And strangely – quiet. Not just a physical silence, though there was that. Instead, an interior stillness (dare I say it?) a peace. Not angry. Not filled with lust, for there was no hurt that needed medication. All strange, foreign... Other.

"Before she was your mother..."

"Before you were his victim..."

"Before he was your father..."

Before.

God did not shout me down. He did not belittle me. He did not rebuke me—truly, not even a little. Nor, however, did He change to suit me. He did not suddenly answer my "Why?" He calmly, steadfastly refused to stop being God in order to accommodate what I thought I needed to resolve my pain.

The big, hairy, religious word used at this point is Sovereign. God continued as He is—before, now, forever, Sovereign. In control. "Unyielding, unhasting, God only wise." That's a line from an old hymn. That hymn writer must have met God as I was meeting Him now.

Strangely, at first, I wanted—felt almost panicked—to find a way out of that prairie reverie–that endless expanse of uninteresting, apparently useless space that resisted being discerned. I wanted a way back to reality. I needed a compass, a path. But I was deprived of both. And the counselor was no help. He was the instrument of God who led me out there into that emptiness. He seemed almost pleased with himself.

In truth, I was deprived of nothing. Instead, the realization slowly dawned over many days. In fact, I had been given a gift.

Earlier, at the outset of the sabbatical my church had granted, me, my wife, and I planned to take the first full month out of four and do exactly nothing. We went to the ocean so that I could just stare at the expanse. She could read and write and work on projects for church. My only rule? She couldn't discuss anything related to the church with me. That was the agreement.

For me, it needed to be a complete radio blackout. But for the first two weeks there, even without outside interference, I couldn't shut off. The noise of my fears, insecurities, and anxieties filled the recesses of my mind. But then…

Two weeks into that first month, at dawn's twilight I awoke to three statements, three very clearly articulated statements.

Be of good courage.

Your youth shall be renewed.

Rest.

At first, I couldn't decide if I was awake or dreaming; and if awake, what was I hearing? I came fully awake, realizing that the statements were clearly evocative, almost verbatim quotes, of Scripture.

Understand, please, that as a Presbyterian, I don't really expect direct, personal communication from God. In fact, suggestions that I may have had such would draw looks of skepticism, even scorn from some colleagues. So, to admit to myself, much less to others, that I had had an encounter with the Holy Spirit… Listen, can we just keep that between us? I am telling you this only to help you connect the dots of my thinking between that time and the moment of what? Catharsis?

Too Freudian? Okay… a moment of realization, Revelation. Whatever you want to call what happened in my counselor's office was connected to those moments early in my sabbatical, especially with the word, Rest.

"Rest."

"Be of good courage."

"Rest."

He—God— forced me, over the course of 58 years, to this moment. A child, a warrior, and now, a man. An older man. An older man whose anger made him a warrior as a young man; whose anger resulted from a betrayal of his childhood. An older man whose anger forced him–finally–to seek peace, to seek respite from the rage fueled by the pain I felt from the most profound wound.

The mystery of a time before, which is now

> *I write to you, little children,*
> *Because your sins have been forgiven for his name's sake.*
> *I write to you, fathers,*
> *Because you know the one who is from the beginning.*
> *I write to you, young men,*
> *Because you have overcome the evil one.*
> *I have written to you, little children,*
> *Because you know the Father.*
> *I have written to you, fathers,*
> *Because you know the one who is from the beginning.*
> *I have written to you, young men,*
> *Because you are strong, and the word of God abides in you,*
> *and you have overcome the evil one.*
>
> 1 John 2:12–14

One day I was working on a sermon for a completely unrelated topic when I read these lines in 1 John. It's a small letter toward the end of the New Testament written by one of Jesus' original followers. As I read them, I was transported back to my spot in the prairie's formless void.

I was stunned, as I had been the first time I "went" there, though not as abruptly. But it felt just as powerful as when I heard, Before she was your mother, she was my daughter.

The words leaped off the page and into my heart.

Little children…

Those who are meant to be safe, meant to be protected, meant to know that they're able to screw up and still be loved, and still be welcomed home. I was once a little child, before...

Fathers…

Those who are meant to know that eternity is theirs, that meaning has been fulfilled and their purpose—raising their children—has been sustained by Him who is from the beginning, before…

Young men…

Warriors meant to fight with confidence, courage, and determination. Those who are meant to overcome evil; to know the parameters of the battle and to be certain of the outcome – because they know the One who has already overcome the evil one, before…

Before! God is before all things and through all things. He is Sovereign, as the Good Book says, "the same, yesterday, today, and forever." He does what He says He will do. How do I know this? Because He showed Himself to me as the One who has been before, during, and beyond the events of my life—in the things I heard and saw that day in the counselor's office—when I finally hit the limits of my ability to figure out, reason out, the unreasonable that had happened to me. He showed Himself to me in the strange, but healing calm of the vision of myself sitting in the middle of the prairie. Sitting perhaps for the first time, at rest.

You might assume that my routine sermon preparation was dramatically interrupted that day, and you'd be right. I sat pondering the significance of these words for me. I was the little child who was robbed of innocence. I hadn't been safe. And once, I was the young man, a warrior, fighting with everything in me to make mom better, but failed. Now I am the father, an older man, who came to the brink of despair. In every eon of my life I have come up short. The hurt I have felt has created a snowballing anger that turned into an avalanche from which I could not escape. I saw it, I felt it's cold, choking weight pressing down on me.

As each phase of life has more quickly revealed the limits of my competence to cope with it, I have finally collapsed from sheer exhaustion, overtaken by the very thing I have alternately tried to control and outrun. So, here I am today, finally fallen from the tower of belief in my ability to subdue life's most threatening challenges. But instead of falling into despair, quite inexplicably, I've fallen into a realm of peace and rest. A realm that is devoid of the A+B=C rationality to account for the causes and effects which have taken their toll on me. No, now I am in the quiet of the prairie.

Of course, I know well the wounds that threatened my existence, in body and soul. They have become second nature. But the wounds which inflicted the deepest pains I could ever imagine no longer define me. Yes, they have certainly contributed to the outline of my life. But there is something more, something deeper, something I cannot explain, which has cast everything in an entirely different light.

God is after all, finally answering my boyhood cry for understanding, for insight, for wisdom. He is calming my roiling anger. And out of that calm, He is transforming monster lust to beautiful, life–giving desire.

I still struggle. Too often I feel ripped away from my prairie sanctuary. When I feel that displacement, I scratch my head asking if I can return to it, or whether the original experience was only intended to be a temporary respite from the ongoing primal struggle of my life? I don't have an answer.

Genius discovery: order out of chaos when chaos persists

Today, writing this, I have been able to return to my prairie sanctuary if only, perhaps, to take you with me. But this is no small thing, for either of us. I've lived long enough to know that I am far from being I alone in needing the refreshing wind of His grace and mercy. It blows away what is transient and nourishes the soul, stirring simple, pleasant peace. It has been my hope that some kind of good might come out of the hellish things I've experience.

Perhaps you have already taken heart from what I've told you, that everything in and about your life is not all despair and futility. And trust me, nothing about being a minister has given me a leg up on getting to where I am. In fact, my public persona as a Rev. has made it harder for me to land where I am. Why? Because I've spent so much time beating myself into a life of calm resolve with the theological information that I was sure should have enlightened me faster than others. Was I ever wrong. And my journey is far from over, far from finished. There's more in store, though I couldn't tell you today what it is. I just know that He is, and He is for me, just as surely as He is for you.

Mom's journey was tough for her and hard for me to watch. But now, this portion of it, as we know it in this flesh and blood realm, it's over.

I am convinced, that she is more fully and completely experiencing what it means that she is His daughter than she ever knew before. Now she knows what role her disease played in His cosmic narrative for all those who were touched by it, perhaps including you.

Her pain shaped my soul. He used that pain just as deftly as a sculptor wields his spatula on clay to reveal something of unique, breathtaking beauty, something that was not seen by others before it came to be. In the meantime, I'm looking forward to the day when I will know as fully as I ever will that I am His son. But I'm not passively waiting. I'm hopeful, expectant, in a new kind of calm rest. He is teaching me to rest in the knowledge that He is before.

Imagine me… angry, wounded, abused, lost child letting go of seeking justice! It's not what we do. It's not what I've done. But I'm doing it now. Not because I talked myself into it, or because I'm an old man who's out of gas. I rest because He took me to the end of myself and showed me that I can exist secure in Him. Does that mean bad things don't happen? No. Or that they won't happen? No. But my life is no longer defined by the "what happened" or by "what's happening."

I told you one of my heroes was Martin Luther King, Jr. The kind of peace I experience now is echoed in the last, and perhaps greatest speech of his life, delivered in Memphis, Tennessee on April 3, 1968.

> *Well, I don't know what will happen now. We've got some difficult days ahead. But it really doesn't matter with me now, because I've been to the mountaintop. And I don't mind.*
>
> *Like anybody, I would like to live a long life. Longevity has its place. But I'm not concerned about that now. I just want to do God's will. And He's allowed me to go up to the mountain. And I've looked over. And I've seen the Promised Land.*

God who showed King the Promised Land has shown me that it's alright. I've seen that He is before, and that's changed my perspective on everything. He has given me to know that the child whose security and joy was robbed, is actually safe, and can still know joy. All is not lost; it never was, because He is before, and I am His. The One who permitted my mother's disease, my abuser to abuse me, my father to grow through his frustrated missions to fix what he could not fix – that One whom I have so deeply resented at being asked to trust Him… I am learning that He is worthy of my trust because He was and is

Before. He is Now and He is Who He will be. He has resolved all my questions even though I don't know what all the answers are, yet. He did it Before. You and I will discover it later. It's alright with me. I don't mind anymore.

You and I aren't alone in our wondering, let alone our quest for relief from our most urgent anguish. We're not the first and we won't be the last. Consider Job who lost everything. Consider Jonah who was swallowed by a whale and coughed up on the shores of a town who rejected his message. Consider Peter, who after being convinced that Jesus was the God–man, denied him three times. And there's Paul who officially persecuted the first Christians—I mean imprisoned them and arranged for their torture and executions. He was transformed from henchman to holy man and became the greatest preacher in the history of the world.

There are saints and sinners from every age, in every land, in every culture, who, like me, have known pain. But all of us have in common our Father who is Before; and we are his sons and daughters. He loves us. He is wise. He knows. He leads. He has plans, purpose, meaning, destiny, dignity–in store for us all. Nothing... nothing that has happened, is wasted, and our pain is not the end. In my case it might have been the beginning.

I am learning to trust Him more – more, at least, than I was able to while I nursed my wounds, continually reopened them as if I could examine them more critically to get to their cause and somehow fix them. My counselor pointed out that pattern. He reminded me that as long as I kept opening them, my wounds would never heal. And, even though there will be scars they are not only reminders of the wounds but of my healing from them. Now when I see and show my scars, I do it as evidence of something life–changing that happened in the past which has actually led me to where I am today. It's all possible because of the One who is Before it all.

So, for now, as a veteran warrior, I fight for beauty. I'm turning toward others wearied by the changes and chances of life, offering a listening heart and a place of respite from the hurt, anger, and disappointments. I'm finding that instead of siding with the wounded in their offense, I'm offering kindness—born from insight I never knew was possible while I was writhing in pain and clamoring for justice. Oh, I hear and feel the wounds of other. But now I can offer hope–not because I figured anything out, but because He showed me that He is before.

I cannot fix anything or anyone. I couldn't fix myself. None of it is mine to fix. But I can walk with you, listen to you, pray for you… that He will show you Himself as the One who has always held you in His embrace from before. Before that happens it's possible, you'll reach the end of yourself. With the utmost care and respect for who you are, what you've been through, and what you are going through right now, I hope you do come to that end because that's when you'll be able to see Him like never before. And when the time comes, as we travel together, perhaps we can arrive at our prairie rest together, where Before becomes Now–Forever.

Reflections

Groundhog Day could be called Dave's rape day. Waking up to the same old story with more nuances discovered day after day is simply hell. The cycles Dave has repeated eventually landed him, well… at the end of himself. In my experience, those who are most deeply wounded almost invariably come to some kind of unbearable crisis moment that unbelievably supersedes the power and pain of the original wound.

As I write this I'm struck by the similarity, even if there is a vastly different nuance, between the phrases original wound and its distant cousin original sin. Theologians believe that it is the original sin, the defiance of God, that puts us at risk of eternal hell. I'm not here to argue the point. But what I'm seeing in our storytellers and so many that cross my path is not so much the effect of a willful decision to do things contrary to the Almighty's prescribed way. No, what I'm seeing are lots of people who are undone by the original wound. Certainly, they can be one and the same thing. But how can we sit in judgment of anyone, say like David, who lost so much at such an early age as a result of choices that were not his to make? As I say, I'm not here to rebut or defend whether or not it is the original sin that throws the monkey wrench into the working gears of our lives. I do know this, thousands, millions of people are suffering under the weight of their original wound. And I also know that I am seeing God redeeming, renewing, restoring and healing Dave, and countless others of us, from a life which has been twisted and gnarled by so many things over which we have little, if any, control. Is there anyone of us who can't identify with the feeble and faulty efforts Dave took to make things right. All the kings horses and all the kings men (and women) can't put Humpty Dumpty together again.

No, I suspect Dave's almost never–ending nightmare had an unseen drive that joined his yearning for relief with the intent of God to reach into his life. God entered into Dave's suffering. By my standards, perhaps yours too, this is not the way life should be. But that's my friends is the way it so often is.

So how do we go forward? Doing the best we can with what we know of God who knows us through and through. As Dave says, trusting, hoping. And, by his own example, being willing to go to the mat, facing the most hellish things that drive us crazy. You know, we aren't alone in this. Every character in Dave's story played a role in his transformation.

So, here's one minister who, when he speaks to his flock, isn't just rattling off what might be called theological gossip – talking about things he's heard about but never experienced firsthand. No, Dave, my friends, is the real deal. He's been to hell and back. I'm sure there are moments when he is circumspect, working to convince others of God's love while at the same time seeking to live in the experience of that love, that quiet, sitting in the prairie grasses blown by the wind which is nether hot nor chill. In other beginning chapters I spoke about firing where we wire and wiring where we fire. This is how Dave experienced life for decades, trying to find a way out of his wound.

Where are you in Dave's story? Are you in it?

His Genius, his superpower, does not often or always directly benefit him. But when he watches and profoundly hears and walks among people, sensing their hidden wounds and their own incessantly annoying time loops, his Genius awakes... "BEFORE." He gently reaches over into another's suffering in the most sensitive, perceptive and insightful ways allowing the voice of God to repeatedly speak to the wounded soul saying, "I got you, babe."

Dave's epilogue

I have a Genius, I'm told. Personally, I think (well, I've told him what I think–the one who told me I have a Genius. I won't repeat here what I said to him.) My indecorous response notwithstanding, he made me think about my wound–even convinced me to write about it. After two years, he showed me what I'd written. Oh, so embarrassing–just awful writing.

Yet, I read it through again. And buried in that very tacky prose, I vividly recall what I was going through when I first wrote my story for this collection. I was transported back to my counselor's office and lifted into the images that emerged in the critical moment when God broke through to me. I'm "there" now, if you will. The fact that I'm sitting at my table writing about it, is testament to the power of that "place" to which the Lord took me.

That "place" is grounded in reality. That is to say, the mental image I am inhabiting is not abstract. It is a realistic image of a place on the American prairie–flat, grassy, sky and horizon sewn together as far as the eye can see. And I sit in it, staring–feeling the breeze on my cheek, the warmth of the sun, the rustling of the grasses, the firmness of hard turf underneath. This imaginary place has all the benchmarks of reality. Except, I've never been to the prairie. I'm drawing on photos, and film sequences, and descriptions from history books.

It is thus intriguing to me that such an image would be what God would use to move me, so to speak, away from my pain in the first place then, and now, these two years later, return me there–and at a time when I feel the need for the respite it provides. My friend could not have known my need right now, not so specifically, anyway. But the fact that I'm now transported back to this mythical refuge... well, it's all very interesting...

And soothing. When I first "went" to this imaginary retreat, I wanted to guard it from intrusions–and yes, from intruders, people. It was people, after all, who drove me to it; it was people who harmed me, people whose own harm I could not "fix." People were/are the problem. Back then, I was sure they would cause whatever was soothing in my prairie, to evaporate like mist. Why? Because I was afraid I'd be forced to address their clamoring needs and my own wound be ignored, yet again.

But today, having reread my story—which was just now surprisingly thrust under my nose by my friend—I have to admit that there's a new dimension opening up in me. There's a new desire emerging–small, perhaps tentative–but a willingness to open my solitude to other wounded hearts who may themselves need a place to find rest. That's not at all where I was before. Before I was afraid that the mere presence of someone else's need would demand that I stop to "fix" it. I cannot fix. I am slowly making my peace with that. Being in the presence of needs that I knew I could not fix used to feel like impotence, like vulnerability. I could not prevent injury to myself or anyone else, no matter how much I wished and worked to stop it.

But in this new moment, I don't feel impotent or exposed. No, not at all. Instead I feel clothed by the expanse of the prairie that surrounds me. Now, all I want to do is to share that comfort with anyone who might need it.

Share that comfort. Share the comfort. That's my desire now. God be pleased to grant it. Amen.

Chapter 8: The Man Behind the Mask

I met Fred at a bar in DC that has blues music every Monday night. He's about 80 years old, playful, self-deprecating, and loves to dance with the ladies—but always at a safe distance. His hair and dress are stellar silver, perfect sartorial splendor. There are usually 15 to 20 dancers in the back of the room, and Fred would often be in the fray, except when the music slowed. Slow dancing isn't Fred's thing. There's nothing slow about him.

He seemed bigger than he should be—not in physical stature, but in presence. I started wondering as I watched him. He became a friend who I saw almost weekly. When my wife and I hosted a Halloween party at my home I invited some friends from the bar. Fred came in a devil's costume that was well conceived. He even carried a pitchfork and spoke in character with timely devilish humor. But Fred seemed to be more than a guy who was having a good time at a party. With all the pomp and circumstance, he observed in his dress and his chosen role it was as if Fred had discovered a stage to act out a side of himself, he dearly wanted to but needed the mask to do it.

I almost told him, "Fred, you didn't need to take this party so seriously." But I was wrong. The very next year Fred dressed as the puppet cowboy, Howdy Doody. Once again, the hair, clothes, character, and humor were big and loud–an otherwise muffled voice shouting from behind a mask. But what was he saying? What did it mean? Over time we became better friends and had many quick hellos in the bar in-between songs. I liked him and sensed he enjoyed me, and my wife, as well. He would often scold me for not bringing my wife to the Blue Monday event. When I did, she delighted in his request for a dance.

One time a New Orleans style jazz band came to the bar. When Fred walked, I saw a visceral change in him. It was as if they were playing his music. I didn't know then, that Fred was from New Orleans— ground zero for Mardi Gras, the French and African hybrid of the ancient festival of Carnival with its masks and parades.

Carnival takes its name from the Latin carne levare meaning "removal of meat." The Catholic Church's observance of Lent was a time of spiritual emphasis on the need of humans for a savior due to our sinful character, driven as we are by our carnal, fleshly needs and desires. Among other practices of Lent, the church required abstinence from eating meat. So, before the somber period of self-denial, carnaval came to be a popular festival of fleshly excesses in anticipation of the "farewell to the flesh" that would be the theme of Lent's 40 days. In a word, Carnival is the ritualized adult spring break, in which social norms and behaviors are completely upended, reversed. It's as if someone said, "You know we really are perverse. Rather than hide it, let's just go all out and admit it. Let's party!" But the risk in partying that hard is having to own up to who you really are afterward. Thus, the need for masks and costumes which are supposed to disguise the revelers. If there is any redeeming value to the tradition of Mardi Gras/Carnival, it's that by the time Easter rolls around, the need for salvation from our debauched lives could not be any plainer.

Masks and parades allow people to be anyone they want, safe from the constraints and consequences of ordinary life. The mask provides anonymity. The parade? The safe gathering of its masked participants to party like there's no tomorrow.

Why the mask, why the parade? Maybe you will get more answers as you explore Fred's world and his wound. His wound has a Genius that took 71 years to be revealed… and it's a wonder to behold.

Who I Was

I was born in New Orleans, we moved to Dallas, then to Baton Rouge and back to New Orleans. Shortly before returning to New Orleans, after 9 years away, a grammar school teacher groped me in his office. He pulled me into him and told me it was not a sin to have an orgasm, as long as I did not "spill the seed." I was confused. I didn't understand his advance. But I pulled away and left quickly. He was not one of my regular teachers and I never saw him again.

I was the youngest of five children. I was a surprise; my mother was 45 years old when I was born. She was glad to have me, however, and expressed it in many ways. Soon after my birth, my dad lost his job due to the Great Depression and the family moved away for a while; to Dallas then Baton Rouge. Shortly before the outbreak of WWII, dad found work as a traveling industrial rubber salesman there. Every week he left home Monday and returned on the weekend. He did much of his work in restaurants and bars.

My oldest brother and my sister, both late teens and young adults, shared the parenting role with my mother. They taught me how to pitch and play baseball, how to dress and mix colors, and how to dance. Along with my father, they helped instill a long-term interest in residential architecture. My oldest brother, a star athlete at LSU, left to become an officer in the Navy. My sister, a beauty court maid at LSU, left to marry a decorated soldier with 253 combat days and multiple wounds.

My mother had a free-fall in her life style when dad lost his job and we left New Orleans, though I never heard her complain about it. We did not eat out in restaurants; we did not take vacation trips. I recall staying in a cabin in a park once; I recall driving at age 12 from the Big Easy to Boston for my oldest brother's wedding. I count those as our only family vacations.

We lived in a small Craftsman house with a dirt yard. My two older brothers and I slept in the same bedroom. The war was on and we had not yet received the benefits of its technological advances. These were "ice box, wringer washer, clothes line, steam iron, hand-washed & dried dishes, victory garden, and chicken coop" days. New personal goods were not being manufactured. Everything we had — bikes, cars, appliances—constantly needed repair. We all had daily household chores to do to keep the household afloat.

Because we were recovering from the Great Depression and supporting the war, people were much more focused on one's duty rather than on one's rights. I recall living comfortably as part of my family, my neighborhood, and my parish, and school. I was never conscious of expressing individuality the way most people are today.

When I was ten dad got a job in New Orleans as the office manager of the industrial rubber company he had worked for before the economic downturn. So, we returned to New Orleans to live in the large 1840s Greek revival cottage my father inherited from his family. The house was situated in an upscale part of the city. It had been enlarged and converted from gas to electric lighting in the Victorian era. Some electric appliances were installed but few additional improvements had been made. His sister had operated it as a boarding house for several years before we moved there in 1947. Both my dad and I were in love with the house and together we made many improvements to it. I lived there with my parents until I graduated from college.

When we returned to New Orleans, at first, I was the only child who came with my parents. My sister stayed in Baton Rouge with her husband. My older brother moved away after the war, got an engineering degree from MIT and moved to Long Island. My middle brother who is six years older, stayed with my sister to complete his last year of high school. He returned to live with us in New Orleans a year or so later. He lived with us until his marriage in 1963, except when serving in the Army in Germany during the Korean War. He was good to me, sent me gifts from Germany, loaned me his motor bike while away, and his new car for dating when he returned.

A popular New Orleans book is titled, "Who's Your Mamma, Are You Catholic and Can You Make A Roux?" There, your lineage is all-important for social acceptance. My parents had good blood lines, but no money to go with them. And, they were only high school educated, living in a neighborhood full of medical, legal, and financial professionals and business owners. My mother was very religious but my father, not so much. She was Catholic; he was Anglican. He attended Catholic services with us. I was very conscious of this patch work lineage and it embarrassed me.

Mom ran the household; dad insisted that we treat her with respect. I think he suffered from depression and low self-esteem but with no awareness of his condition, and certainly no outside help. My friends loved him. Mom wished he'd spend less time at the corner bar. My parents didn't entertain at home, though mom had outside social activity through church, civic organizations, and her bridge group. We were supposed to look good and be good. Having good table manners and knowing formal place settings was very important. "Don't talk about family matters outside the house." "Don't cry, nobody will like you; get over it!"

I entered a Catholic parish grammar school and made several close friends. We were average kids; not the tough guys, not the smart guys, not the rich guys. We were average students, academically. Five of us remained friends for life. In a city where everybody was defined, I knew my place, I was just one of the guys

What happened to me

Like a lot of other boys, I signed up to be an altar boy in my parish church. A group of us were daily servers at mass assisting about 20 priests on the Loyola University faculty. I became friends with one of the priests and, over time, became his dedicated altar boy. He took me on overnight trips, gave me expensive gifts, took me to restaurants and expanded my social horizons and skills by including me in dinners and parties in the homes and country clubs of his prominent, wealthy friends. In many ways he was a surrogate father and mentor. He had a warm social relationship with my mom and dad and spent time in our home.

At puberty, when I experienced sexual arousal and ejaculated for the first time, I knew I had sinned and needed to confess it. I went to my trusted friend and mentor, my priest. We were in his apartment. He said I was no longer a virgin. To mark the occasion, he wrote the date on a poster hanging on his wall. The caption read "Just a boy."

After that conversation he gradually—and I now know—deliberately moved in on me. Whenever he got me alone, he kissed, groped, and fondled me. He may have abused me even prior to my conscious awareness. On several trips to Spring Hill College in Mobile, Alabama he took me swimming naked in a pond on the property. Occasionally he examined my circumcision, saying he was concerned that it might have been done improperly and he wanted to be sure it would not affect the growth of my penis. Every one of these events echoed the original sin I experienced at the hands of the Dallas teacher. The disgust I felt reverberated through my entire being. And this was just the first of many cuts that would wound my conscience.

The dark side

I could not make sense of what was happening to me—that a priest was doing this to me. Nor could I reconcile what I felt was my inability to do anything about it. I was pretty sure my mother would never believe that anyone, especially a Catholic priest, was doing this to her son. So, I told no one. I was afraid of being chastised for spreading lies about the Church and creating a scandal. I reasoned that I'd be worse off if I spoke up.

When I was about 15 my priest was transferred to Mobile for two years. I don't know for certain, but suspect he was sent to a sex abuse rehabilitation program. I received a letter from him telling me that his behavior toward me had been wrong. He hoped that what happened would not deter my interest in the priesthood. But it was too late. When he came back to New Orleans, I was a junior in high school. We resumed our friendship, but I made sure we were never together alone. He was instrumental in getting me a scholarship to college and helped me join a fraternity he favored. Shortly after graduating from college I was engaged to be married. He was going to officiate the ceremony but died of heart failure.

My adolescence had been stolen from me; my emotional and social development were arrested, or at least severely retarded; I had been scarred for life. The effects of the wound only deepened over time. As my friend the priest abused me, I developed tactics to cope, but these became a way of life; a way to survive the trauma that effectively neutered my ability to feel and experience anything. These efforts to protect myself set the stage for a life-long battle with clinical depression and alcoholism.

Intuitively knowing that what was happening was wrong, but feeling powerless to do anything about it, I prayed that I would not have a sexual response. I forced myself to freeze, to suppress the sensations and emotions, and to mentally flee the scene. Living in desperation, I cultivated a vigilance that dominated me. As an adult, I have unconsciously applied these reasonable, but childlike autopilot responses to everything that my soul senses is unsafe. I am self-focused and self-conscious. I freeze in conflict and fear, suppressing action, incapable of responding in healthy, self-nurturing, free, open, and appropriate ways. I am neither focused nor interactive in conversation; I don't do small talk well. I have difficulty staying connected to what's happening in the moment. I can't sustain being present because everything in me was stuck in overdrive to keep me from being where I was. Why? Because it was so bad. In male-female relations I'm guarded, fearing my contact or comments will be interpreted as inappropriate.

By the time I entered high school, I was obsessed with a pathological guilt about moral and religious issues. I was conflicted by what my priest was doing to me, by his advice that I should not go steady with my girlfriend, by the admonishments of the nuns that touching girls is the "near occasions of sin," and the inclinations and movements of my own body. Because I couldn't talk to anyone about any of this, I got my own copy of a Catholic Moral Theology (published in 1948). It was a guide to help priests provide spiritual counsel to the penitent in the confessional. But I had to find some way to process what was happening to me. So, I secretly studied it, particularly the part about the Sixth Commandment, "thou shalt not commit adultery." At the time, Catholic moral theology was all about defining sins, counting them, and confessing them. This merely reinforced what I was already experiencing.

I have no recollection of my Catholic high school religious education. I know that we were not encouraged to read the Bible. Our guidance about the Bible, Christianity, and the Church was found in the Baltimore Catechism, the standard handbook for all K-12 American Catholic school religious education since the late 1800s. What the church was committed to us knowing and believing was presented in a series of questions and answers that we memorized. Know this stuff inside and out and you knew what was important in life, about yourself, God, the world, heaven, and hell. Pretty convenient.

The persistent guilt over the condition of my soul was like a toxic stew that fed an insatiable, high-performing perfectionism. I tried to live distant from and above the crowd. I developed a talent for sarcasm and off-color jokes that strangely left me with the sensation of being connected to others and simultaneously removed from them at the same time. In order to quench the self-condemning awareness of my sexual abuse, to try and hide it from myself and others, I became very busy. I got involved in many school organizations. Adrenaline was my drug of choice to numb my feelings. I have vivid memories at age 12 dressed in a business suit and my mother's friends saying that I was "such a responsible child". That pleased me, my efforts were noticed and affirmed.

When I started high school, I got a part-time job. I worked as a neighborhood electrician's helper, installing electric circuits, duplex outlets, light fixtures, and outdoor TV antennas in many of the old Victorian homes in the area. This provided me the money needed to buy a more effective drug to numb my feelings—alcohol. A fifth of Ainsley Scotch cost $2.50, about one Saturday's earnings. Around age 18, I bought a used tuxedo and a set of tails, the requisite uniform for to participate in the social scene as a "Debutante's Delight." This insured many months of free liquor at endless parties each year during the Debut and Carnival season.   Achievement was my goal. Public recognition meant everything to me. At my high school graduation, I was awarded Outstanding Student not only by my senior class peers, but also by the school's faculty.

The foundation for success firmly set, I repeated it over and over again. In college I became student council president. Four years later I was named Outstanding Male Student at graduation. As was customary at the time, I married one of the debutantes at age 22; by age 26 we had three of our four children. At age 24, I graduated first in my Nuclear Weapons Officer's Class. After serving in the Army, I joined the country's largest, richest, and most successful computer corporation. At age 27, I wrote the application control program for the Gemini Mission Control Center. In my early 30s, I played key roles in the Apollo 11 Lunar Landing mission and in the Apollo 13 rescue mission. At age 37, I was managing a 750-man Space Shuttle Software Development Laboratory in Houston. At age 43, I was Director of Software Engineering and Technology for my 10,000-man division.

But these accomplishments had served to insulate me, protect me from genuine intimate relationships. I was slow to trust and cautious about getting too deeply involved with others, professionally or socially. As my family and my job expanded, I was required to be in more and more social situations where I felt unskilled, inadequate, and frankly threatened. In order to cope, my use of alcohol expanded to daily drinking. On weekends it was all day. I was an egomaniac with an inferiority complex, but the alcohol and adrenaline kept things in balance.

The lifetime efforts to compensate for wounds that were too great to handle cultivated what I suppose was the inevitable fruit—depression. Beginning in 1974, I've experienced a recurring cycle of major depressive episodes. Initially it seemed to be triggered by unresolved conflict in a very stressful job. In the midst of a major design review of my group's work with other NASA contractors I experienced a surprise panic attack. That event unleashed an almost immobilizing period that ebbed and flowed, lasting almost 40 years, ending in 2011.

In September 1980 I was hospitalized for nine weeks with clinical depression. Until recently, I chalked up this breakdown to my promotion into a new and unfamiliar job, my perfectionism, and the stress of being the sole breadwinner for a family of six. The hospital adjusted my medications and suggested that I stop drinking. I decided to stop for two years but I didn't feel any better. I missed the fun of the weekend binges. As soon as the two years were up, I started in all over again. Finally persuaded by my psychiatrist, I stopped drinking at age 51 and it's lasted to this very day.

The first two and a half years were extremely difficult. Without alcohol to smooth out—or blot out—the realities of my life, I experienced panic attacks in unstructured situations—where I couldn't control or orchestrate things—like holiday family gatherings, business marketing functions, and charity events. There was no escaping the feelings of depression. I couldn't maintain my workaholic pace, so I began to reduce my job responsibility and hours at work. Though my bosses seemed to understand they really didn't. I was continually pressed to take positions with even greater responsibility. If I worked anything less than a 60 to seventy-hour week I felt disoriented and guilty. When I was not actively engaged with co-workers on a specific project, I was self-conscious and uncomfortable around them. I wasn't used to taking a lunch break in the cafeteria and eating with other employees. I knew nothing about their personal lives.

A byproduct of reducing my work hours meant I was spending more time at home. But my role there was changing. Our children were adults, no longer living with us, and my wife had begun building a successful business career. Just at the moment I was being drawn into the home, she was being drawn out of it. Never having been able to initiate or sustain an intimate relationship with her it became obvious that we were moving in opposite directions, like the proverbial two ships passing in the night. At age 53, we decided to separate and end our 30-year marriage.

I moved out of our large home in a wooded area near two country clubs to an apartment next to the parking lot of a large suburban shopping center. Except for the few months I had lived in a boarding house just after graduating from college I was living alone for the first time in my adult life. It was terrifyingly lonely.

At first, I was unreliable in my personal commitments because I did not know how to keep a calendar or manage my schedule. This had been done by my mother until I graduated from college, and by my wife and secretaries thereafter. I was having difficulty adjusting to my changed role at work. I was no longer the center of attention. My depression was increasing. I was adrift. In 1991 my company created incentive packages to encourage long-time employees to retire. Somewhat fearfully, I decided to accept the buy-out, one year's salary, and a significantly reduced pension. So ended my 32-year career at age 54.

Everything that happened, culminating with the early retirement, stripped me down to basics. At age 51 I had a nice house, a nice wife, and a nice job. Three years later I had no house, no wife, and no job. I was all alone for the first time in my life.

The Genius

With few responsibilities beyond taking care of myself, I started to explore aspects of my own being, my personality, and character, all ignored, and underdeveloped in adolescence. As a young boy I had to suppress the pain that flowed from terrifying experiences I didn't know how to handle, and so I leapfrogged over some, maybe most, of the important developmental phases of life. And that crippled me. I've had to go back in time and revisit chapters of my life to discover and fill in the blanks that were created by all the props I put in place to avoid feeling the searing pains that I was sure would overwhelm me.

Without work I am alone, unaccountable, and unattached. The performance-based, image-projecting, professionally superlative life has come to a screeching halt. I've shed my 3-piece suits, monogrammed, button-down shirts, repp ties and cap-toe shoes to pick up where life left off, from the place where—out of desperation—I abandoned my younger self.

I've made a conscious, no longer reactive, decision to try to open up—to myself and others. I've begun to see the layers of self-protective defenses and unconscious behaviors that were imposed to assure I'd safely live at arm's length from anything that could threaten me. I've grown so weary of hiding behind a masquerade. I want to experience and know the real me. So, I've decided to become unmasked, risking life beyond the boundaries and fears—with its unpredictable joys and pains. Doing life the old way, tightly controlled, has been deadly. And though I am now far more vulnerable to what can, and often does, happen, I'm also freer, more present, more in the moment, more in touch with myself, than I've ever been. For the first time I feel like a human being instead of a human doing. After a lifetime of living in control, convinced that I could guarantee every outcome, I have accepted the fact that being human means I am and must be vulnerable to things far beyond my control. And that means I am risking feeling pain. Who, in their right mind, wants to voluntarily sign up for that! But I vowed that I'd find a way to let go of my perfectionism and let this new life, my real life, unfold as it will—not a moment in time event that I can manipulate, but a journey. Who knows what might happen?

In my tentative openness to a new way of life I thought a try at sowing my wild oats would be a good place to start. Why? Perhaps it was because the most tender and deepest wound has been in the conflicted and confused moral, sexual, sin-conscious sense of myself. For most of my adult life, I attributed my lack of social skill and fear of intimacy to my perfectionism (religious scrupulosity) conditioned by the strict Catholic moral teachings of the 1950s and undergirded with a heavy dose of guilt that wasn't created by my abuse, but which was certainly intensified by it. In my adolescence I was awkward around girls and afraid of getting too close to them; and I didn't want to run the risk of developing friendships with socially-skilled boys for fear of committing sin. On my first date, in this new-found adult freedom, I discovered just how far gender roles have changed in the 30 years since my last date. Near the end of our dinner out, my she made it clear that she wanted to return to my apartment. It nearly scared me to death!

On another occasion a friend mentioned I should approach someone who he'd learned was interested in me. Her husband had recently walked out on her, her birthday was coming up soon, and she was lonely and disoriented. I called her, took her out dining and dancing on her birthday and surprisingly immediately fell in love with her. That was the end of my dating; and once again, no oats! We spent the next 20 years together. I realize now that it wasn't my religious training but my personality that caused me to seek out a monogamous, committed relationship.

I had long planned to become a "Renaissance Man" after retirement. My liberal education had stopped at the end of my freshman year in college. Being a science major in a Catholic university meant that I filled my elective slots with theology, philosophy, and extended laboratory courses. Now years later, I began a reading journey but soon experienced it to be a weighty task. I read very slowly and became tired quickly. Discovering that I suffered from Dyslexia I abandoned serious reading with great disappointment.

Not long after that, I discovered The Great Courses audio lectures and Amazon audio books. Listening has given me the opportunity I thought had been lost. Whole new worlds of interest have opened up: the history of Western thought, the Enlightenment, Church and Bible history, and the historical development of American values. It's surprising to me that after listening to several hundred hours of material I retain few of the facts I encounter. But my views and attitudes have changed from the information I've been exposed to.

I joined an older men's discussion group at Church, attended twelve-step meetings, volunteered as a driver for a community ministry, and as an information technician for a medical clinic. At first, it was difficult to make these commitments, and keep them. After a few false starts, I learned to accept failure. But instead of approaching life as an all or nothing contest, I've moderated my approach. Now I accept jobs only if I had talent in the area and if I enjoy the work. I realize I have likes and dislikes, strengths, and weaknesses. I don't have to excel at everything, not that I ever really did, but I thought I was supposed to. Imagine the unnecessary burdens I carried for years that were of my own making. I don't have to be perfect; I just have to be me.

Volunteering has exposed me to a broad cross section of people, some of them have become great friends. I'm finding it easier and more rewarding to interact with men and women, not based on our triumphs in life, but based on our common weaknesses. I'm practicing honesty, integrity, and trust in my relationships. Operating in non-homogeneous, diverse communities is giving me the skills to participate more fully in life on its terms. I've become less isolated, less rigid, and more intimate with others. The more I accept my limitations the more I've been able to accept other people just as they are without imposing judgements that used to keep me safely walled off from people. That used to happen all the time, born out of my narrow understanding of myself. I'm not afraid of people like I used to be. Now I can risk just being, and that's given me the joy of listening, listening to the naked truth that flows out people when they feel safe and respected.

In a word, I've been reborn. The insatiable curiosity that was stunted in my adolescent years has been resurrected from the grave of shame and self-loathing. I feel more alive in this end stage of life than ever before. It's as if I get life for the very first time. Do you know how wonderful it is to feel useful, living with purpose, contented?

In a one-eighty polar opposite from my button-downed professional days, I now go swing dancing, biking with a group, and I socialize with friends after church. I had no time for this —actually, no real ability— when I was working. In fact, professional life was the only place I could hide from trying to do life as a fully prepared adult. But because the foundational pieces I needed to be whole were virtually absent, I was running scared, even at work. Now the relationships I enjoy are no longer measured, controlled or calculated on the basis of how I can stave off being found out as an insecure, emotionally delayed man.

Because the masquerade I used to survive in life could never take the place of real life I now see that it—the mask—had to finally crumble. Yes, I was terrified when it did. There was nothing familiar to hold on to. Though I haven't experienced an earthquake, I'm guessing that the terror people report when buildings and roads and houses begin to buckle and fall apart is a lot like what I felt when the things my life was built on collapsed right in front of me. There was nothing I could do except to hope and pray there'd be something of me left once the dust settled.

I'd put so much effort into presenting a picture of competence to the rest of the world that when it all came tumbling down, at first, I didn't recognize the me that was lying in the ashes. But now there's a spontaneity about me, an immediacy that isn't worried about what anyone else thinks. It's as if I've been released from the prison cell of self-consciousness. This recovery of adolescent naivety comes rushing out of me sometimes in sarcasm, sometimes in humor laced with off-color innuendo. It takes others by surprise—here's an old guy whose seasoned appearance communicates wisdom and social grace, but whose boyish antics, never properly expressed when I was young, come tumbling out, raising more than a few eyebrows. At times it comes across humorous and endearing; and sometimes as crude and off-putting. Add to that the flamboyant, demonstrative character of my New Orleans roots and I can be downright showy. I love to celebrate special occasions in costume and decorate my front door and balcony on public holidays. Even though this new me—actually the real me let loose—runs these risks, I'm now living more honestly than ever before. I like the me who has finally emerged from a lifetime of repressed (and depressed) personality. Now I am known for who I really am not, for what I try to manipulate others into believing I am.

No longer religious, but spiritual

During the four years prior to my retirement I was feeling conflicted about my work life and my depression was increasing. I was trying to connect with God, so I could turn some of the crap in my life over to him. I felt the need to pray but didn't know how. I asked my pastor and a lifelong friend for suggestions; they suggested books about how to pray. Those books defined, discussed, and explained all kinds of prayer, but not how to pray! After several frustrating years of trying, a friend wisely told me, "The way you learn to pray is just do it - start small."

So, I started this new approach by praying in my car on the way to work. I would ask for guidance in my work and help for handling my depression. I'd end every time with the words, "Thank you" which I had been instructed to do. When my self-consciousness subsided, I moved my praying into the house, and I started reading from a book of daily meditations. But I wasn't able to retain what I read, even after reading a page several times. When I finally retired, I had more time for regular prayer and meditation. One day, by grace or by chance, I brought the book into the bathroom with me during my hot bath. That daily ritual became my home chapel for the next 10-15 years. I found I could focus and pray and connect in the confined space, with a minimum of distraction. The hot bath added to the peaceful experience.

Daily prayer, meditation, and spiritual reading, reinforced by occasional discussions with people of similar interests, has helped me internalize more mature spiritual insights –my truths about non-material realities. Here are some of the discoveries which have changed my life:

- Misery is optional; I can't get away from pain, but I don't have to add misery to it.

- God is not a puppeteer. He does not directly modify or manipulate me, others, or the physical world. He guides me in dealing with all of life.
- My prayer should be directed to seeking God's guidance; not asking for specific things for myself or others.
- God uses both good and evil (joy and pain) for my benefit.
- I must act my way into new ways of thinking; I cannot think my way into a new ways of acting. We learn from experience. For me theology is an academic (thinking) exercise; not a spiritual one.
- If I follow the physical laws of nature, I will be healthy; if I follow the spiritual laws of nature, I will be happy.
- Prayer is the pathway into the kingdom of God (his rule, his mind, his way); Thankfulness (gratitude) opens the door.
- I should only give advice if a person believes they have a problem, they believe I have an answer to the problem, and they ask me for it.
- The fundamental thing I should (can) know and internalize about God is that I am not him. My grandiosity and procrastination are driven by my subconscious idolatrous belief that I can do things perfectly (and on my own). My humanity propels me to want to do the next right thing, but my idolatry wants me to do the next thing right!
- I am human, I am flawed, and I will make mistakes. My scope of influence lies in the present moment. The result of my action is in the future, in God's domain.
- Mood follows action. Just do it!
- Holding resentment is like drinking poison and hoping the other person dies!

Insights from experiences that changed me

I now see that my priest seduced me, using the abuse for his pleasure and to become my surrogate father who gave me many material and cultural gifts. Strangely, though the abuse obviously wounded me, many of the gifts I received from him formed me in ways that enhanced my life and my effectiveness in the world. While I love my natural father greatly, he could not have given me these things. He was a loving, high school-educated, alcoholic with low self-esteem.

For most of my life I didn't believe that my abuse had any significant impact on me and so I haven't obsessed about it. Even now I don't hold any major resentment against my abuser. The attention that my alcoholism received as a cause for so much upheaval in my life hid the actual underlying the cause of it. In fact, I don't recall the subject of sexual abuse ever coming up during my therapy sessions or hospitalization for depression. Over the years, a few different confidants and several professionals who reviewed my medical history were alarmed that I had not been treated for the sexual abuse. Until recently, I have not felt the need to process this issue in therapy. After all, I didn't believe I was seriously affected by it. Since I hadn't been raped—physically penetrated—I was not even sure that my experience qualified as "sexual abuse." The reason I held this secret for 60 years is that I could never answer the question I knew would be asked, "Why didn't you stop it?" But the 2002 Boston Globe's exposure of extensive sex abuse by clergy in that diocese enlightened me and freed me to explore my situation with others. I now believe the alcoholism, depression and hospitalization were directly and indirectly caused by what happened to me with the school teacher and my priest, and I have begun therapy for abuse I experienced.

Until recently, I blamed the Church—the Catholic Church— for my fears, distorted attitudes, and self-protective ways of living. But now I'm beginning to understand that it was the abuse that was the more significant factor. Unfortunately, it was two people in whom a youngster should be able to have the greatest trust—a teacher and a representative of God—not the school or the Church, who wounded me.

It's taken a long time, but meditation has dramatically calmed me down. The practice didn't come to me easily. My mind often races, turning over many people and events. I became aware that even before I woke each day I was filled with anxiety and worry. So, shortly after retiring I started to meditate with a variety of efforts and techniques. After five years I was able to quiet my mind for a minute or so as a prelude to morning prayer. But for another 20 years I made no progress. My most recent attempt in the last six months has been very rewarding. It is a directed, 10-minute meditation and it's having a significant impact in lowering my anxiety. I especially notice this in conversations and in my improved ability to listen, to myself, to others, and to God.

Reflections

Fred has come to me, again and again in our shared bar, initiating little sidebar conversations that profoundly touch me, each time deepening our relationship. When I invited him to consider sharing his story, I wasn't sure he would. So, whenever I'd see him, I'd gently encouraging him to stick with it. I felt that he had something important to share—maybe even more important to experience as he wrote—if he wrote. But pretty soon I discovered that Fred was way ahead of me. It took a while for me to realize that he'd actually taken on the challenge. I could tell when he was in the throes of fighting with his demons; he'd yell and curse at me, with a feigned air of frustration. When his momentary tirade quieted, he thanked me for the opportunity to be part of the Genius project. I'm in awe of the cathartic, healing effect that Fred and so many others experienced who bravely accepted the challenge to explore their wounds. The writing project is itself a therapeutic tool that unlocks a profound, often new, self-understanding. Turning over the events of his life, Fred has discovered his wound, and its effects on him, including the Genius gift of adolescent naivety in the last chapter of his life. At a time when many people despair over the past and fear the future, Fred is experiencing a delight in himself that appears to have conquered depression.

It's hard for us to wrap our heads around the profound effects that happened when Fred was touched the wrong way. You'll see this in some other stories as well. It's likely some of this is going to be too painful to read. So, you might ask, "How could so much carnage happen from someone's hands touching someone else's private parts? After all, it's just skin, right?" Not that we are oblivious to the repercussions that come from inappropriate touch, but on the other hand, it's difficult to accept that a life could be so tormented by such an event for so long. Shouldn't a person be able to get over it?

The same kind of doubt about the event and its consequences is evident in the story of The Fall. I've heard it; maybe you're thinking it. "Really, all of humanity fell because Adam and Eve ate an apple (or whatever it was)—Really? It was just an apple!"

Here's what I would say to you. It appears that God created our sex organs and the fruit on the tree of Knowledge of good and evil especially holy, sacred, and reserved for particular purposes, not all purposes. There is a specific kind of knowing that the use of the fruit and our genitalia were designed to communicate. So, the use of certain parts of the human body and the fruit of the tree can only be properly expressed by observing the purposes for which they were created. In contemporary Western culture, society is saturated with sex. As if it was just another piece of fruit to be plucked from the tree, there seems to be a sense in which we want it both ways—on the one hand, a no holds barred celebration of sex as the height of human expression, and on the other, a denigration of it by making sexual expression and our genitalia into things that are too common, stripped of anything special, to be consumed with anyone, anyway, anytime, for any purpose.

Argue with me if you like. But here's the rub—everyone agrees that when a child, a man, or a woman is touched in certain ways, such as rape, incest, adult-child, unwanted, and uninvited sex—the wound sustained is one of the most devastating and long-lasting of all. We find it abhorrent and repugnant. Why? Because there are some things which ought not be done. There are some things that violate the purposes for which they were created. There are some things which are special, sacred, holy and to be reserved for those purposes only. Why do you suppose that invading armies that want to finally subdue a population rape their victims? In order to defile, to intentionally break the boundaries of civil, humane relationship, so that by committing the most depraved acts the perpetrator can establish his power over his victim. Be it a marauding army, Fr. Joe, Uncle Jim, or your high school English teacher, the effects and the results are the same. There are lines which should not be crossed.

In this time and space of the "me too movement," sexual and gender identity debates, natural boundaries, and questions about the relevance of the church in today's world... every school of thought agrees... there's a sacred space and surface. The violation of Jerrys sacred space wounded him for sure. But it also led to a genius discovery. And you?

I didn't tell you that the night Fred walked into the bar and the New Orleans jazz band was playing, he popped open a silly little frilly girly umbrella and began to parade around, trying to entice other patrons to join in his joyful, carefree strut. I could tell I wasn't the only one embarrassed for him. I remember thinking, "I'm not joining THAT!" Too silly, too Mardi Gras, too adolescent."

But now, after our three-year friendship, I realize that is his music, his way back to a place, a time, a person that is the authentic Fred. His Genius is his ability to recover and reclaim the adolescence he lost in the first quarter of his life and revel in it in the final quarter. This could so easily have become the eighth and final round of a lifetime of pummeling by demons too great for him. Not so! The innocence stolen from Fred in his adolescence has resurfaced with a shiny confident polish in the eighth round of his life. That night, as Fred paraded around, and around the bar, and I watched, he no longer needed a mask to survive. Fred's Genius is his ability to play, to release the whimsical ways that are part of being a child who is preparing to live as an adult. The silly play of his grandchildren bring him joy and healing laughter. But he doesn't just delight in their innocence as an old man observing what used to be; he's living and loving his own lively self for the first time.

Fred, it's been a joy to be with you as you have slogged through the story of your life. I just have one question. What's your costume for this year's Halloween party? I know you're already thinking about it.

Chapter 9: The Cigar

Steve is a like a good cigar. Each phase of his life a puff of thought, a moment of introspection, a discovery. But he hasn't always known this.

There is such a thing as a cigar phenomenon, a sub-culture of cigar aficionados. People, mostly men, who savor the experience of selecting, smoking and enjoying the company of others who revel in the slow burn of bundled layers of cured and dried fragrant tobacco leaves. It was none other than Christopher Columbus who discovered the widespread use of tobacco among the natives of the West Indies and Central America in the late 1400s. In fact, a form of the modern-day cigar may have been used by the Mayans as far back as the tenth century. In 2012 researchers from the University of Tampa discovered 800 pre-Columbian cigars in mint condition, buried in Guatemala, dating back 600 years!

In the 1500s Spanish and Portuguese explorers learned the use of tobacco in the new world and capitalized on its popularity throughout Central America, Cuba, North America, and Europe. In 1869, in an attempt to preserve his dominance in the tobacco industry, Vincent Martinez Ybor moved his production from Havana to Key West, Florida to escape the effects of the Ten Years War in his island homeland. In 1885 he came further north to the fledgling city of Tampa where he erected the company town named for him, Ybor City. Thousands of Cuban and Spanish tabaqueros came to work the industry which by 1929 peaked in the output of 500 million hand-rolled Havana cigars, earning Tampa the title of cigar capital of the world. Now today, more than 40% of the world's most traded cigars are made in the Dominican Republic.

Aficionados are particular about their cigars, preferring them to be hand-rolled, not machine produced, and properly humidified. Though one of these can be purchased anywhere from $2 to $50, specialty cigars are the pride of the well-heeled. The 8.5-inch Gurkha Black Dragon prices out at $1,150. But that pales in comparison with Gurkha's Royal Courtesan made of rare Himalayan tobacco which is irrigated with Fiji water, infused with Remy Martin Black Pearl Louis XIII, wrapped in gold leaf, banded with diamonds, and hand-rolled by blindfolded artisans in order to heighten their sensitivity to the creation of these rarest of all smokes. A cool one million dollars will provide you the ultimate experience, hand delivered by a white-gloved messenger. By 2025 cigars are expected to be a $23 billion industry. There is such a thing as a cigar phenomenon. But why?

While millions smoke alone, there's nothing like sharing a good—or even better, a great—cigar in the presence of others. True aficionados don't simply smoke for the individual tactile pleasure. It is a bonding, connecting experience, whether you know the name and life story of the guy across the room or not. Cigar smokers are often cave-dwellers, comforted by the fragrance and ambiance of a walk-in humidor that attractively displays and carefully preserves the texture and flavor of the hundreds of varieties, shapes, sizes and prices, from all over the world. But the humidor is just the beginning of the experience. Stepping inside you remember old smokes, recalling past cigar memories while simultaneously enjoying the search for new sticks... new smokes... new flavors, and... new moments of reflection that will inevitably transport you into a timeless flow, a stream of consciousness, a connection with an awareness of the lasting things in life. This moment is what matters. Trust me. I know. I am the aficionado I am describing. I've spent countless hours with others who tell of the same sensorial experiences.

The cigar experience—I have to call it that. It's not an inanimate object that you pick up and light—it's a realm you enter, like going into a deeper state of consciousness, an experience. This experience is a blatantly mannish activity, though occasionally there are some bold women about. It's a realm of danger, challenge, and possibility. There are lots of leather chairs, and just as often as not, scotch too. Sometimes a cigar lounge is for talking, but more often I find it's for thinking, puffing, letting spaces open up in your soul, where the tempo is marked by slow drags of oxygen through the stogie, and even slower discharges of smoke that swirls and curls, almost as if carrying the unpredictable thoughts and intuitions up out of the places you didn't know existed inside you... except, then you remember, "I felt this way last time, too." And, like the endless variety of cigars, there are many different atmospheres. Some haunts are dive bars... others incite all sorts of visceral responses with their luxurious appointments, and beautiful, lighter-wielding waitresses ready to light your fire.

The three-phase smoke

Among aficionados there is this thing called the "three-phase smoke." In the first third of the smoke you pull a bit hard on the cigar, to get the draw just right, to be sure it stays lit, to be sure you'll not have to stop and restart. Done right, this initial phase sets the stage for the rest of the experience. In the second phase, once the pace has been set, the oxygen is flowing, and the cigar is slowly and steadily releasing its full favor. This is where you enter into the cigar's character, its design, and origin. The final phase is hot and so you slow down the drag because otherwise the end will come too soon. Some smokers even take a tooth pick in order to hold the last inch of the cigar ... seeking the very last possible puff. It's just too good to let it end.

But there's more to the rhythm of the cigar experience which taps into the soul of the smoker. The first phase is the launch, the initiation, the demonstration that the smoker has arrived, is part of the group. It's not just lighting up, it's theatrical, bold talk, bragging, and sending smoke circles into the air to notify competitors, even if no words are spoken. Yes, there is male ego, self-confidence, and testosterone in the smoke signals that imitate potential war-talk. It's fun, cartoonish, and a very familiar ritual. Laughter comes with the one who can land the most humiliating description of a close friend, which often includes mocking the size of his cigar. What's that about?

The first phase eventually quiets as the smoker begins to settle into the second, the beginning of introspection. In this phase the draw is steady but slow as you consider where, what, and who you are in that moment—the questions, hardships, bad day, and stories begin. There's now less about bragging and more about telling what's real, what hurts—often you experience a kind of openness to yourself, in the presence of others, that isn't customary among men. There's a kind of respectful acceptance I often think must have been the norm among cowboys and cattle rustlers as they sat around an evening campfire in bygone times. And that ushers the smoker into an even more vulnerable place.

The final phase of the cigar experience could be compared with REM sleep, that phase when consciousness has moved to another, deeper level of awareness, that our busy, preoccupied, distracted wakeful lives keep us from noticing. I think this is the phase of greatest honesty, true willingness to assess who you are ... even if that honesty is veiled by telling a story about a made-up someone else. In this final phase, there's a lot of questions, some are spoken aloud, others you just notice sitting there in your mind, making themselves known. You don't run from them. They linger. It's safe to play with what they mean, what they're about. While considering, there are long, long puffs, pauses, and a settled silence that signals the mind and heart are letting what's there just be. You see, this phase of the cigar experience can be one of near brutal honesty. Sometimes confession. I think the silence means

that your thoughts can't make their way out into audible sound, well...
because, sometimes they just need to be heard within, by the smoker's
own soul. Sometimes it's better that way.

Steve

Steve has lived the life of a cigar. A bold, bold first third—impressive,
loud, and fearless. No wimp here. A swagger of fast cars, fast women,
and even a fast religion. Then came the second phase. Things started
getting heavy, a little confusing, and lot more chaotic. Sending smoke
signals into the air for potential war partners didn't seem to hold much
thrill anymore. In the final phase Steve has experienced a brutal
honesty with himself. From what I know and have seen of him, I
suspect the point of his life has been to arrive at this place of naked
truth all along. And it seems that his Genius is finally being discovered,
revealed, and known here, as he does the slow, deep drag on the
meaning of his life. The flame of the cigar is burning hot and much
closer to his face than at any other time; like a moth to a flame, it seems
that Steve is being drawn toward authenticity no matter what the cost
might be. Care to enter the cigar bar and wade through the smoke to see
what's going on?

Who am I?

I've been granted a daily reprieve from my alcoholism contingent upon
my spiritual condition. The key is—and this is true not just with regard
to my disease but with my spiritual life as well—everything has to be
one day at a time.

Every morning I pray this prayer. "God, I offer myself to you to build
with me and do with me as you will. Relieve me of the bondage of
myself, that I may better do your will. Take away my difficulties, that
victory over them may bear witness to those who would benefit from
the help of your power, your love, and your way of life. May I do your
will always. Amen."

I was born in Mississippi, the youngest of three children in a middle-
class family. Dad was very much an entrepreneur but never hugely
financially successful. It seems in that regard there were more tough
times than good, but as a youngster I didn't know much about finances.
We were probably better off than I thought or knew.

My brother was five years older, my sister three. I can't say we really
ever bonded. To this day we're not really close. I don't know why and

don't spend too much time worrying about it. I know that I was and continue to be different. Back then, not every kid went to pre-school or kindergarten; most of us started with the first grade. I don't remember having friends before I started school. I just remember playing by myself. Maybe that's where the creative side of me came from. I'm not sure I've ever left that fantasy world, after all, it's safe.

Throughout grade school, middle, and high school I wasn't a complete loner by any means but neither did I feel like I fit in completely. I wasn't athletic, wasn't particularly good looking, and I certainly wasn't wealthy. Can you see my score card developing? Between TV shows and my imagination, it was probably along in here that I began to develop unrealistic expectations of life that would later be central to my undoing.

Fortunately, I made good grades. It was easy. I never really studied, just listened in class, and did my homework. I was lucky to have good reading and comprehension skills. I was a funny kid and learned that using humor got me noticed; it was the way I began to be accepted. I wasn't the typical class clown. I was well behaved and attentive to my studies, but I did say some funny shit and whenever people laughed, I felt good. I liked that and still do.

What happened?

Now, we're changing scenery, lifting the curtain on Act Two. The fantasy life I had created eventually led to the cultivation of some very bad habits. And all of this began infiltrating another very significant part of my life. You see, I had grown up in church. I wasn't just a church kid, I excelled at it. I won a Bible knowledge contest and was president of the youth group. I was the poster boy of the church. Seriously, everything came easily. There was no work involved. What I did and enjoyed just came by way of who I was, my personality. I didn't need to strive for anything. I didn't have any real purpose but assumed this was how my life was meant to be. I thought everything was just supposed to come my way, naturally. I assumed that my life was going to be all the things I had dreamed up inside my secret fantasy world. Looking back, I think this is where and how I was wounded.

Starting somewhere in my senior year of high school and continuing for a year or so afterward, the lure of the world seemed so much more glamorous than the church bubble that I had grown up in. There was a whole new world outside that I needed to explore—new friends to make, new ways to have fun–and boy, did I learn how to do that. Fast cars, pretty girls, and lots of money. It was great, easy, and natural.

Cracking a cold beer and lighting up a joint quickly became my new way of life. And did I mention the girls? I was beginning to see why this boy-girl thing was so attractive. It's been going on forever, causing so much pleasure and so much pain. It might sound odd that a church kid could take to this so easily. But fitting in with this crowd came to me like second nature and my conscience didn't seem to suffer any. The rules were simple: drink more, smoke more, screw more–that's what made you cool, and I wanted to be cool. And oh yeah, if you were considered crazy that was even better. It was during this phase of my life that Muhammad Egob appeared.

In my day everybody in the South had nicknames. There was Fat Jack, Wildman, Pad, Baby Boy, and then there was me, Egob. I created an elaborate story around this fictional character and morphed myself into this super cool, always brilliant, always out on the edge sort of guy. Or at least that's the version of me that was playing in my head. Egob was who I wanted to be. If you asked those who knew me then, they probably had a different version.

In retrospect, these were the formative years that shaped my pattern for dealing with life. Life was coming easy alright; it just wasn't the life I had imagined. When you have no purpose, no ethics, no morals, plenty comes your way–but none of it good. So, I had to learn how to run and hide from the bad things, because the good things were moving in the opposite direction from where I was headed. I told myself it was ok, though, because I was Egob. Being Egob was safe. I was making up my own rules.

There will be an answer, let it be

After a while the shine of partying began to wear off. I hadn't expected that—who would have thought? I was committed to "Can't we just drink beer and smoke dope forever? What's wrong with that? I'm not hurting anyone." But my thinking started to change. I reasoned that there must be something more to life besides having fun. Quite frankly, I wasn't having that much fun anymore, anyway. I started looking for something that would give my life meaning, because there wasn't much of it in me. I wasn't that virtuous at the time, so maybe I was looking for something to make me happy now that the party life was no longer doing that for me.

The first fix I decided to make was to get physically fit. I read an article somewhere that exercise would help depression, and I was experiencing that big time. I started running and playing tennis constantly. I got fit and yes, I felt a hell of a lot better. I don't know that I drank any less or smoked any less dope, but I did feel better... for a while. But eventually this empty feeling of uselessness and self-pity returned.

My next theory was that I could find meaning in my job. "I'll sink myself into my work. I'll be a professional in my sales career rather than a hack. Why not?"

It worked. I studied and invested money in training. I may not have had the talent to be a professional tennis player, but there was nothing keeping me from raising the level in my career. But in time, even that success began to leave me feeling empty. It was like making all this effort to blow up a big balloon only to find the air was slowly leaking out. The distraction that kept me at arm's length from whatever emptiness I felt by devoting energy to my career worked for a while. But I never felt any kind of lasting peace.

I even tried church again. But the harder I worked to find something, anything, that would fill the void, the pain, and size of my wound just grew deeper. Nothing made me feel connected to life or connected to myself.

Leave me the f... alone!

I've begun to tear up as I write this. Not because I'm hurting, but because I am so grateful, so thankful for the grace of God that what I'm about to describe to you is not how I have to live today. As more and more attempts to find peace, to experience serenity failed, I slowly began withdrawing from life.

I was plagued with a mental dullness. That's when I discovered I had a "f...-it" switch. Life would throw me a situation that I didn't like or didn't want to deal with, and I found out I could just say "f...-it." To a certain degree this isn't a bad thing. I think we all have to be careful not to get too caught up in things that really aren't that important. However, as is often the case with our instincts and gifts, it's not the proper use of them that causes problems; it's the misuse of them that gets us in trouble.

I was having fun with my new "f...-it" toy. Something would happen, someone would say something I didn't like, and I'd just throw my "f...-it" switch. It really seemed to work. Don't worry about it, "f...-it."

Being miserable and discontent with my life, I began using the switch more often, faster, and earlier. It progressed to point that whatever "it" was didn't have to be serious. Hell, it didn't even have to be a real time-to-throw-the-switch situation. I fell into the habit of throwing the switch so many times a day it was ridiculous. Finally, I just said, "f...-it all," threw the switch one last time and left it on!

"F... me, f... you, f... everything, and f... everybody. F... you. I don't give a f...!"

De Niro and Pacino did a movie together called Heat; De Niro was the seasoned crook, and Pacino was the down and out cop. De Niro advised his protégé Val Kilmer to have nothing in his life that he could not walk away from in 30 seconds. I was there, or awfully damned close. I was married with four children and I didn't give a f.... The opposite of love is not hate, but indifference, and I had a bad case of it. I never put a gun in my mouth, but I didn't care if I lived or died. I'd lost any shred of hope. Even to this day, many years later, I occasionally have to fight myself over reverting back to that mindset.

The dark side

So, what was this boulder crushing my chest? I'm not sure I really know. There are a lot of things that contributed. The unrealistic expectations I placed on myself. From a very early age I think I lived, and maybe still live, in a fantasy world. Maybe I misused the gift of creativity I've been given. When real life comes along and it doesn't match up with your fantasy, what's a guy supposed to do? I found people, places and things that would help me run and hide from the real things in life that I just couldn't handle.

At one point I went to a psychiatrist who diagnosed me with bipolar II disorder. This is a form of bipolar disorder without the extremes. This condition makes it more likely for sufferers to experience the depression in greater degrees than the euphoria of the mania that comes. Wouldn't you know it, he gave me drugs. Through years of experience I knew how to answer when he would ask how they were working, "Not really good, Doc." And right on cue he'd say, "Well, let's up the dosage a bit." Unfortunately, despite them making me lethargic and zombie-like, they weren't giving me the high I needed, and I started to question whether I should bother taking them at all. So, eventually I quit taking any meds. I continued to experience the mood swings. They continue to this day, although I must say not as often and rarely as severe.

At some point my drinking had moved from fun, to habit, to addiction. I went from wanting a drink to having to have one. Was I physically addicted? I don't really know, and I don't really care. This is what I do know: I had a compulsion to drink. Whatever was happening, good, bad, or ugly, a beer would make it better. But once I had one drink all I wanted was more. The disease of alcoholism is very real. The obsession that comes after the first drink to have another is crazy. It dominates your thinking. Nothing is more important. This feels better than anything else when you don't feel.

The gift of desperation

I was face down in my own shit and unable to get up. I had no hope. I just wanted to die. After a completely embarrassing afternoon with my son at a ball game I was desperate, seriously desperate. Some people call this state "the gift of desperation." It's one of the best things that ever happened to me. The next day at noon I went to my first AA meeting.

God's grace slowly began to lift me out of my pit of destruction, out of the miry clay. He set my feet on a Rock and made my footsteps firm. He put a new song in my mouth, a song of praise to God. There's not enough time or enough words to tell you how good God has been to me and how He's blessed me from the moment I received my "gift."

Almost everyone on the outside of AA has no idea what it is about. It's a spiritual program. The founders had a spiritual experience that helped them relieve the obsession to drink and developed the Alcoholics Anonymous program to help others experience the same thing. There's a spiritual principal behind each of the 12 steps in the program that help guide a person on their journey to recovery. It isn't simply recovery from drinking so that you stop. It's recovery of the life you lost, the life I lost, and maybe never had in the first place. It's becoming alive again, or alive for the very first time.

I was raised in church and went all the time as a young boy. But I never experienced the reality that was described there—the peace, the sense of fulfillment, and contentedness with myself. Looking back, I think a lot of those times when I was trying to find the meaning of life in various things, going through the motions of pretending to want real life, I was really just running in order to hide from God. The answer that I needed, what I was looking for, was there all along; a life surrendered to Him. I know that sounds so cliché, so worn out, so simple. But, if the story of my life is any measure, I'm one of millions who've made the simple so unnecessarily complicated. It's like I heard the church message, I heard that God loves me and has a plan for my life, but it never sunk in. I never let it sink in. Actually, I didn't have a clue what it meant—for me. I mean, there had to be something more that I had to do to make it work, right? But it didn't.

While hiding from God on the tennis courts one day in my mid-twenties, I met a gentleman named Don. He was different. Don walked the walk. He was, I don't know, more real, more authentic. He had a different relationship with God than I had ever seen in anything I'd been exposed to in my church. He wasn't a flamer; he didn't wear T-shirts with cute "God sayings." He didn't brandish any crosses on his tennis gear or fish symbols on his car. He wasn't a commercial for God. But he was real.

Don took me under his wing as a tennis player. I thought I was going to learn techniques to improve my game, but Don helped show me something even better. For the first time in my life I began to see that He didn't want me to follow a bunch of rules. God wants to be in relationship with me, just the way I am right here, right now. Nothing I've done disqualified me from that relationship, and there's nothing I can do to make it happen. It's all Him. But I never knew that before. I didn't know He would come to me in the emptiness I thought it was up to me to fix.

I wanted what Don had. So began my real relationship with God—not the performance I had honed to a T while playing church. Even though I was beginning to turn the corner on an entirely new chapter, I still continued to fight my mood swings. I couldn't escape the pain. I returned to drinking and drugging. Somewhere I must have missed something; somehow, I got off track. But now, I was in worse shape because I'd begun to see hope and had fallen from it. How could this happen? And why?

In time I began to really see the light, as they say. And this is that light. I've been granted a daily reprieve from my alcoholism. But this is contingent upon my spiritual condition. I have to tend to the health of my soul before everything and anything else. So, every morning I pray, "God, I offer myself to you to build with me and do with me as you will..." It starts on my knees, remembering the hell I've been rescued from. I thank God for the abundance of things I have to be grateful for. I am thankful for the hope of a life that will never end, continuing in relationship with Him now and worshipping Him forever.

The epiphany I finally had is that I must be brutally honest all the time–absolute honesty–with myself, with God, and with other people. For me being honest is so crazy hard but it is incredibly freeing. Admitting the obvious things I see about myself is painful. But that is only the tip of the iceberg. What I had to do, and continue to do, is dig much deeper into the hidden parts that I don't want to look at. Those parts that I certainly don't want you to see; my self-centeredness, pride, ego–the list goes on. I have to bring these out of hiding and into the Light. Hidden, covered wounds can't be healed. Unless I expose my wounds to Him on a daily basis they just fester and breed more pain. When it feels like too much crap is building up, I'm likely to throw the switch again. You know the switch I'm talking about! But I can't throw that one so easily anymore because I discovered that everything matters—I matter–to Him.

Reflections

This is not just the story of a recovering addict. Not that such a story is insignificant. Let's be clear, the reasons for Steve choosing alcohol and drugs are many of the same that drove other storytellers in this book, and countless other people throughout history, to choose other responses to medicate, treat, and cope with life's crippling hurts. This is a story about a search for meaning. So much of Steve's life is laced with this sense that what he was, did, or tried to be didn't matter and he has always wanted to matter.

Steve wasn't wounded by a physical assault. He wasn't threatened by an abusive parent. Instead, he suffered one of the most common kinds of injuries, leaving scars on the inside that are hardly if ever seen—the detachment of his soul from his very own life. How did it happen? Hard to say. He felt detached from a very early age. But happen it did, wrenching him apart from life, creating a kind of profound disconnect. The result? Steve not only didn't feel a part of the group, but more significantly, he didn't feel whole in himself.

You heard him; it was as if he couldn't quite feel what he intuitively knew ought to have been possible. He was a child in a family, a student in school, a stellar example of a Christian young man—at least by all outward appearances. But something wasn't right. Steve knew there had to be a way to be more alive than the life he was living. Whatever was going on externally was not touching him internally. He desperately wanted to feel and to matter. He managed to stimulate the feeling part, but that was only short-lived bursts of chemically induced euphoria that left him even more desperately aware of his emptiness than ever. Like so many others, maybe all of us in some ways, Steve had to come to the end of himself, landing at ground zero to begin to claw his way toward a discovery of the man he was and was really meant to be.

Who could possibly receive desperation as a gift? Only someone who has exhausted every other option. Steve realized he was failing at life because life was not fully in him. The old saying "you can lead a horse to water, but you can't make him drink" might have been an accurate picture of Steve up to the moment when he saw how utterly futile his life was. He was one thirsty horse of man who finally admitted he needed the right kind of drink.

Perhaps you wince when you imagine the long years Steve lived through his hellish turmoil looking for love, looking for life, in all the wrong places. Why does it have to take so long? I don't know. Everyone reaches their own threshold in their own time that marks the difference between a make-believe life and authentic being. When Steve crossed that threshold, he made the decision to embrace the brutal honesty that it would take to really find out who he is. And that, I think, is his Genius. Brutal honesty.

When I say brutal, I don't mean rough and mean, or crude for no reason. I mean no more pretending to want life, pretending to want wholeness, pretending to seek healing. When you don't "play at" life anymore you put yourself to the test of facing what's really there in you (and what's really not there) that requires honest to God, gut-wrenching admission. What's brutal about Steve's posture toward himself and all of life is that he has made what looks to me like a profound decision to "call 'em like he sees 'em," regardless of the effect on him or anyone else. No more pussy footing around!

Do I find him uncomfortably honest whenever I spend time with him? Heck yeah! It's like sitting in front of a laser target pointed at my own conscious. Yet Steve gives space for other fallen men and women. It's the fuel his soul runs on ... brutal introspection about himself, about life.

Honesty is incredibly powerful, punching holes through every barricade we erect to can hide from the truths that threaten us. But nothing can withstand honesty. It will take you down if you are unwilling to address what it reveals about you. Steve has this gargantuan gift, this Genius superpower that blows holes through his and everyone else's pretenses. For Steve, brutal honesty simply means he's not going to sacrifice the truth for anything. His dedication to this way of living is off-putting to say the least. And yet, he's not loud, belligerent, or impolite. No, he's a deeply caring man who has decided the best part of the cigar experience of life is living as close to the flame of truth, enveloped by the aroma of real living, as one can possibly be.

There is a day of reckoning for everyone. Some of us come to terms with ourselves sooner than others. But everyone will get there one way or another. When you can see the end in sight, or imagine that it's getting closer, not as far off as it once was, you sit up, and pay much closer attention. Our mortal end will come and that's not all bad; far from it. Our obvious limitations can usher in the phase of life that most powerfully mentors us toward the truth about who we really are, breaking down the barriers which have kept us disconnected from ourselves, others, and God—before it's too late. Living implies a call to integrity, to wholeness, even if we struggle and fail to get what our hearts long for. This is the hero's journey. It's the only one worth taking.

Today, the single medicine that sustains Steve on his journey of reconciliation is the very same power he brings to others—honesty. It's like the key that finally opens a long locked and barred door behind which lies the aching soul that yearns to breathe free, to be connected, to be integrated, to be real. Even though he was raised in church, mimicking what passed for proper conduct and attitude, he was a million miles away from the "act" he played. It did nothing to touch the him. In fact, it was just one of many personas Steve wore on his quest to find the holy grail of his own true self. The goody-two-shoes-church-boy shtick was no more helpful than the fast living, hard driving, party boy role, or the self-disciplined, fanatically driven athlete. But by risking the upheaval of honesty Steve's gotten closer to the flame of true life than ever before.

He's found a new "church family" in his AA community. Here he has discovered the freedom to speak truth that helps open up the rusted out, jammed shut doors that wall off so many other disconnected souls. No, he doesn't lecture—like a converted former smoker. Instead, he tells what he's discovered about the folly of skin-deep living. He knows the way of a sponsor who gracefully offers dignity to the fallen and falling, helping them find the sacred gift of honesty few really want to hold because it will inevitably change everything. But this boldest of actions, facing the truth about the way it has been with himself, has caused Steve to experience the "puff" that begins the most soul-searching introspection which has guide him to a grounded, stable existence.

The final phase of the cigar experience is the one that burns hottest, but it is often the most precious, most savored, because you know the smoke will end all too soon. Brother Steve, you've made a searching and fearless moral inventory of yourself. Brutal honesty is not my strong suit but your example, your coaching is helping. Thank you for sharing your Genius superpower. I need it, we all need it badly. There's something else about Steve, he has one of the best refrigerator size humidors in his house. Why? Well you see...Steve is a cigar.

Chapter 10: The Rescue

On September 1, 2015 a desperate Syrian family attempted the journey they hoped would deliver them safely to the home of their Canadian relatives on the other side of the world. Abdullah and his wife Rehana had experienced too many nights lying awake listening to ISIS bombs exploding, wondering if they would become the next victims. They fled to Turkey with their two young boys, Aylan and Ghalib but the problems encountered there by a steady increase of refugees quickly led the Kurdis to the conclusion they had to get out. Abdullah's sister Timi and other members of the family had already emigrated to Canada. The family thought this would help Abdullah in his efforts to be granted legal refugee status. But when the Canadian government rejected their application the Kurdi family felt a desperation that led them to a fateful decision.

Just three weeks earlier, on August 16, Deseret News published an article about the plight of war-weary Syrians, Migrants mass in Turkey to take shortest route to Europe.

"While tourists eat and drink at Bodrum's upscale waterfront restaurants, migrants carrying their meager belongings in backpacks sit across the street under palm and eucalyptus trees… There they wait to be taken to a remote beach before they are packed into tiny dinghies for the short crossing across a waterway also plied by giant oil tankers, tourist pleasure cruisers, and coast guards."

Smuggling Syrians into Europe had become a flourishing cottage industry all over the Mediterranean. Turkish authorities reported that in the week just before the Deseret News story nearly 3,000 refugees were caught in the Aegean. By that point in 2015 over 33,000 migrants had been caught or rescued at sea.

The Greek island of Kos is just under three miles away from Bodrum, Turkey where the Aegean Sea meets the western Mediterranean—a thirty-minute boat ride. Once in Kos, Abdullah was sure the world of war would be left far behind. Such a tiny distance to go to secure a home with food, beds, and a hired police force that keeps people safe at night—luxuries this family had never known.

After paying nearly $6,000 for the four of them, Abdullah scurried with his wife and two boys to the beach under the cover of darkness and climbed into a small inflatable rubber boat rated for eight people, but there were 12. Five minutes after pushing off from shore the engine stalled and the flimsy craft flipped, spilling everyone into the sea.

Despite his efforts to save them, among the dead were Abdullah's wife and their two sons. Conflicting reports emerged about what happened. There were life jackets, but it turned out they were fake. Some reports said Abdullah himself had captained the fated dinghy. Others said an unknown man piloted the boat but abandoned it when the engine died. The details of what happened that night are as confused as the reports about the human calamity which has befallen millions caught in the tangled web of the international crisis that is the middle east.

Had it not been for the images of the boy on the beach, lying lifeless in the sand as if he had fallen asleep there, the fate of Abdullah's family would have been buried in one more statistical report about the Syrian refugee crisis. In the early morning hours of September 2, three-year-old Alyan's body was spotted by locals. Pictures of him being carefully and respectfully lifted into the arms of a soldier deployed to recover the drowning victims flashed on TVs, smartphones, and computer screens around the world. His clothes were those of any little playful boy, put on by a loving and attentive mother only hours before. The world cried. The picture won't leave my head; it's permanently etched. Four years have passed. Thousands more have perished. Nothing's changed. Somebody's got to rescue the innocent children.

The story that follows is about a set of eyes and broken heart that were drawn to a lost and vulnerable child who might have become another casualty of a family's desperate efforts to survive. Why would a middle-aged, middle class woman, defy the norms, be so naïve, and say yes to a situation that would put her and her family at risk?

Sometimes Genius care is expressed in small increments. The sight of an orphan child evokes an instant of compassion that moves a person to help out with a donation, adding their signature to a petition, or a momentary pause from life's routine to offer a sincere prayer. But there are others who when they witness the same scene… well, they become the life raft. See if you can detect the superpower in a rather average, ordinary, suburban mom who intervened to prevent a body from washing up on shore. She saw it coming and stepped in… not knowing why or how.

My story begins like this

I had a modest upbringing in a small town in the Midwest. My siblings and I never went hungry, we always had a roof over our heads, and we lived a relatively calm life. We didn't have a lot but neither did most people around us.

I moved to the big city in my early twenties. I married a successful businessman, had children, and lived in the suburbs. I was happy. I was busy raising my two children. I was involved in my community and in my church, where I eventually became a deacon. A deacon is a formal position with responsibility for helping the church do its mission. Little did I know what could come across the path of this deacon! After all, I had reasoned, this is a safe position where I make decisions about church and help to serve communion. For me, it was mostly about caring for people in need.

What happened to me

Deacons don't do their thing alone. There was a group of us who work together. One of the other deacons at my church was a man who had two children; a six-year-old daughter, and a baby boy with severe disabilities. I didn't know Joel when I joined the deacon board. But that changed on September 11, 2001. Along with many others in our community that day, we sought out the same place to pray and weep—our church sanctuary. We were both deeply distraught over the unbelievable terrorist attacks that had taken place that morning, some of them not far from where we lived.

I was weeping for many reasons. Looking back, I was probably suffering from postpartum depression. I was heart-broken over the loss of life that day, which seemed even more unbearable in light of what felt like my overwhelming life. Joel sat down and listened quietly, trying to provide comfort as I talked and wept about my baby boy; how life was so hard as a new mom, that I never got any sleep, and how the baby fussed all the time. After I had calmed down, Joel began to talk about his life, about his handicapped baby boy who was diagnosed with a heart defect. The baby had just gone through open heart surgery and wasn't expected to live long. Our sons were both nine months old.

Joel and I became friends that day, though we were never close. We attended the same church and birthday parties, but we didn't have much in common: he was a single dad raising a six-year-old girl and a nine-month-old, very sick baby basically on his own, and I was in a stable marriage with a healthy son and daughter.

One day, quite unexpectedly, Joel asked my husband and I if we would take guardianship of his daughter should anything ever happen to him. We agreed without hesitation, never thinking that there would come a

157

time when we would be called upon to keep this promise. Such crazy things never happen in real life, at least not in my shiny new deacon's role.

On Mother's Day, 2014 I got the call that would change the course of my life forever. Terry was at the hospital with her father. She asked me to come and get her. I thought about it and I went. I went because this teenage girl needed someone to walk with her. The drive to the hospital was full of panic and so many unknowns. I like stability. But my life was changing along with hers and at a rapid pace.

His death was sudden. There was no way that I was prepared for the role that I had promised to take on—it had been theoretical, not something that would actually happen, but it did. The so-called stable life I was enjoying when Joel asked us to help out in the event of an emergency had become an emergency all its own. My husband left after 21 years of marriage. Now I was a single parent of two kids, but I had to make good on my promise to Joel. How could I do this, and on my own?

Despite the shock of it all, the beginning of this baffling calling into something I was ill-prepared for was the easiest part of this journey. I helped this lonely, confused, and grief-stricken 15-year-old girl say goodbye to her father at the hospital. I supported her through the funeral. I went to court to help determine the best placement for her. Her mother lives in the neighborhood but would not have been an appropriate choice.

I was able to arrange therapy for her and help her graduate from high school. I tried to protect Terry from her half-siblings who weren't kind people. I did everything I could to foster an improved relationship between her and her mother. But mostly I provided her with a stable home—well, as stable as it could be—during what was probably the most turbulent time in her life and mine.

My home went from having two children to three in one day. No preparation—like the stork just dropped a baby on my porch... just boom! A man died and his daughter was in my house. Now she was... my daughter?

There have been so many challenges. Honestly, there were moments I have resented Terry in my home. She tested me on a daily basis. We fought—oh did we fight—we screamed, and cried, and yelled, and even laughed. It's been a journey of hills and valleys. I've lost count of how many days I carried the most unbearable load of guilt about my feelings toward her. The resentment and anger that boiled inside is so not like me, but I was feeling it, so I guess it was me, but a me that repulsed me even more than the unmanageable world of chaos I was now in. Why me? What naivete had tricked me into this quicksand that was swallowing me and my family?

My anger wasn't reserved just for me. No, I was I furious that Terry's own brothers and sisters haven't stepped in to help. Whenever any of them dared say anything against her, I was more protective than the most perturbed momma bear. And speaking of mommas, I've been beside myself with outrage that Terry's own flesh and blood mother hasn't lifted a finger to help her own daughter. Here I was, a virtual stranger rescuing a child whose mother should have known better, who should have done more. How could this woman simply let her child drift off without a care? A whole tribe of people who are her relatives could have supported this rescue mission but didn't do a damn thing.

For a time, I was concerned about the safety of my son when I wasn't home. This feeling has since dissipated because Terry and he have grown into being sister and brother. Brothers and sisters never fight right? Wrong. And I've anguished over what I'm supposed to do for each of my kids. Is it right for me to have the same loyalty to my children as my foster-daughter? Shouldn't they be treated equally? But then shouldn't my own kids get preferential treatment? I've been tortured with self-doubt. Am I a good mother... to any of them?

I didn't realize how hard the transition would be to open our home to another child. We live in the same zip code, under the same roof, but the character and quality of our lives is miles apart. Our personalities— and our core values—are very different. We struggle—I struggle—to find some kind of workable mother-daughter relationship. Sometimes we aren't physically comfortable in each other's presence. Okay, let me be gut honest—sometimes we haven't been able to stand each other's presence!

It has been five years since Terry came to live with me. When she first came, we didn't even have a room for her. But the biggest challenge for me has been finding room in my heart for her. And it turns out, she's had the same struggle. We've celebrated Christmases, graduations, and family celebrations together—some she attends and some she's been absent from. Yes, it's been a psychological, and spiritual yo-yo existence.

She's 20 now and continues to live with me. She's working full-time and going to school online part-time. I have struggled with the next step. As with all children, there comes a point when they must move on and be self-sufficient. At what point do I tell her, "You are an adult now. You need to be on your own?"

Our story isn't over yet and I'm afraid the next step is going to be the hardest. My prayer is that we will always be connected, but that she will become independent and self-sufficient. I guess that's what all of us parents hope for our children. Did I do right by her? Did I do right by her father? I hope so. With all that's happened, I don't know. Maybe I'm just too close to the day to day grind of trying to be a faithful mom.

Is there a Genius?

A lot of people have asked me why I agreed to take on this challenge, and why I have continued on this journey. Was there something in my past that led me to this calling? Despite the weight of the task, I see it as something I was called to do.

My first response was, "When I saw a frightened young girl who didn't trust anyone, who was rejected by her half-siblings, and who in the course of one day no longer had parents or a place to call home, I was led to help her."

But over time, I've realized that it wasn't just empathy for Terry's situation that drew me to her. I discovered that we share the same wound. Terry has never had a loving relationship with her mother and neither have I. I recognized myself in her and seemed to know instinctively how to reach into her pain and find ways to grow through and beyond it. I think it has been a growing awareness of the effect of having a mother who, in a sense, hasn't had me. Oh, she was physically there, but I never felt like she had me, like I was really cherished by her. It might sound silly to hear a grown woman with her own family say such a thing. But it's true. I guess it's this gut instinct that I could have floated away, and it wouldn't have mattered to my mother one way or the other that made me so keen about giving Terry a shot at knowing she mattered to someone. I think this is what gave rise to what I can only describe as a surprising Genius that helped me intuitively know how to step into this volatile, and complex relationship. I recognized her wound because Terry and I have experienced the same kind of hurt, disappointment, and suffering from our mothers, who couldn't or didn't want to love the way we so desperately needed.

Terry and I have sat, comparing stories about things our mothers have said. It's scary to discover that some of the same words were spoken to us, triggering the same feelings and hurt inside us. In some ways my journey with Terry has been so hard because watching her recoil from the pain of broken relationship with her mother is like watching a movie of myself. It can get confusing sometimes. Am I mother to Terry? Is Terry me? Is there a way that I can mother myself by how I respond to Terry's need for understanding and care? I suppose this is an area that can be peeled back and studied.

One difference between my past and hers is that my father continues to help minimize the negative comments that my mother throws at me. Watching Terry, I see how having dad in my life has been such a help to me. My foster daughter lost her dad and doesn't have that voice. I'm trying to find a way to help her with that.

Reflections

Long before the tide of life deposited an orphan child into her arms Regina was straining to experience the loving embrace of her own narcissistic mother, a parent who either couldn't or didn't want to see her child, struggling for life. And yet, despite being overlooked and disregarded, Regina has survived, perhaps out of desperation not to be sucked down by the incessant undertow of her self-absorbed mother.

Did the events of 9/11 that unfolded that day for a young mother awaken or inspire something that has lived deep inside her wound, that altered her perspective? She talks about weeping for the loss of life. Could that event have unleashed a grief and empathy for the little girl who was always on the verge of drowning in the wake of her mother's own self-obsession?

Many of us are captivated by stories of Genius found in headlines and history books, but miss the heroism found in the small stories of ordinary lives. I can't help seeing the Genius of a rescuer flowing out of the depths of Regina's own wounded soul that was clamoring to be seen, to be noticed, to be regarded, to be wanted, to be cared for, and to be loved.

When she said yes to Joel's life and death request—something a lot of us would have asked for time to think over as a way to run from such an audacious invasion of our ordered lives—it was as if life was presenting her with the opportunity to be healed by the rescue of herself through the dire circumstances that faced young Terry. And notice that it was a father asking Regina to care for his daughter that Terry's mother could not or would not do. Regina's natural desire for her mother's love seemed to evoke a Genius ability to persistently love Terry in all the self-sacrificing ways that a parent is called upon to do. Someday, Regina's father won't be around to buffer the effects of her insensitive mother. Did God give Joel to Regina now, so she could exercise hidden wisdom in the care of her own life by learning how to do it for Terry?

It's striking to me that Joel didn't reach out to just anyone to take his place. Out of something that happened in their exchange on September 11, as they prayed, talked, and grieved together, Regina and Joel touched a profound treasuring of life. Both of them knew that no one should go unseen, unloved, unprotected, or unaccounted for. Maybe this is the Genius that was awakened in both of them—which would be called upon to mount the rescue of not one, but two orphaned girls, Terry and Regina.

A young Midwest mom with a new baby boy answered her 9/11 moment with a simple, yet naïve, "Yes, we'll take her if you die." No baby should be left alone on a beach. Genius!

Chapter 11: Funny 'cause it's true

-Homer Simpson

Stanley Kubrick's film Dr. Strangelove or: How I Learned to Stop Worrying and Love the Bomb blends a dangerous moment in time with humor that is powerful, revealing, and piercing. It was produced in 1964 against a backdrop of international tension, a time when the cold war between Russia and the United states was precipitously close to becoming hot. In 1962 the two superpowers had only narrowly averted mutual annihilation over the Cuban Missile Crisis. Nuclear weapons were prolific, the risk of miscalculation was only a hair's trigger away, and diplomatic paranoia was ubiquitous.

Behind the genius satire of the film loomed real-life, impending doom of Biblical proportions. Yet Kubrick presents humanity's most frightening prospect with humor, allowing us to look in the mirror and defuse the feared unknown. Humor breaks open closed vaults inside of us in ways that no other weapons are able to penetrate. How in God's name could nuclear holocaust and humor be woven together? Dr. Strangelove does so with brilliance.

The iconic British humorist Peter Sellers plays three roles in the movie—a Royal Air Force officer with an easy but hilarious British accent, the neurotic President Muffley of the United States, and the quintessential mad scientist, a former Nazi, Dr. Strangelove. All three are forced to contend with what people living in the 1960s were certain was the world's worst nightmare.

Acting on his own authority, U.S. general "Jack the Ripper" orders an unstoppable bombing raid into Russia. President Muffley intervenes by warning his Russian counterparts that a squadron of B-52s carrying nuclear bombs is coming their way. The Russian ambassador angrily returns with a message that a doomsday machine has been activated by his nation. It will destroy all of life on earth in retaliation for the U.S. attack. Remember, the audience watching these scenes was living with this load grade fear about this very scenario every day. The well-known actor George C. Scott played the role of General Jack, convincingly caricaturing the popular Communist paranoia of the time about hawkish American military leaders. But the audience couldn't help laughing.

The movie handles a timely end-of-the-world scenario from a cartoonish, almost blasphemous angle that gets a message into viewers' minds, that what they witnessed on screen is possible and may be true if we don't defuse the situation and find the damn code! This awkwardly comic but disturbing movie was named by "Entertainment Weekly" as one of the 100 funniest ever made.

Dr. Strangelove was brilliant because it took the obscene, made it funny, and helped its viewers come to grips with what they felt was the most threatening reality of their lives. And, there is no doubt that the movie was viewed by diplomats from around the world, perhaps even influencing geopolitical policies, contributing to a world that became just a little bit safer than it was before. Who has this kind of a code?

Judie didn't just live with the threat of potential devastation. In her life the bomb was released, and it exploded! When your father up and leaves, well, it's like a nuclear blast. Everything is shattered. This isn't supposed to happen. And who would fault anyone faced with Judie's fate for withdrawing into a hermit-like existence, or for carrying a life-long, boiling rage that seeks vengeance, or even for killing the inexplicable pain by answering it with suicide. But she's done none of these. Instead, in the face of the obscenely unfair and outrageous disruption to her life, she's made a skit out of it and laughs!

When he left, Judie's idyllic life evaporated into a deceptive mirage that would never be recovered. Like everyone who faces the disorientation that life throws at us—and there are too many permutations of disordered existence to name here, that subvert what we assume ought to be the ordered, predictable life—Judie responded. She reacted. You don't face disruption without changing, whether you like it or not. Even the most outwardly stoic folks who look like they're unmoved, unaffected by life's traumas—even they are changed. Perhaps working harder than ever to impose the sheer force of their will over the inevitable threats to their existence. Whether it was conscious or not, Judie's instinctive will to survive stirred into germination a seed that was sown in her darkness and despair. That seed has become for Judie a plant with big, broad leaves that offer cool shade and relief from the searing heat of life that could have easily scorched her alive.

Two lives

I've lived what I call a double life. No, my dad was not a spy, but he left when I was 14. So, there was my life with him and my life without him, two lives. His leaving cut a wound deep inside me. It's as if I can trace my fingers across the jagged line of an indelible scar that will never go away.

I was always desperate to please him. I wanted to be near him. If he did it, I wanted to do it too, not for the pleasure of the activity, but for the pleasure of being with my father. I kept score at the Little League games he coached, sitting right next to him. I raced as a skier even though I hated every minute of it. I was afraid to fall and break something, so I always came in last. He taught me how to sail; he even built a boat so I could learn. I didn't really embrace sailing, being afraid that we'd tip over. But I wanted to be with him, and so eventually I learned to love it. There is this favorite memory I have of just the two of us sailing on a crisp, late October day, the wind at our backs and me at the helm. Long after he walked out of my life, he told me, "I never really knew what to do with girls, I was better at raising a boy."

I'm the middle child, born in Rochester, NY. I was delivered by Dr. Snow (yes, Dr. Snow) during a January blizzard. I'm told he was dressed in a tuxedo because he'd been called away from a post-holiday party that evening. There I was, all five pounds, four ounces of me on the delivery table, taking my first breath at 12:01 am.

"I always knew you would be special," said my mom every year on my birthday as she retold this story. "Mom, no one except Jesus has had their story told as many times as I have!" But I loved her for it; it was our thing every year until the day she died. I felt special because she made it so. I've continued this tradition with my own children and can safely say that boys are not as enamored with this as girls are.

When he left

Even though he left me, I didn't leave him. Over the years I tried desperately to include Dad in my life, but when he remarried, she wanted nothing to do with us, my brother, sister, and me, and so I finally gave up and let it all go. Just at the moment when I was on the threshold of the most exciting time of my life, I was abandoned to a bunch of angry divorced women in our neighborhood. Mom's new friends would come over on Friday nights, drink, and ask me to play the piano and sing Liza Minnelli songs. I became an entertainer. I thought everyone was doing the same thing, entertaining. I figured that I understood them. Divorce was new, they had all fallen from the yacht club, country club set, now having to find jobs after being moms, having to navigate weekend fathers, with less money, and all of the bills.

Compared to life before he left, I was not just materially poor, it felt like the wind had been knocked out of me. Now I was really at sea, but Dad wasn't in the boat with me. This was now my normal. I escaped by babysitting every chance I got. Lost father, lost family, lost adolescence—just a few of the wounds that complicated life—all leading to my downfall, but in the end, to my win.

I'm definitely competitive, sometimes even with myself. Over the years I learned that I can do just about anything I set my mind to, except math! I can't do math. I'm an artist. I am so over-the-top right brained that my report cards were Mom's least favorite day. I dreaded it too, but managed to get to college, get a degree, and eventually find work. I had always wanted to be a teacher. From the time I was little, I taught my stuffed animals in the basement and I taught my friends, but I graduated with a degree in graphic design.

I had many a failed relationship, and two engagements. I could not fill the hole that was deep inside me. I searched for a way, but it just lurked there, never satisfied, always hungry, always a vacuum that seemed to suck the air out of life. Eventually I did get married, had two wonderful kids, and settled into what I wanted to be normal—church, sports, work, dinner, lunch, travel. It was a good life on the outside, but I was unfulfilled in my marriage; we couldn't connect emotionally, and so I decided to divorce.

But something's wrong

I was trying to be this perfect person, this Stepford wife. But it didn't work, and I knew after one very long hard night, that my problem wasn't my husband, it was me. I watched a hundred re-runs of "Eat, Pray, Love," until my girlfriend said, "Give it up, you're not going to get your word." She was right and I knew it. I personified the lyrics of the 70s Stealers Wheels song, Stuck in the Middle with You.

"Yeah, I don't know why I came here tonight, I got the feeling that something ain't right, I'm so scared in case I fall off my chair, and I'm wondering how I'll get down those stairs..."

When I finally sat with a therapist, I began to discover just how many hidden traumas had affected me and made me into who I had become. It wasn't the journey I wanted to take.

By this time, I'd been in my job for 12 years. I loved being a teacher of art. I was loved by my students and well respected by my peers. Perhaps out of a need to go back to the past I started reconnecting with old friends through social media. On its face this can be good but, in my case, it turned out to be very bad. One evening after enjoying dinner and drinks with an old high school friend I realized that I wanted very much to get home. I had a busy week ahead. But getting home that night was not going to happen, at least not the way I planned.

I remember blue lights flashing. I remember refusing a breathalyzer. I remember my hands being tightly bound by zip lines. I did not speak after being pulled over and arrested for Driving Under the Influence. I knew this meant I'd lose my job, but I did not know just how serious the next year would be.

You know what's funny about jail? Nothing! Except the interview with a nurse which lasted about an hour. I asked her why they needed my medical information, she told me, "We don't want you to hurt yourself." I laughed. Seriously? How much can you do to hurt yourself when you're wearing a red jumpsuit and flip flops? It wasn't funny, and yet because I was tipsy, it was.

Finally, I'm all alone in a white cell, with no clock, no sense of time, no pillow, or blanket, just me, and the only prayer I can remember is, "Yea, though I walk through the valley of the shadow of death...." Funny, when you suddenly notice that you're praying you're shocked into an awareness that this is really, really serious.

You can't leave jail until you blow a zero—not that I wanted to learn this tidbit. They test you every hour. At this moment I don't realize that I will be court ordered to do this breathalyzer for the next eight months in my car, every three to five minutes. I get one phone call and the only number I know is my ex's. One of the best things we ever did was remain friends. He arrives. I'm finally released. He takes me home, and it slowly but painfully dawns on me what I have lost, but I do not know and will not know what I have gained until much later.

In the state of Virginia, a DUI costs over $15,000 in court fees. You lose your license, then get a restricted license, and a breathalyzer in your car. You attend mandatory alcohol classes for 30 weeks, weekly AA meetings, and report to a probation officer who is never kind, and it's forever. And the whole thing is public knowledge. To top it off, I was forced to resign from the job I loved. I walked in shame, away from the school and students I had poured my heart into and wondered, where do I go from here?

Grace is amazing

The vague jail cell memory of the twenty-third Psalm turned out to be the first step in turning all my attention to God, and His saving grace. At the same time, my intuitive fallback posture toward life kicked in, telling me, "I can win this!" And so, I threw myself into landscaping, gardening, finding a job. I eat, pray, and love - my God.

I survived the first year, healing from the damage caused by my drinking and the DUI. And the serenity I was learning, taking one moment at a time, opened me to appreciate the gift of grace. I'd been told "You will never teach again." And I assumed that was it.

One day I received a phone call that led to an interview. Afraid that once my story was known I'd not only be denied the opportunity for the job, but I'd be humiliated as well, I decided to face my fear head on. Near the end of the face to face meeting I was asked if there was anything that would hold me back from being hired. I swallowed hard and told the truth. As I did a flood of tears rolled down my face because it was so hard to admit what had happened. When I finished, the headmaster said, "Let the first sinner cast the first stone. That's not how we roll here." I was stunned and cried the whole way home, no longer out of shame, but out of joy and thanksgiving for this enormously gracious gift.

After a year of grieving, and praying, and digging deep—into the earth and within myself—I was set free from the shame of my failure. Not that the experience of being stripped of everything and monitored like a convict on work release didn't leave its effects on me. Sometimes, when I hear a beeping in the car, like Pavlov's dog, I still look for the breathalyzer thinking I only have a three-minute window to blow into it. And then I realize, it's just the seatbelt warning.

Laugh and the world laughs with you

There is power in prayer, there is grace from above, there is goodness, and kindness in every day. There is humor. When someone says, "One day we will laugh about this," they're right, you will. I do.

I love my friends fiercely. When they tell me they are suffering, I bring homemade lasagna, the good kind with lots of cheese. I weave stories and help them laugh because, just like the movie Patch Adams, I believe laughter is the best medicine.

I want to laugh until I die. I want to help others see how silly the hard of life really is. Don't get me wrong. I wasn't laughing when the officer booked me on a DUI. And I certainly wasn't laughing when my father left me. But because of these breaking experiences, today I see my life as an opportunity to share another approach to living. Make no mistake about it, life is hard, damn hard. Ask me. We've got depression, drug overdoses, epidemic rates of suicide among kids who can't cope with their hard. All of this upsets me greatly. But if you look at it from another point of view, life is filled with joy. In fact, it can be downright funny. All depends on how you look at it.

Am I the comedian on stage? No, I'm terrible on stage. But does my humor carry me through? Absolutely! On any given day I can sing a Liza song and bring a smile to someone's face. I don't know how this happened. I just know it did. It's as if, in the face of all the most hellish things that can happen—and they do—there's this impish streak inside me that says, "Come on, laugh a little. It can't make things any worse, right?" I've decided that this is either the sign of brilliant genius, or a definite indication of mental illness. Anyone who knows me knows that if I heard one of them say it, I'd fire back, "You're right. It's the mental thing. Better get that checked out."

But why? Why in the face of all the crap that happens should I laugh and play when everyone else is moaning and groaning? I choose the I can beat this attitude, because I know where this is all going. I know where I am going. I've seen Him; I've seen how He works; and I know that with all my faults, I am loved, cherished, and celebrated.

> *He will wipe every tear from their eyes.*
> *There will be no more death or mourning,*
> *or crying or pain,*
> *for the old order of things has passed away.*
>
> Revelation 21:4

Though you won't see me performing at the comedy club or on an HBO special—at least not anytime soon—I guarantee you'd love to have me in your car after an 11-hour trip to "who knows where" because we'd be laughing all the way. Perhaps you'll find me squished in between two very funny men on a dance floor singing "stuck in the middle with you." You might see me imitating my sweet friend with her wonderful Spanish accent when she tells me about the benefits of medicinal marijuana at the age of 82.

My sister and I laugh at just about anything. Growing up, our favorite TV show of was Carol Burnett. She is a comic genius, with her facial expressions, her wit, and the unmistakable brilliance in her classic "Gone with the Wind" routine, complete with curtain rod. Hilarious! She took everyday life and made us see how silly it can be. What I didn't know then was that her parents divorced when she was young, and she went to live with her grandmother. That's why she closed every show by tugging on her ear. She was saying goodnight to Grandma.

Carol had three divorces; her daughter suffered from drug addiction and later died of cancer. Do we extract our sense of humor from such tragedies? I believe we do, not because we're laughing at them as if they aren't real and have no power, no. We are laughing THROUGH them. Laughter gets me through the ugly, the brutal, the incomprehensibly awful of life. I see it, I feel it, I reel from it just like you do. I'm not ignoring it. It's just that laughter gets me through.

While I don't claim that standup comedy is in my future, I can weave a good story, especially with my sister. One time, we were driving through the rolling hills of England, and I noticed that the sheep had different colors on their behinds. "Is that so they know whose farm they come from?" I asked. She nodded answering, "Yeah, at first I thought that too." She kept on, "When the sheep are impregnated, they have a paint pack that explodes so they know which ones might be pregnant." As I continued looking out the window, I suddenly saw one that had lots of different colors. I blurted out, "Well that one over there must be the whore sheep!" We couldn't stop laughing. This became our private joke and a theme neither of us has let go of. To this day, my sister and I send each other pictures and figurines of sheep with many colors and laugh uncontrollably at the memory of that car ride every time.

One time my sister called me complaining, "I have no idea what to get my husband for Christmas, he has everything." I replied, "Get him what mom gave me—a real unicorn, remember?" She laughed and said, "I got mine the next year and you were so jealous. He had a rainbow tail and a glitter horn, and I rode him all through town." We weave stories to heal our sorrow; we weave stories to help us treasure memories but also to remind us not to take life so seriously. I told my lawyer, "We should invest in a fleet of Barbie jeeps, and line them up at the jail so people could get home the next day. It might be a slow ride home, but at least they would have transportation!" We laughed together at what that would look like. Once he sent me a picture of Buzz Lightyear saying, "The beeping, the beeping. Will it ever end?!" I had to laugh because that's exactly what I ask myself. Maybe I should just disable the seatbelt warning!

My journey is far from over, but I am careful each day to play by the rules. I make sure to take care of myself especially when I start feeling overwhelmed. The past is in the past and each new day is a fresh beginning. You do get to choose how you respond to what was and what is. I choose to see the lighter side.

Reflections

I was getting ready to go to my favorite bar on a Friday night in the spring of 2017. I asked my wife to go with me. She asked if she could bring along her friend, Judie. Sure, why not?

You now the old adage about first impressions? When Judie appeared, my brain said "BLING!" Her clothes were really loud, silly, even a little clownish. I don't think the fabric was battery-powered, but you would have thought so from the colorful sheen that seemed to blink. I'm not ridiculing her, not at all. Judie had pulled off her flamboyant costume with masterful ability, like you'd expect from an artist. She is her own canvas. For Judie dressing is dress up day every day. This is a well-educated, highly-respected, obviously confident woman. But my brain reacted to her as BLING and so that's been my nickname for her ever since.

So, there I was sitting in my overcrowded bar, with these two conservative Christian high school art teachers (one of them my wife). A bunch of 60-year-olds were dancing like… um, happy, carefree, 60-year-olds. The music changed. It was the 70s tune by Stealers Wheel, "Stuck in the middle with you"

Judie was idling and tapping and finally jumped to up to dance with the rest of the crazy people who were now singing the lyrics. "Well I don't know why I came here tonight. I got the feeling that something ain't right. I'm so scared in case I fall off my chair, and I'm wondering how I'll get down those stairs. Clowns to the left of me, Jokers to the right, here I am, stuck in the middle with you."

I quickly caught my friend Ken's eye. I could tell he was thinking the same thing. We jumped onto the dance floor following Judie, on in front and one behind with Judie "stuck in the middle." Yes, it was silly, adolescent satire, a ridiculous space we would never want filmed or to have our children see. Yes, the band did four refrains, so of course we went along with it.

My wife Deb laughed so hard the hard cider she was drinking came out her nose. I didn't know that Deb and Judie had just come through a particularly hard day. This sandwich dance with Bling in the middle was a picture of us all laughing out loud at life and enjoying it while the obvious pains, insults, and accumulated woes of life vibrated just underneath the surface. But we laughed anyway. This was medicine Judie's taken many times before, using her Genius ability to make people laugh, neutralizing the explosive possibilities that seem to threaten us every day.

Solitude
By Ella Wheeler Wilcox

Laugh, and the world laughs with you;
Weep, and you weep alone;
For the sad old earth must borrow its mirth,
But has trouble enough of its own.
Sing, and the hills will answer;
Sigh, it is lost on the air;
The echoes bound to a joyful sound,
But shrink from voicing care.

Rejoice, and men will seek you;
Grieve, and they turn and go;
They want full measure of all your pleasure,
But they do not need your woe.
Be glad, and your friends are many;
Be sad, and you lose them all,—
There are none to decline your nectared wine,
But alone you must drink life's gall.

Feast, and your halls are crowded;
Fast, and the world goes by.
Succeed and give, and it helps you live,
But no man can help you die.
There is room in the halls of pleasure
For a large and lordly train,
But one by one we must all file on
Through the narrow aisles of pain.

Chapter 12: The Girl Who Came in From the Cold

Hansel and Gretel is an ancient German fairy tale about two little souls, a brother and sister, who were neglected and abused by their parents and then, of course, by a wicked witch who threatened to devour them. Well known over five centuries, its popularity grew exponentially when it was put into print by the Brothers Grimm in 1812.

Between 1315 and 1317 most of Europe and part of Russia was in the grip of the Great Famine. Times were extraordinarily hard in the mostly agrarian nations. The story of Hansel and Gretel was not unfamiliar to millions of families who were sometimes forced to send their children away from the starving farms and villages, hoping they might discover good fortune elsewhere.

The fable's main characters were the children of a poverty-stricken woodcutter and his wife. Overhearing their parents' plan to abandon them in the forest, the children take matters into their own hands. Hansel fills his pockets with white pebbles that he carefully drops along the pathway in order so he and his sister can find their way home after being left in the woods by their mother. But when they returned their angry mother takes them again into the woods to fend for themselves. This time the breadcrumbs Hansel leaves are of no use because they are eaten by the birds. Young children can't prepare for all contingencies because they are children. They have not been exposed to the harsh realities that in time all of us come to realize can and do happen in life. Yet, despite being lost in the woods, Hansel assures Gretel that God will not leave them.

The challenges these two children have forced upon them are too painful for most adults to consider without anguished heartache. I can see Hansel telling Gretel… "It's going to be ok," even though he had no plan. After many days of wandering they follow a beautiful white bird who guides them to a clearing, and to their eye-popping surprise, there stands a treasure to suite any child's imagination, a Ginger bread house. Tired and hungry, they rush to eat parts of the roof and candy picture frames. An old woman appears, perhaps the grandmother they never had? Could their luck have changed?

But now their fortune turns even worse. The old woman is a blood thirsty witch who cages Hansel and enslaves Gretel to feed her brother so that he will be suitably fattened for cooking and eating. The calamity that the Great Famine spread across the continent is reflected in this fable's unthinkable plot. The diabolical circumstances described in this story underscored the utter helplessness experienced by families and children. There was no way out!

As she prepares the oven for cooking poor Hansel, the witch is tricked by clever Gretel who asks the witch to show her exactly what to do to make sure the fire is as hot as possible. When the witch leans in to stoke the fire, Gretel pushes the old hag inside and locks the door. The evil witch is burned to a crisp. The two children are freed from their impending and terrifying fate.

As Hansel and Gretel look around the witch's house, they find a vase full of jewels, fill their pockets with them, and set off once more to find their way back home. A duck ferries them across a large lake where they meet their father on the other side. In their time away their mother has died. Safe from witch and mother, and having discovered riches at the point of death, Hansel and Gretel live with their father, as the saying goes, happily ever after.

In the story you are about to read, Gretel has become Janet. She was left out in the cold, victimized by parents who suffered a kind of famine—the absence of any humane parental inclination. Though she escaped the fires of a witch's oven she was literally burned by ice-cold hearts.

Janet's story

When I was four years old, my mother locked me out of the house, literally leaving me out in the cold. I remember sitting on the step and seeing my sister peeking out at me from inside. By the time I was let inside, the toes on my left foot were too frostbitten to be saved. They had to be surgically removed. Though I tried to be brave I was terrified lying there waiting for the operation to begin. The doctors told me to count to ten as a black mask covered my face to anesthetize me. Afterward, I remember that my aunt and grandma visited me in the hospital, but mostly I remember feeling alone and having to trust the nurses to take care of me.

I was born on April 11, 1967 and have survived a half century—quite a feat considering how my life has gone. Imagine trying to teach middle school children for 38 years with the past that I've had. Oh, there's more to tell. My frozen foot is just the tip of the iceberg! Though my journey has strangely equipped me to be able to tap into the minds and hearts of my students differently than someone who has not persevered through the wounds I've experienced, I am not sure I always believe—or accept—that the pain I've suffered was for my best.

I was the second child in a family of four girls, a mom, and a dad. From as far back as I can remember I was always sad. There was harshness, a gruffness in the way I was treated. As a result, I was always on guard. Most of the time I was afraid.

When I was in kindergarten, I was standing on the floor of the school bus, waiting for it to stop in front of my house to let me off. When the bus braked, I lost my balance and hit my lip on the back of the seat in front of me. It hurt. I was embarrassed. But as I stepped off the bus, my pride wounded, Mom was there to greet me, not with comfort and concern. No, she scolded me in front of all the other students who were looking on. In fact, I don't remember her ever comforting me. She made me feel that I couldn't do anything right. And Dad was no better. He would not stand up for me or my sisters; I could never count on him protecting me. It was clear that I was a disappointment to my parents. I could not escape the pain of this loneliness intensified by being in a family that should have loved, cared, and protected me. Isn't that what parents are for?

One afternoon when I was seven, no one was at home when my sister and I got off the bus. We were confused. Why couldn't we get into our house? Where was everyone.?

As we stood there not know what to do a strange car pulled up. People we'd never seen before got out and told us that we needed to go with them. Our parents had been taken into custody and my sisters and I were put into foster homes. When the dust settled it was determined that I and one of my sisters were the only two in danger. I thought, How can only two of us be in trouble? What about our other two sisters? My parents were charged with abuse and neglect for two of us.

Though I was removed from the daily abuse and neglect inflicted by my parents, my emotional state remained the same. I had been incubated in a home occupied by people who were disconnected, by parents who were adults in age but not in responsibility. My heart and mind were constantly wracked with the pain of knowing I was unloved, unwanted, and worthless. At best I had been tolerated. There was no place where I belonged. In a word, I felt abandoned. Just writing that one word, abandoned, stirs up memories of the terrible emptiness that is too pervasive, too excruciating to describe.

Over the next couple of years, I moved in and out of different foster homes, including moving back into my home with my parents whom the authorities had previously determined were the cause of our troubles. But after a short time back home we were taken away from my parents again. My sister and I ended up together in another foster home. I really liked it and felt safe there. I played and felt loved. I remember actually being happy. But the couple divorced, we had to leave, and my world was turned upside down again.

Now, my sister and I entered our third foster home. After a while life began to settle down. I spent the next three or four years there, enjoying my childhood up until I was about 13 years old. Perception is everything. My young mind constantly struggled with the feeling that I was not the preferred child—that I was a "foster child." While I was in this home a lot of other foster kids came and went, based on their circumstances and frequently based on their behavior. It wasn't all good. But even though I didn't feel completely loved or chosen, I didn't want to risk moving to another new home, so I tried to "earn my keep" by working hard, doing well in school, and staying out of trouble. If I wasn't a chosen child, I had to make sure no one had a reason to reject me. This is still something that I have to be aware of.

When I was an adolescent, I and my foster siblings sometimes visited and played with cousins of the family I lived with at their favorite uncle's house. A few times we stayed overnight there. This uncle singled me out, paying special attention, and even giving me a nickname. But it was not the kind of attention a child who is loved by an adult should receive. I felt trapped. Because I didn't want to leave my foster home and start my life all over again, I didn't tell anyone that this man molested me. So, I tried to keep my distance from him. But because of the secret I was hiding I became more isolated, sinking more and more into myself. I was always looking over my shoulder because I didn't feel safe.

Around that time my sister and I were given the opportunity to move back to our original family home again. We were offered a trial period of a month to see if we wanted to remain with our biological parents. When I was there the last time, I never felt comfortable. I always had to hide my foot to avoid ridicule. My toeless foot must have reminded my parents of the day they left me out in the cold. So, I decided not to go back. I stayed in my foster home. Because of how I understood the instruction I'd been given by the judge I thought I had to keep this decision to myself. So, I didn't tell my sister. When the day came for her to leave, she looked confused when I didn't get into the car to go with her. As she rode away, I think a part of my heart died because now I felt even more alone than ever. Later on, I found out that my sister continued to have bad things happen to her. I felt it was my fault because I wasn't there to protect her. Writing this now, decades later, still brings tears to my eyes.

A few years later, My foster parents got me a job with one of their friends. She managed the local airport and gave flying lessons to my foster mom and dad. I liked her and enjoyed working with her. She was interested in me and took me under her wing. As we grew closer, I felt safe talking about myself and how I felt about things. It was good to have a confidant. But, as chance would have it, wouldn't ya know, she physically molested me too. This really messed up my young mind. Yet, even though I had been violated again I didn't want to risk having to move. So, I said nothing and let the abuse continue for some time. I reasoned with myself, After all, she really does care for me, doesn't she? Because my boss repeatedly apologized for her actions toward me, I thought—and foolishly hoped— that our relationship would eventually become healthy. But it never did.

My life continued on in emotional silence. There was a lot I was ashamed of and had to hide. I tried to make things right by working to change the people who were hurting me. I would alternately distance myself from them or try to point out things the Bible said that would convince them that our relationship had to change. I could not understand how people who said they loved me could treat me this way. Nothing I did changed the situation. I grew extremely cautious. I couldn't trust anyone and was always on the lookout for hidden motives. I had hardly any close friends and was always sad and lonely. Even though there were people all around, I couldn't talk to anyone for fear that opening up would put me right back in the same situations again. How could I be vulnerable and not be violated? So, I prayed, a lot.

Fast forwarding several years—my toeless foot required additional surgery. During recovery I had a lot of downtime to think. Alone in my thoughts the more I took stock of everything that had happened the more depressed I became. Eventually I told my foster mom about the uncle who abused me. I felt it was safe to do this because he had died. But because the flight instructor was still living, I kept those episodes to myself.

You can probably appreciate that with the insecurities and fears which had grown up around the repeated experiences of being mistreated, humiliated, ignored, objectified, overlooked, and unloved, it was impossible for me to trust anyone. Even though I was grateful for the relative safety and stability I had at my foster home I wasn't really close to my foster mom. And so, I think I kept her at a distance. Being emotionally close had way too many consequences for me. I learned to protect myself by not getting too close to anyone, including her. Under the circumstances I really do think she did the best that she could. How could she really understand me? I mean, when you're trying to keep secrets, it is a hard road for other people to know what's really going on, even if you want them to know. I was afraid to tell anyone how I really felt. When I did it turned into a nightmare. On top of that I had been constantly told There is always someone else worse off than you. So, it wasn't my foster mom's fault that she couldn't connect with me the way both of us probably wanted to. I finally decided that if I told her about the uncle, we might get along better, and be closer. She was shocked when she heard what had happened. But she didn't blame me. I think she has a much different understanding of me now. I certainly respect her more than I did growing up.

Though this conversation with my step mom was a breakthrough, the depression that was triggered during my recovery from surgery led to nine months of counseling and a lot of hard work. I finally came to grips with everything that had happened to me because I was able to get it all out in the open with the therapist. Since then I have confided in a handful of some close friends. But still, deep down inside, I have to say that I continue to struggle to accept that I am truly loved and truly chosen. I rarely feel it.

I've been through a lot. Trust me, I'm not complaining. I know I'm not alone. I had it pretty well drilled into me that there are a lot of other people who are worse off. But that backdrop has made it all the more difficult for me to see and understand what I've been through. So, I'm often at odds with myself. It's hard to get out of my own skin and look back to see the effects of what has happened. I guess no one can really do this since we all live the unique experience we've had without the benefit of an objective view.

But that doesn't mean I have no perspective at all. Even though there are millions of orphans and foster children, there is no one else who lived my experience in the depth of my soul, except me. Of course, if you ask anyone else about what they see in another person, you'll wind up hearing some things that overlap with your own self-perceptions, but a lot that does not. Some of what others will say about you takes you by surprise, because it comes from another perspective that it was impossible for you to have. It's just hard to see yourself when you are as close as you are to your own life. That's just the way it is.

So, I'm not sure I can see and appreciate myself the way others can. What I do know is that while I can't and don't see all there is of me, the crazy, sad, unnecessary, and unfortunate things that happened to me have hit me like repeated body blows. And those body blows have left their indelible impressions on me—emotionally, psychologically, physically, and spiritually—making me someone different than I used to be. I'm not sure where that little girl is anymore.

Sitting where I do today, knowing I cannot erase the past and start over again, I realize that I have a heightened awareness from these events that it's likely I might not have had without them. Like a sixth sense, that others don't possess, I am keenly aware of the details of my surroundings at all times. I can tell when things are even a little bit off. I am a quick study of people as well. It' like I was unconsciously trained by my experiences to become expert at sensing and knowing the motivations, intentions, and purposes that are at work inside of other people. Sometimes I can detect that in what they say. A lot of the time I just know it from their behavior, their body language, and facial expressions and the sound of their voice. It's not something I wanted to know, but I do.

I said I am a teacher. Somehow, despite all the messages to the contrary, I have found meaning, value, and purpose for living. The sensitivity to my own drama has given me a way to see into the lives and circumstances of my students. Unfortunately, the similarities between my life and theirs is way more common than I wish it was. Perhaps the reason for my seeing and knowing is because of how life has wired and rewired me; perhaps it's because there are more kids who are experiencing the kind of life I did—maybe it's some of both. In any case, I'm aware of a deep need in them that transcends their learning readin', writin' and 'rithmetic. Tuned in to this deep need, I am in my element when I'm working with them. Loving, esteeming, celebrating, and nurturing these tender lives fills me with energy. And though I'd never want anyone to live what I did, there just might be a meaning to it all. Other folks, maybe like those who didn't know what to do with me, seem to want to run from these challenges, as if there's something too hot to handle with these kids. I look at such people and think, Really? How hard can this be?

I've mentioned it before, but it is important for me to say again—I was not chosen. I was not selected as special. No one in my family of origin, certainly not my parents, instilled in me any sense of joy about my existence. In fact, it was just the opposite. I didn't have to be told in so many words—I learned that I was not wanted, not desired, not cherished—I was just here and in the way. The most profound evidence of my parents' conscious decision to ignore me is the absence of my toes. I struggle inside to make sense of what happened and why. In the end there is no acceptable explanation that doesn't reinforce the experience of personal rejection. As long as I live, I will have this constant physical reminder that my life meant nothing to the very people who brought me into the world.

And, other than my foster parents—for whom I am incredibly grateful—it seems that the people who said they loved me were so twisted by their own tortured experiences of life that I was repeatedly met with their perverse version of what it means to be human and to be in relationship with someone else. I was a child who was obviously wounded, and broken, and needed protecting. I've wrestled with God over that—and sometimes, still do. What is it like to be truly loved and truly chosen? It is a journey that I'll probably be on for the rest of my life.

> *Sing to God, sing praises to His name...*
> *He is father of the fatherless, and*
> *a defender of widows...*
> *God sets those who are alone in families;*
> *He brings out those who have been bound*
> *into prosperity*
>
> Psalm 68:4-6

Reflections

What Janet didn't tell you is what I see of her, and what many others experience from her. Out of her story, her own tortured fable life, Janet has discovered jewels in the witch's house. Treasures she didn't know existed, wasn't looking for, and never intended to find. Genius is like that sometimes. It just happens. Out of the wildly awful, calamitous episodes of our lives something that we would do anything to avoid comes crashing in on us, changing life in ways we never imagined, delivering us into realms we never knew existed or wanted to be in once they were shown to us. For some, like Janet, these disgusting, vile, inhumane, mutated experiences that we are given in place of the life our soul cries out for, strangely crack open insight, strength, resilience, and perception that defy the very threats that breathe against us.

Janet has been intuitively drawn to those who are disabled, those who lack the everyday abilities that you and I take for granted. There are many such people in our midst and yet they are invisible to us, made so by the kind of life-negating revulsion we feel, a reaction that must have been at work in the lives of so many who tried to deny and ignore Janet.

She volunteers to serve children and adults who attend special camps and programs designed to provide tangible expressions of support, love, care, dignity, and humanity to those whose souls are crying for the same. She uses her vacation time to find, hold, be with, and listen to the groans and grunts of the disabled who can't speak words that I can understand. But she does.

She was left out in the cold woods alone. No older brother, sisters that were cut off from her, no pebbles, bread crumbs, or ferrying duck to guide her safely home. Like the children in the German fairy tale Janet repeatedly fell from one level of hell into another and yet the very wounds that pierced her soul seem to have released in her a laser-like focus of knowing what Being really is, what it means. Though few ever bestowed on her the gift of recognizing and affirming her own existence, it's as if Janet has been given the ability to distill out of her life one of the highest concentrations of awareness of Being, I have ever seen. This dear soul has been miraculously abled to personify the promise of God present in the most ignominious circumstances of life. And that is Genius, beholding the image of God in another person. I think she is poised to see and receive even more of what the four-year-old sitting in the cold has always been seeking. Godspeed in your journey my friend.

Epilogue

Dear Al, thank you for helping me on my journey and finding the good in me when I can't see it myself.

Chapter 13: The Visitation

It was Easter Sunday. The family of five had just gotten home from church and the annual egg hunt. The kids were worn out from the extra-long morning, in fact, it was already afternoon. To top it off they'd gorged themselves with candies and sugary frosted goodies all morning. Their glucose high had just peaked and judging by the rising bickering he was hearing between his two daughters and son; the crash was evidently on its way. He was feeling kind of a letdown too.

This wasn't the first time Manny wondered why. After all, he was a minister. And this, well... this Easter celebration was the crown jewel in the whole structure of his career. Without resurrection from the dead there wouldn't be any Christianity, Church, or his job as the local pastor! So why did he feel so down? He decided he must have been worn out, tired from all the extra services he was responsible for creating and conducting over the last eight days. As he sat dozing in his favorite recliner—that was once his father's but now his since his father's death—the liturgical back and forth between him and his parishioners earlier that morning echoed in his brain, "He is risen... Christ is risen!" His eyes almost closed for the final count as he wondered before drifting off why he felt closer to death than life.

Who knows how long he'd been asleep. He awoke to a commotion just beyond the living room, outside the front door. "Those kids again. Damn it, can't I get a little rest!" As he cranked the La-Z-Boy's arm to vault himself back up on his feet, he was more than a little woozy, like maybe he should just ignore whatever was going on outside and slink back into the chair. But then he heard the kids again.

More awake now, this time he realized what he heard wasn't bickering; it was... laughter, wonder, delight—as if their sugar high had been miraculously transformed into... what? He didn't know. As he stumbled toward the front door Manny's wife was standing in the porch looking back at him as if he'd better hurry up because he was missing out on the parade. But they lived on a dead-end street. What the heck was going on?

The aluminum storm door creaked open as his oldest daughter shouted to him, "Dad, look at this!" There in front of him was the cutest little puppy, frolicking with his son and his little sister on the shivering grass that seemed to be wishing it was midsummer and not this brisk upper Midwest winter day that was masquerading as spring. Before he could utter a word—and as the father Manny always had something dad-like to say—his mind raced. "Whose dog...? Where did he...? Oh crap, the kids are gonna want to keep him!"

But faster than his synapses could process his fatherly protocol for dealing with unexpected puppy sightings, his three children glanced up from their spontaneous joy, looking at mom and dad with eyes begging for their parents to set aside their customary roles of responsibility and just dive into the moment.

Manny felt guilty when he noticed a boyish grin start to cross his face as found himself recalling the time he came home with a dog who had followed him for three miles, right up to his house. Manny was 10 years old and had immediately fallen in love with this abandoned—or was it lost—companion. His heart instantly leapt with joy when the dog first responded to him. But his mother would not hear of it. There weren't going to be any stray dogs in this house.

The scene in front of him now was a black and brown fur ball jumping all over his kids. They were giggling and laughing with a beauty and purity that washed over him. Every so often one of them would informatively instruct the others about being careful with the little guy as if they had suddenly become seasoned dog handlers. Just then the pup lost his balance as he crawled over his son who was lying spread eagle on the ground. He took a cute tumble and wriggled on his back as he struggled to stand up. Everyone laughed in adoration.

Manny forgot that he wasn't the boy who had to give up the dog who found him. That boy was now the parent who could give himself and his children the gift he'd always regretted having been taken away. But he didn't exactly let on to anyone that's what was happening to him. So, he didn't make any promises he couldn't retract. But then, just as quickly as that, Manny was bending down and talking to this little fury bundle of energy, running his hands through the smooth black coat. Well of course that just encouraged the kids all the more. Pretty soon there was an unabashed love fest happening right there in front of God and everyone, and none of them cared a wit! Time stopped. They were all wrapped up in the happy surprise that just shown up at their door, slobbering dog drool and all.

In the midst of this unplanned encounter the suddenly childlike father still had enough of a grasp on reality that he knew the idea that he or anyone could separate his kids from the puppy—or himself for that matter—was patently absurd. No matter what parental misgivings he might have momentarily considered, Manny realized he was in way over his head with this one. Neither his formal preparation for professional ministry nor life itself had prepared him for this kind of Easter joy. There wasn't any script to follow.

As he was quickly adjusting to the fact that it was more than likely he was about to become a dog owner, his son shouted, "What should we call him?" Manny chuckled. The kids asked what he was laughing at. He told them the story of a family friend he had when he was growing up. His name was Chester. One time, Chester came to visit on Easter Sunday. When it was time for him to leave someone in the family shouted, "Happy Chester, Easter!" I know, it's one of those silly family sayings. But that seasonal greeting had popped to mind many times over the years. Now here he was with his own family and Manny was laughing about it again. "Hey kids, should we call him Chester, after all, it's Easter?"

The kids didn't exactly respond with a rousing ovation. The two oldest just looked at each with puzzled faces while their baby sister played with the dog. He could tell they were just barely hanging on to his suggestion while their brains kicked into gear searching for something better. That lasted about 30 seconds, until his oldest girl blurted out THE name. "Buster!" "Yeah," the other two said. "Buster!"

Of course, it had to be Buster. Their only other favorite dog in the whole world was the neighbor's—Bear. They knew there couldn't be two Bears in the neighborhood, especially when the two families lived back to back across the alley from each other. How confusing would that be? So, his wonderfully smart daughter came up with a contraction between Bear and Chester! Okay, so Buster it would be. Manny shouted out as if he was baptizing a new baby, "Happy Buster, Easter!" This time the kids laughed.

They all ran up the front steps and into the house, the littlest struggling to carry the squirming Buster inside. Manny cautioned them that while it was quite likely that someone had abandoned this little guy, it wouldn't be right for them to just assume that's how Buster landed in their laps. And so, he told the kids "First thing Monday morning I'm going to put an ad in the paper's Lost & Found section." Their faces fell. "No, now listen," he went on. "If after a week there aren't any phone calls, you can keep him." Their eyes grew wide. Manny was sure he'd never seen his kids pray so hard over the next week. Day after day passed. No calls. Even Manny was hopeful. By the weekend Buster was a full-fledged member of the family.

Unplanned, unexpected, out of the blue happenstances take us by surprise all the time. Whether we can see and accept them is a completely different matter. And even if we can, what we do with them may be more of a question of what they do with us, what they portend for us.

Let me introduce you to Frank who, like Manny, was dragging himself through his quasi-deflating routines of life when something quite strange happened. Unlike most of the other storytellers who've revealed a chronology that led to a discovery, what you'll read next are snapshots in time, vignettes, puzzle pieces that, no matter how you arrange them, seem to bring a flat, two-dimensional picture to vivid life, even though some of the pieces are still missing. Here's Frank's story.

Guardian Angel

One day I was pulling my work van out to go do an estimate across town. A neighborhood teenager I'd waved and said hi to a few times suddenly appeared on his bicycle, blocking my path. With the biggest most confident grin I ever saw he slapped his hand on the side of my truck. I stopped and rolled down the window to hear him confidently declare, "I bet you're looking for a good worker." This guy had obvious physical disabilities and some mental challenges, but I decided to play along with him.

"So, are you the good worker you are referring to?" He just looked at me and continued grinning. I knew that meant "Yes, of course it's me!"

"You seem pretty confident; what exactly can you do that I might be interested in?"

"I can do anything you show me how!"

I thought, "Here I am flat broke with a failing contracting company. I need back surgery but don't have the insurance or the money to get it taken care of. I'd like to help this guy but I'm not even taking care of myself!" Next thing I knew I heard these words tumble out, "Listen Buddy, I don't have much for you but if you'll come by around nine o'clock on Sunday morning, I'll give you $5.00 to get the trash out of my truck and put everything back in its right place."

I wouldn't have believed it was possible, but his smile got even bigger. He became very excited and started telling me how he had been through a special maintenance training course at the Earl Pulley Center.

I thought, "Wow, I obviously made this kid's day. Now if he shows up, I hope I have the five bucks I promised him."

He did show up... early, well before nine. We marched over to my truck. I opened the side door and boxes of electrical wire fell out along with a bunch of trash. His eyes got really big but not as big as his smile. His body language spoke volumes, Disabilities or not, I am up for this challenge.

I explained to him how I always seemed to be behind schedule so at the end of a job I would throw everything in the truck and rush to get to the next one. I just never seemed to catch up enough to stop and straighten things up. We dove into the project together. Before long, my truck was cleaner and better organized than I think it had ever been. I paid him his $5.00 and we arranged to do this deal every Sunday as long as it worked for both of us.

The next day, Monday after work, I pull up to the house. Guess who was sitting on my front porch? "Hey man," I said, "This week has really flown by, and I can't believe it's Sunday already!" He about fell off the porch laughing. Buddy was now my sidekick whether I liked it or not!

That's how it all started, when he was about 18. I was 36. I've known Buddy now for over 30 years. He calls us "The Gruesome Twosome." As unlikely a relationship as anyone could ever have, and yet Buddy is probably the most influential person in my entire life, and I'm no kid anymore. Do the math. Despite his own challenges, he maintains a positive attitude that I find absolutely contagious. Through our friendship he has caused me to realize that making a positive difference in somebody else's life also brings enormous benefits to me. Buddy is living proof that a smile makes everything better than it would have been without it. At a time in my life when I was feeling very sorry for myself and defeated, was in a dangerous downward spiral, and starting to become more and more bitter, I found myself standing at a fork in the road. I feel very fortunate that Buddy was there to influence the direction I chose. I'm sort of agnostic when it comes to religion. I don't believe or disbelieve. But when it comes to Buddy, I have no doubt that guardian angels do exist!

Glass Angels

Buddy and I regularly hit all the thrift and Dollar stores. It's a great way to spend time together. One day we went up to the local Dollar store to shop. I entered first, Buddy followed me but soon we were separated, each of us absorbed in the search for the treasures we just hadn't found yet.

When I was well into the store, caught up in my quest, I heard a loud crash. It was obvious glass was breaking, lots of it. I looked around, no Buddy in sight. I backtracked through the aisles to see where he was, acting on a gut instinct that he had something to do with what just happened. I found him and I was right.

Buddy is blind in his right eye and so he'd walked right into a large shelf filled with glass angels. There on the floor, all scattered about as if they decided to dance in the aisle were eight or ten glass angels that, just seconds before, had been quietly perched on the shelf, their wings extended like they were getting ready to take off. Well, they did take off with Buddy's help. Now they were strewn across the floor, broken in pieces with their heads and wings mostly shattered.

I immediately ran over and apologized to the store clerk. I told her I would pay for the damages. She didn't say anything, just looked over at Buddy and began cleaning up the mess. I threw my arm around Buddy's shoulder and took him to another aisle. We continued our shopping and then went on our way. We didn't buy anything that day although money did leave my wallet.

This particular store is one of my favorite haunts, so I stop in often. The next few times I stopped I was by myself. Every time I walked in and made eye contact with an employee, we'd both silently sort of look over at the flying glass angels on the shelf, the new recruits who'd been called up after Buddy had bumped into their predecessors. We'd smile back at each other remembering the glass crash.

One day Buddy and I decided to return to the Dollar store, the scene of his unintended crime. I walked on ahead as usual. As we were approaching the store, I saw the employees beyond the plate glass windows, pointing, and laughing between them. They'd seen Buddy trailing behind me. As I opened the front door I yelled over toward the employees and said, "I see you noticed who I brought with me today!" Buddy entered behind me. I said, "Ok, you remember what happened the last time we came here!" As I turned to point at the shelf with the glass angels, I couldn't help but crack up. Apparently, the angels remembered him too because now instead of preparing for flight, all these angels were kneeling and praying!

Buddy's Philosophy

Buddy and I were in the car taking a day trip. As we drove on, I noticed he was not in his usual good mood. So, I asked him a few times what was the matter, but he kept saying, "Nothing." After a while I decided to try a little psychology, so I asked him if he would be willing to help me if I had a problem. He perked up, "Of course."

"So, Buddy, how would it make you feel if you helped me?"

"Good!"

"But what if you knew I had a problem and I wouldn't let you help me. How would that feel?"

He grew glum again, "Bad."

"Buddy, that's how I feel today because you obviously have a problem but won't let me try to help."

He thought about it for a moment and then opened up, "The kids are making fun of my disabilities." He sat, starring ahead as we rode.

I told him "Buddy, my philosophy is that we should do our best with whatever abilities we have and that's good enough. If someone has a problem with that it's their problem, not ours. Besides we all have some disabilities. Guess what? Theirs is their attitude." He sat quiet.

A long period of silence passed. "Frank, what does philosophy mean?"

I explained it this way. "Your philosophy is what you believe so much that you actually live your life by it."

"Frank, what's my philosophy?"

"Well, let's figure it out."

It took quite a while, but I started by asking what was the most important thing in the world? Buddy said, "To be myself."

"What is the most important thing to have?"

Immediately, "Good friends!"

I told him, "Good! So far, we know your philosophy is to be yourself and have good friends. Let's find one more thing, What should you always remember?"

He said excitedly, "I know! What you told me Winston Churchill said. Never, never, never give up."

"So, Buddy, your philosophy is to be yourself, have good friends, and never, never, never give up!" It was like watching the sun rising at dawn, casting its rays on a dark landscape. He suddenly came to life, like the happy, contented Buddy I'd always known. He snapped out of his funk and we went about our day.

A few weeks later I ran into a friend who is a breast cancer survivor. "I saw Buddy the other day." She went on, telling me she'd been in a terrible depression for weeks, feeling sorry for herself. Even though she tried she just couldn't snap out of it. Apparently, Buddy noticed her, walked up and asked, "Linda, what's the matter?" She said, "I don't know, I guess I'm in a bad mood." Right then and there, Buddy described his philosophy of life to Linda exactly as he and I had figured it out weeks before. She lit up, "Miraculously and immediately, my depression transformed into optimism!" I recognized the feeling she described because this was the same effect Buddy had on me the very first time I met him. Over the years too many people to count have been touched by this same disarming but profoundly wise character that lives inside of Buddy, a guy you'd never expect it from. When he's with you, everything changes. When he walks away, it's like, well... like you've been touched by an angel.

Gotta Get the Girl

From the first day Buddy smacked his hand on the side of my truck and announced that it looked like I needed to hire a helper and he was it; we've been a team. He wanted a job and well, it seems I needed a purpose for living that was bigger than the burdens that were quickly, almost permanently, driving me down. Buddy is my alarm clock. I assigned him the task of calling to wake me every day at 8:00 am. Why? Because he knows I've gotta get going to work if I'm going "to make the green stuff." What he doesn't know is that I'm usually up by 5:30 or 6:00.

Over the three decades we've been together—about half my life and three quarters of his—we've spent a good chunk of it riding around in my truck. One day I noticed something tucked into his shirt pocket. "What's that Buddy?"

"The DMV rule book."

"What's it for?"

"Frank, I wanna get my license." I thought, "Oh, this is never going to work."

"So, Buddy why do you need a license? You can ride with me."

"To get a girl. If I'm going to go on a date with a girl, I've got to be able to drive." Well, I couldn't argue with that. But given his serious disabilities, there's no way Buddy's ever going to have a license.

"Okay Buddy, well if you're going to get a license you have to know the rules and the road signs and that means you need to know how to read."

"Oh, yah."

"So, how about I teach you how to read?" He agreed because he wanted to get his license to drive a girl on a date. Let's just say he was motivated. I started putting him through the paces on simple words related to driving. "Buddy, how do you spell STOP?" He didn't know, so I taught him. We'd be driving along and pull up to a stop sign. I'd say, "Buddy, we've stopped because there's a stop sign, see it? How do you spell STOP?"

"S-T-O-P, stop."

"Right. Great!"

We did this with all sort of words. Buddy's spelling graduated from words related to traffic signs to other things. "Buddy, how do you spell Bob?"

"B-O-B, Bob. Hey, it goes both ways!"

"Yup, that's right."

He was catching on pretty well. So, I decided to expand his vocabulary. I taught him how to spell a whole bunch of words, but the spelling game was getting boring to both of us. Then I came up with a new idea. "Buddy, I'll say the word and you spell it backward, okay? Here goes… Mississippi. Spell it backward."

Buddy thought for a second. Then I heard, "I-P-P-I-S-S-I-S-S-I-M, Mississippi backwards."

"What? Wait a minute." I pulled to the side of the road and got out a pencil. Well I'll be damned. He did it! "Buddy, you're amazing." He answered, "Well, duh—you just turn it around!"

So, we kept this up for a while spelling all sorts of words backwards. He loved it. But then this exercise became a little stale too. I had to find another way to engage him.

"Okay Buddy, here's a new test. I'm going to spell the words you've learned, and you tell me what they are."

"Okay."

I thought I'd give him an easy one to start off, so I said, "R-E-D." He cried out "Mississippi!" I just lost it.

The Gruesome Twosome

This is the title of a 1940s Warner Brothers cartoon starring Sylvester the cat and Tweety bird. In it two cats vie for the affections of a femme fatal but Tweety bird manages to expose their deficits in one calamity after another. The Gruesome Twosome very badly want the same thing but nearly destroy themselves and each other trying to get it. Over the years of our friendship I think I've come to see that Buddy and I are two cats trying to get the same thing. But… we don't work against each other.

Imagine it. Two broken down cats like us meeting at the edge of my driveway. Here's me—pretty strong ego; athletic; former EMT. Things came easy. Then a failed marriage that ended before it got started; took over my family's business but then my father died; struggling to make ends meet, suddenly realizing I used to make a difference in other people's lives but took that for granted at the time. Now I'd gotten to the point I really wanted meaning and purpose, but I was so consumed with making money to keep all the balls I was juggling in place, there was no meaning left. I was broke; my construction business was a shoestring operation, teetering on non-existence; my body had been broken down by all the punishment I gave it when I was younger, my back was killing me; I had no one in my life, sometimes not even me.

And then there's Buddy—a kid with more challenges to overcome than ten other people combined. He's afflicted with cerebral palsy; is paralyzed on the right side, blind in one eye; he suffered a brain injury when he was a child—his father is dead and gone. Buddy lives with his mother, completely dependent on the two of us. I'm not sure where he'd be—no, that's not right. I'm afraid of where he would be if I wasn't in his life.

Two broken down cats—one in spirit, the other in body. But between the two of us—wow, it still blows my mind. The greatest joy in my life is to see the pride that Buddy takes from knowing he's made such a difference to me. I'm not sure which one of us rescued the other, but here we are. I can tell you this, I know I wouldn't be the man I am today had Buddy not stopped and smacked the side of my truck telling me to hire him. There's something in him that is irrepressible. If it hadn't been me, I'm sure he would've wound up on somebody's front doorstep who was desperate for another chance at life.

Trust me, I was low, so low when I met Buddy. But there was something about his spirit that said to me, "You've gotta give this kid a chance." He's been wounded, abused, incapacitated, pushed aside, and ridiculed all his life. Even so, you'd never know it by the way he introduced himself—I should say forced himself into my life. I was the last guy he should've stopped that day. I didn't have anything to live for, but this kid did. I simply just could not ignore him. What do you do when life smacks your truck and grins at you?

Reflections

Frank and Buddy are each other's Genius. It's as if two half-lives have become one whole, and yet these two lives that are far better together than they were alone. What's that old adage, more than the sum of their parts? By the way, I know Frank. He understated his condition by the time Buddy showed up. He was sorely depressed, not sure life had any meaning, not sure how long he'd go on if this was the trajectory of his future.

Buddy? My goodness, Buddy is the guardian angel with wisdom that comes from a place that is just as mysterious and unexpected as the little puppy that trotted up and transformed Manny and his family on a chilly and abrasive spring day.

Friends, there is hope in the dullness of life. There is resurrection from the corpse of lifeless dreams. There is a superpower resident inside us that seems to want so badly to come out. But it seems that many, in my experience, most—though not all—are consigned to wrestle with life and themselves in the process of the Genius's release. And even when that superhuman quality comes out, our wrestling goes on. Except, when the Genius appears, the arduous journey is transformed from dismal, tedious decay to the promise of something new. Not just the recovery of some kind of safe and comfortable respite from the onslaughts of life. No, something beyond the limits we so often regard as the boundaries of a normal life. Something of purity, delight, surprising beauty, and a joy that defies description. So, Happy Chester, Easter! Happy Buster—Buddy—Manny—Frank, Easter!

Chapter 14: Rest for the weary

Known for its breathtaking beauty and wildlife, Yellowstone became the world's first national park in 1871, primarily for it's incredibly unique geothermal features. 500 geysers, more than half the number in all the world, are found there. The famed naturalist, William Muir said that Yellowstone's geysers "splash and heave and roar in bewildering abundance."

But of the hundreds of geysers found in Yellowstone, only six of these have any kind of predictable pattern. Thus, the name of the most famous, Old Faithful which belches every 60 to 110 minutes, or 20 times a day. The rest? You never know when they will blow.

After sitting dormant since 2004, and only erupting four times in the last 60 years, the characteristically quiet Ear Spring geyser blew to a height of 30 feet on September 15, 2018. But what's more amazing is what Ear Spring coughed up—80 years' worth of human trash shot into the air, propelled by the pressure created when volcanic magma super-heated the underground water. After the historic eruption was over, park rangers collected the unexpected contents which had been buried deep inside. They included cans, part of a cinder block, crumpled foil, a plastic cup and spoon, cigarette butts, a sign that seems to have something to do with bears, a whole lot of coins, and, unbelievably, a baby's pacifier that dates from the 1930s. I wonder where that baby is today.

Like unpredictable geysers, fueled by disturbances deep underground, there are eruptions of the human soul that take us by surprise.

I had just finished a sermon as the guest preacher at a church in Chattanooga. I was there for a weeklong conference. To get people's attention I spoke on Genesis chapter 3 and what is to me God's all-time most important question.

> *Then the man and his wife*
> *heard the sound of the Lord God*
> *as he was walking in the garden*
> *in the cool of the day,*
> *and they hid from the Lord God*
> *among the trees of the garden.*
> *But the Lord God called to the*
> *man,*

"Where are you?"

Genesis 3:8,9

After the service ended, I made my way from the pulpit to the narthex where I had a book table. This would give me a chance to engage in conversation with people and listen to what was inside them as I prepared for the week ahead. But before I could get there, I was accosted by a group of jolly African women whose enthusiasm and warmth wrapped me in their loving hugs. Frankly, I wasn't sure I wanted to escape the embrace of their effervescent spirits. Eventually though, they did let me go.

When I got to the table worshippers who'd beaten me there were curiously fingering the books and picking up the workshop handouts. But in the crowd that was forming one woman wasn't looking at the literature. I sensed her presence and looked up.

"You don't know me. I'm Elizabeth. Chris is my husband. [The pastor who'd invited me. This was my introduction to his wife.]

"So, here's my answer to your question, where are you? My son died and it's not making any sense to me why we are trying to plant a new church."

Whatever else was going on around us suddenly evaporated. The only thing that mattered was Elizabeth's naked suffering. Even now, to call her experience a wound feels like I'm dishonoring her, because the loss of her child was a death of herself, a repudiation of everything that once had meaning. Though I didn't know the details, I didn't need to. For whatever reason—the sermon, the upcoming workshop on church planting, the agony of unanswered and unanswerable questions between husband and wife—Elizabeth's wound had been super-heated and shot up in the face of the visiting expert. Out popped the evidence of a child she once carried, her child, her flesh and blood. I just sat in silence, listening to Elizabeth's soul erupt with a force that demanded my attention.

She didn't say it, but I heard Elizabeth's soul cry out, "Unless there is some purpose in Owen's life, I can't do this. I can't do pastor's wife. I can't do church planting. I can't do life as if he never was."

Sometimes, all you can do is sit and listen and let yourself be scorched by the boiling fury that flows from someone's soul. Trust me, it's an understatement to say this is uncomfortable. As soon as I was splashed by Elizabeth's experience, her questions became mine too. Had I tried to stop up her geyser I'm pretty sure we'd never know what was inside. Listen to what has since come from her soul.

My nightmare

We were running. Quickly moving in the dark woods, our breath ragged and our feet stumbling. I didn't look back, but I could feel them behind us. There were too many to count. Whether man or beast, I couldn't tell. It was dangerous to run through the trees in pitch black, uneven dirt beneath our feet. If we stopped or rested at all I knew we would certainly be lost.

The night was long and after what seemed like hours of running, we cautiously slowed to a stop. I chanced a glance behind us and felt relief. The threat seemed far behind us, and maybe we had outrun them.

My hands felt the soft bundle wrapped on my chest, comforted by his weight. I moved the blankets from him slowly. Time stopped. His face was blue. His face was blue! In our haste to outrun the danger, I had brought the danger with me. I had smothered him in his blankets, in the very things I had brought with us to keep him safe and warm.

I awoke with screams.

My husband spent the rest of the night holding me as I sobbed the bitter, ugly tears of a mother whose only child had died within her.

Eleven years later, I still wonder if there is a part of me that will never forgive myself.

Owen. His name is Owen and he is our eldest. Most of the time we speak of him in past tense. In terms of was or had been. But he is, and he was. Both are true. And that's what makes this life so difficult.

In the early months after he died, I lived a half-life. I would spend hours half awake, half asleep, moving from the couch to the bedroom and back again. I was terrified of my dreams. They tormented me with visions of dead babies. I spent hours in a dream-like state, daydreaming of another world in which Owen did not die. You might have wanted to commit me to psychiatric care had you known me then. I could see in my mind's eye another apartment still full of his things. Our bed and his crib still smushed next to each other and a baby laughing just out of sight in the next room.

About a year later, I listened to a news interview with Joan Didion about her book The Year of Magical Thinking. She recounted when, after her husband died, she could not throw out his shoes. "He would need his shoes," she reasoned. In her mind, there was a place her husband still needed his shoes and she, of course, could not get rid of them. She knew he was dead and would not ever need his shoes again… but she could not throw them out.

"Yes," I remember thinking when I heard her interview... "he will need his shoes."

Owen is our eldest, and he's dead

It is a harsh reality to hear, to live. I was exactly one month away from my due date. My belly was swollen and aching, full of kicks and elbows thrown into the decreasing lack of space. My husband and I were young, "too young to bear the weight of such a tragedy," someone carelessly remarked to us in an attempt to comfort. We had been married for almost three years and my 25th birthday had passed a few months earlier. Owen was a sweet surprise early in our marriage, coming at a time when we were still figuring out how to argue without throwing remotes and how to cook dinner by ourselves. I loved him with my whole heart, and I cherished his company, even if I was still wrapping my head around what it would be like to care for another human being.

I was at work when he died. I know that now. The next morning when I walked into the doctor's office with anxious hope that they would tell me everything was fine, I knew then. It took all of 15 minutes for two doctors to confirm there was no heartbeat. 15 minutes to change our lives forever. I carried him 36 weeks and it took 15 minutes for everything to fall apart. How would anything ever make sense again? How could life go on when everything was broken?

"People don't just drop dead for no reason." My OB laughed nervously, leaning against the counter in the exam room. She furrowed her brow as she took in my pitiful face. She had just told us our baby was dead. I still don't know if this was her attempt at compassion or humor. She said more to us before we were sent home… using words like autopsy and blood work, but never "I'm sorry." I had three doctors during my pregnancy with Owen. And not one of them told me "I'm sorry" when they came in to check the ultrasound that day.

I was told to call the hospital when I was ready to check into labor and delivery to be induced. When we called a few hours later, I was told there were no beds ready for me and I would have to wait at home another day. I thought my body was going to split open from the pain of knowing my child was dead inside me, and another day's wait until I could deliver. If I could have run away, I would have. If I could have unzipped my body to release the life that was no more within me, I would have. I didn't know how I was going to brave the drive to the hospital to deliver knowing I would be delivering my dead baby. That night, I was sure I was going to die. It did not feel like a mercy when I woke up the next morning.

I walked into the birthing suite in the labor and delivery unit and collapsed into the chair next to the bed. Women in labor, women nursing their new arrivals, and rooms full of excited visitors surrounded us. I cried, not in the throes of labor, but in the throes of grief. A nurse walked in to take my information and explain the induction process to my husband and me. He held my hand as I tried to breathe through my sobs. He held me up as I quietly asked for a c-section. Everything in me wanted to be put to sleep and to wake up when it was over. This is not how it was supposed to be was all I could think in my haze.

Owen was born the next morning… three days after he had died. He was born much like any other baby is born, except when they placed him on my chest, he made no sound. He was beautiful, our son. Ten perfect fingers, ten perfect toes. Long skinny feet and reddish-brown hair. I had never held such a tiny and perfect newborn before. I couldn't take my eyes off of him. We held him all morning, and into the late afternoon. Family came. In and out of the room they came to meet our son, and to say goodbye.

We spent the remainder of the day trying to squeeze a lifetime into a few hours. We held our son, admired his precious face, and lovingly stroked his perfect chin and nose. Pictures were taken, though not nearly enough to satisfy a lifetime. My husband cradled his son in his arms and wept. There would be many more tears to come, but the tears we shed on Owen's birthday are seared into my memory. I will never forget what it felt like to hold my baby boy, feel the weight of him in my arms and know that he was not there anymore. This was not how it was supposed to be.

I never wanted this life

In the days following his death, my breathing was shallow. It took great effort to breathe, to stand, to be. The surface of my skin was raw, electric. I felt like I would burst wide open if I moved too suddenly. If I breathed in too deep, I would collapse from the pain of it all. The shock. The trauma.

He was alive. I knew him. I loved him. He was real.

And then he was dead. No warning. He was still... so very still and quiet, so much heavier than the day before... the day before when he had been alive.

I can imagine what these words are like to read. Every word I write is etched in sadness. Painful. Uncomfortable. Tragic. Pitiful. Heartbreaking.

As the days turn cooler and the nights come earlier, I feel that familiar ache that reminds me so bitterly that all is not right in this world. Can you feel it? Do you see it too?

Eleven years later, I breathe in and the sadness stirs, going further down. I breathe in deep and let the sadness wash over me. I breathe in deeper still and feel the sadness fill the tender ache. He would be eleven this November. He was my little boy. He is my little boy. He was here and he is still a part of me.

After Owen died, my husband and I went into survival mode. There weren't very many plans made or at least none that I made. I had no energy for anything except my grief. I lived, breathed and consumed grief. It was everywhere and in everything; in the clear blue skies outside our window, in the sounds of children playing down the street, in the aisles at the grocery store. Nothing was innocuous. Everything was a reminder of what was lost.

I could barely stand eating at restaurants or shopping for groceries. There were always babies. There were always pregnant women. I did everything I could to avoid them. In fact, I hated them. I hated them so intensely that I lost many friends. I was angry all the time. I remember our pastor coming to see us the day we spent waiting at home before Owen was born, and I remember telling him I wasn't angry. Tears poured from my eyes, but I wasn't lying. Then, I wasn't angry. I was in shock, deep in shock. Looking back, the shock was a grace provided before the bone crushing grief assaulted me.

Slowly as the days passed, the shock wore off in waves. They threatened to drown me. Big waves, small waves... they were everywhere. They were as constant as breathing. They came in many forms, and the only surprise they offered were the form they chose. Babies in strollers, children named Owen, babies crying at church, pregnancy announcements, diaper commercials, expiration dates on cans of food with his due date, and well-meaning people offering the cold sympathy of 'at least we could have more...'; 'at least we didn't know him yet...'; 'at least we knew we could get pregnant again...'

The world felt dangerous and cold. How could the sun continue to rise when my life had ended? How could people talk of anything else? I was indignant and confused when close friends announced pregnancies, as if pregnancy could be joyful... as if they thought their babies would live? Didn't they know that babies could die before they ever got the chance to breathe? Didn't they remember Owen? I hated them. Friends, strangers—anyone who crossed my path with the audacity to be pregnant after I had lost my son so unfairly.

It is not easy now to admit that I wished their babies would die too. Anger burned all my bridges. Anger burned within and threatened to burn me alive.

I spent most of my days alone. Chris would get up and go to work, leaving me in bed all day. I ached for Owen. My whole body longed for him, my baby. He was missing... couldn't other people see that? Nothing would ever be the same, no matter if I could manage to have another baby or how much time passed. I was so hurt and angry that no one could understand how I was feeling. My anger and resentment further isolated me, at a time when I needed connection and compassion.

I stopped going to church, fearing the well-meaning comments that so often came. I was hurting, the gaping wounds visible all over my body. I didn't understand that they only wanted to comfort me. I didn't understand that my gaping wounds frightened them, even repulsed them. I couldn't see myself how they saw me. Their words, their hope felt like an attack, and I was ready to defend myself. I chose an armor of anger, a breastplate of bitterness, a helmet of hatred.

In the year following Owen's death I was convinced that I had done something wrong and it was my fault that he had died. I spent hours recycling the same conversation with Chris. What did I do? What didn't I do? What did God see in me that was so wrong that I should suffer this way? What did He want me to learn? How could I learn what He wanted of me so I would never ever suffer like this again? I felt sure there was something I needed to learn, some hidden thing I needed to uncover to guarantee I didn't cause us to suffer another loss.

Six months after Owen died, I suffered through the pain of an ectopic pregnancy. The utter devastation of this loss was enough to keep me from ever, ever stepping foot back in church again. Chris would leave me at home as he worshipped alone, sometimes leading the church in song. I didn't care. My heart was hard as stone, my self-insulating armor complete. God's goodness was for other people. People who hadn't angered him the way I must have. People whose children didn't die.

Six months later, I was pregnant again. Fall had come at last. The air was cooler, the days shorter and it was time for Owen's first birthday. For the first time I had a whisper of hope that this world could bear something besides heartache. I held the hope of this new baby in my cold heart, feeling something resembling joy beginning to creep in. The anniversary of Owen's death and the celebration of his first birthday were heavy, full of longing and sadness. I imagined our life and saw visions of a toddling tow-headed boy filling up my days. I ached for him, and what might have been.

One week later, I began to miscarry our precious little baby. That night was long and painful, compounded by the devastation of the whole prior year. I laid in bed, wracked with pain and sobbed. Chris held onto me. He had been holding on for the both of us for a year. I remember yelling at him, "Why??" And begging him to tell me that God had not abandoned me, that God had not forsaken me…

It was the loss of our third baby that cracked my armor. Where else could I go? What else could I do but collapse at the feet of the One who promised me hope in the midst of the graveyard of my life. There was no life, no peace in this world, in a world that buried babies. The world was dangerous and cold, but maybe… maybe the One who promised He would never leave or forsake us could also give us hope and peace in His promise of making all things new… in His promise of coming again to bind up brokenness.

Maybe I could hope again. Maybe I could even feel joy.

How can life go on when everything is broken?

That night… when I thought I was dying of a broken heart, God revealed Himself to me and I have never been the same. It is nothing short of a miracle that I am still here.

> *…few of us enter the tragedy of living in a fallen world and simultaneously struggle with God until our hearts bleed with hope. We either give into pain with a hopeless cynicism, or we settle for an artificial resolution that insists that things really aren't too bad, and we need not muck around in the 'negatives' of life.*
>
> The Healing Place by Dan B. Allender, PhD.

He has made my heart to bleed with hope... and I haven't stopped bleeding since.

What if the Creator of this world, the world I found dangerous and cold, had not abandoned us because we messed it up? My head was spinning, and I found myself thinking about things I had never considered before.

Almost overnight I felt a quietness in my soul that I could not explain. It was not mine to figure out the whys and hows of Owen's short life and death. This world is full of sorrow, brokenness, death. If you live at all, if you love at all... you will be touched by grief. But... the story does not end with grief. It does not end with death.

How could life go on when everything was broken?

The only way I can manage to get up in the morning is to be reminded anew, with each sunrise that my story—that this world's story—will not end in mourning.

Owen's death buried me deep in the ground, but instead of more death, I have found life... new growth has bloomed and given life to a beautiful awakening within me.

Go on
Cover me with dirt
I'm not dead.
I'm blooming.

It has not been easy for me to trust the Lord since Owen died. When things take a turn in my life and I am faced with one brokenness or another, I often feel a familiar panic rise in my throat. PTSD, depression, and anxiety became real to me eleven years ago. I have found healing in therapy and in quietness with the Lord, but I do wonder if anxiety and melancholy will be with me until the Lord returns to make everything broken whole again. I have seen too much not to worry and ache with the brokenness all around me. But I have experienced too much of God's faithfulness not to remain dependently at my Father's feet.

I struggle openly with all of this, even as a pastor's wife... especially as a pastor's wife. It may surprise you that three years after Owen died, my husband and I drove with our three-month-old daughter 500 miles to attend seminary in the Midwest. My struggle with life and with the Lord did not end when the long days of pregnancy gave us a baby who lived. It did not end when we were in seminary, learning and growing in knowledge of the Lord. It did not end when we accepted our first ministry call.

Israel means "wrestles with God" and oh how I have wrestled with Him... and I will wrestle over and over again with the Lord, if only to bleed with hope again and again. Hope in the Lord will never put us to shame, though you may think that we should be able to trust with no help, without a struggle. I don't think the Bible teaches us that. There is no shame in falling at your Father's feet in desperate need of help. He knows your heart better than you, and He knows you are no more able to make your heart trust than you are to make the sun rise each morning.

Horatius Bonar, a Scottish preacher from the 1800s, teaches that faith is a resting. He has an illustration of a man, too tired to keep going, but too tired to lie down and rest. "What folly," he says... "if you are tired, lie down and rest!"

Faith is a resting, an empty hand raised to our Father. Rest, he calls. Rest in what I've done, in who I Am. Rest in my never-ceasing love and pursuit of you. Rest in what I have promised to do.

In the early years after Owen died, before our living children were born, my head instinctively turned to the backseat almost every time we got in the car. There was no child to buckle into a car seat, of course. We had stored his infant car seat at my parent's house, deep in the far corner of their basement storage room. My heart felt his absence so tangibly that my body couldn't help but to look for him. My eyes scanned the room for him almost everywhere we went. He was a real part of me for nine months and it would take a long time for it to sink in that he was gone. Even still, eleven years later... four living children crowd our van and my head turns again to the backseat... looking, searching for the little boy who would be the oldest. After our third baby was born alive and healthy, the grief of Owen's absence would take me by surprise in moments of counting children in the attempt to keep track of them all. Where are the others? my heart would ask. The depth of grief has found no limit. I am still searching the world for them, only to find that they will not return to me—but I will go to them.

All our bodies are riddled with brokenness. We are broken people. Some of us (more than others) are reminded of our brokenness from the moment our eyes open in the morning. Our bodies ache, our hearts grieve and the undeniable not-rightness of this world screams for attention.

But some of us ignore our brokenness—content to go days, weeks, months or years without thinking much about our broken state. We can exercise, eat healthy food, and convince ourselves that this is enough. We can deny the hurt in our hearts, and keep busy with work, school and play. Maybe we can fool ourselves into believing that we have our stuff together, that things aren't so bad. But the fact remains... we are broken and dying. Our bodies need more than healthy food and exercise. Denying the hurt and needs of our hearts will only suffice for a time.

Our bodies, our souls need regeneration. And this broken world, the one where babies are stillborn, and people die, and marriages end, and people knowingly and willingly hurt each other, this world needs regeneration. And that is why the Good News of the Gospel is so good.

The wind whispers His promises. Jesus has promised to come back. And when he does, he will set all things right. He will mend our broken bodies, heal our broken hearts, and separation will be no more. This world will be remade, and it will no longer be broken.

We don't have to ignore the brokenness in the world or in our own lives. Sugar-coating the hurt and ginning up a positive attitude will not heal hurting hearts. Only Jesus and his promises can fix what is broken.

When we pretend that the hurt doesn't run deep, we are denying ourselves the comfort of the Gospel. Jesus did not smile, pretending that things aren't bad here. He wept. He overturned tables and was angry. He died in and for this brokenness, this struggle, this suffering.

There are a lot of hurting people in this world. We're all part of the broken masses. We need Jesus, and that's a good thing because He is real, and He is bigger than we can even imagine.

You might conclude I'm a pessimist. But I'm not. After everything— and God knows there are many more things than the burdens I've born—you could say I'm sobered by life. Some will take comfort from this point of view I suppose. Others, who are trying to force suffering into a formula that resolves to joy might be put off by my perspective. If, like me, you are uncomfortable with the sober view, think about how the willful decision to ignore reality skews everything. The life you're living and the ability to appreciate just how magnificent our Savior Jesus is, and what an awesome Father God we have. Opening ourselves to experience, even actually embracing the depth of our brokenness, will lead to such joy and sustaining hope in the Lord, I promise. More importantly, Jesus promises this.

We wait with eagerness and joy because He will return to make all things new.

> *I lift up my eyes to the hills*
> *from where does my help come?*
> *My help comes from the Lord*
> *who made heaven and earth.*

Psalm 121:1-2

I've always run towards my grief with my arms open, ready to feel the hurt. Whatever grief needed me to do, I was ready. I knew it was the right thing for me to do. I knew I needed to feel every part of my loss. I needed to grieve. Even if I'd tried to, I couldn't put my grief in a box and hide it away pretending to be some kind of paper-thin Christian who floats somewhere above what happens in real life as I mutter a self-hypnotizing mantra, "Just let go and let God." That's no more real than those who want to credit Jesus with some kind of superhuman powers that freed him from His actual flesh and blood suffering and death on the cross. Lots of doubters hurled insults at him, "If you're really who you say you are, if you're really the Son of God, then just snap your fingers, call out to your father, summon the angels to take you off the cross!" Didn't happen though did it? He died, like Owen died. No rescue. If your faith depends upon a miracle show it's not faith. "Faith is the substance of what we hope for and the evidence of what we do not yet see." I know, it's a mystery. But I believe it because through death, the death of my stillborn children, I have experienced this hope. Did you hear me? I didn't hover in some realm between earth and heaven and talk myself into hope. He came to me in the midst of the grave.

It's been suggested to me in more than one conversation, in looks, and in other sorts of nonverbal cues that I should just move on, get over it, and stop dwelling on the past—as if Owen is my past and not a part of me.

We shouldn't—and don't need—to throw the blanket of God's sovereignty over our suffering and pretend that we aren't hurt, deeply affected by our grief. No, if I've understood anything it's our need to open our hearts to whatever is our pain and sorrow, taking it all in, and take it all to God. Run to Him with our arms open and fall at His feet with all our baggage. He's not pretending our grief, our pain, our suffering, our sadness doesn't exist. He sees it more clearly than we do. He sees the whole picture; the beautiful story working itself in our lives and in the lives of all His children. And He is making all things new and beautiful.

I found out that grief changes a person, whether we like it or not. It peels back the layers of innocence much more quickly than time or age can. I've heard it said that you want to become a better person, not a bitter person because of what you go through in life. Mostly I've been bitter. I hid from friends who didn't seem to understand, and I felt anger and bitterness towards people who didn't seem to have any struggles. I carried the torch of unfairness high for all to see, and I intentionally shut people out of my life because they would not or could not grieve with me.

No matter how much I wanted NOT to feel what I was feeling, the truth is that I couldn't change my heart. I couldn't let go of the weight of how I felt my life was unfair. And, I couldn't let go of the unfairness of people asking me to be someone I couldn't be, and to feel things that I wasn't feeling.

It was only the Holy Spirit who could change my heart, who could show me grace in the way I longed to experience. It was grace that changed my heart... grace, that indescribable balm of relief poured out upon me from somewhere outside every effort I could ever muster to heal or soothe my soul wracked with pain. His soothing grace that penetrates my weary soul that feels misunderstood, judged and even now and then sometimes still struggles with bitterness.

I am the wife of a pastor. I am a mother to four living children, and three who are just out of sight. I don't have all the answers and I won't pretend I don't struggle with the Lord's providence in my life.

I praise God that He is so abounding in patience, in mercy, in faithfulness, and in love for me. He will never abandon us, never let us go.

An unexpected gift

The Genius which has been released beyond the life-threatening borders of my wound is rest. I've found rest in Him. He is before all things, and in Him all things hold together.

In the dark, scary, unknown places we can trust Him... oh, the hope we have! This is our Father's world and one day, He will renew all things here. He will make all things right. For now, my soul waits in hope, not a hope dependent on the breadth of human knowledge and experience, but a hope inspired by God Himself.

As the years have passed, some slowly, painfully, and others rather quickly, I have felt my hands loosen their grip around the dream of what life was supposed to have been with Owen. I can't explain how, but I have felt the Lord bestow rest within my heart, trusting in what is to come.

> *We will see our wounded Savior,*
> *We'll behold him face to face;*
> *And we'll hear our anguished stories*
> *Sung as victory songs of grace.*
>
> Wendell Kimbrough

Reflections

"My son died, and I can't make sense of it...." Every time I hear someone's confession of their bone crushing, soul-searing experience of life, I am moved to holy silence. There simply are no acceptable answers to the pain of loss—at least not in this three-dimensional life. That would be like trying to explain why our hearts hurt, as if we could turn off the instinctive nature of love that draws us toward life. And this is why Elizabeth's disclosure to me of where she was had such a disarming power. "Where are you?" is God's all time most provocative question because it asks us to be completely honest. She may have been angry when we met, but that's not what I picked up. And even if she was, who could argue with that response? Of course, you now know by her own admission that anger did factor into her story. But that was only a piece of it. No, what stands out to me about Elizabeth is her tenacious quest to find out what her experience means. If life has meaning, then Owen's life must have purpose—there's got to be another dimension where there will be an answer.

I'm impressed that unlike many people who suffer unspeakable violation and loss, Elizabeth didn't settle for a life of grief over the life that was taken from her. Memorializing losses, no matter how large or small, has crippled too many of us. While she will never, and can never forget her loss, Elizabeth is persevering to find its meaning in the context of her whole life—including parts of it she hasn't known yet.

Her unspoken declaration to me on that Sunday morning in Chattanooga, "If there is no meaning to Owen's life then there is no meaning to mine," is one of the most profound invitations I have ever witnessed of a person seeking understanding beyond the bounds of their own knowledge. Frankly, she was asking God to remove the veil of separation between where she was and where He is. Think of it this way. By saying where she was—stuck in meaninglessness because life had not delivered what she believed it ought to—she was actually asking God the same question He asks all of us, "Where are you?" Over the years of her persistent desire to find out where He is it's as if Elizabeth has experienced the outstretched hand of God take hold of hers and lead her to new insight, new depth of knowledge, and a new kind of relationship with life which has inspired a transformation of her whole person.

Has she escaped the torment of suffering? No, no more than the evidence of Jesus's passion has been erased. When he appeared to the disciples after resurrection it was the marks of the nails in his hands, feet, and side that convinced them who He was. The marks of her cross will always be with Elizabeth. But now she lives a different life than the day her baby died.

Out of her suffering she's received a Genius gift... the ability to rest, to live with the effects of her loss and not be overcome by them. But this is not simply coping. No, Elizabeth has seen into life beyond what she had ever seen before. It's as if through her loss she has been ushered into a new country few seldom travel to. And among those who've been there, few can appreciate what they have discovered. You ask, how is it possible for Elizabeth to be okay with where she is unless she is medicated or self-deluded by the platitudes of a religion that betrayed her? It is possible because when she was in free fall, she grabbed hold of promises made to her by the God who made her, and Owen, and her husband and their life together. Yes, it was out of desperation that she held on, waiting for revelation. And she has apparently received it. What good, what meaning, or purpose can possibly come from such a powerful loss? The faith to urge others who are in free fall from the wounds of life to grab hold as well.

"You don't know me, I'm Elizabeth and my son died..." She was telling me, "and I've died too." Perhaps you've suffered a death that has left you feeling like the walking dead. With all the sincerity I can express to you, friend, if that's where you are, I urge you to ask God "Where are you?" My prayer is that He will take hold of your hand and lead you into that realm where He is. Whatever your wound, I pray you will be found where He is, with Him.

Epilogue

He is so beautiful to us. After 11 years I can see how it must be to look at him from a different perspective, but I felt like what I wrote was so exposing—it didn't make sense to me to hide him in the same breath. I think it's really important for our society to continue to get more comfortable with death and grief. One of my close friends back when I was skipping church told me that the church needed to see me. Not to hide because the church needed to see us grieve. I definitely understand her now.

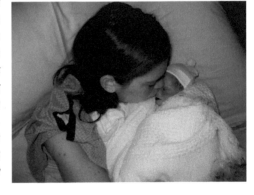

Chapter 15: The Elephant Man

Joseph Carey Merrick lived a life few can imagine. You know him better by the freak show name given to him—the Elephant Man. Fate—or some other power—chose Victorian England to serve as Merrick's stage. To be born at such a time with his deformities seems cruel and mysterious. However, Merrick instinctively understood his time and place, and though he only survived 27 years, used his unimaginable challenges to become far more than anyone could ever have predicted. He used his wound to advantage, actually embracing the spectacle he realized he was to so many who couldn't stop looking at his deformities.

To all appearances, Joseph was born a healthy baby boy on August 5, 1862 in Leicester, England. But when he was only 20 months old there were some visual cues that something was odd about his development. His parents, Jane and Joseph Merrick, raised him alongside a younger brother and sister. Before he was three, he witnessed his brother's death, the same year that his body began to change; it twisted, becoming misshapen. When he was 8 years old his sister died. By the time Joseph turned 11 his deformities had become grotesque. Heaping cruel insult upon injury, his mother died that year, stripping him of the only person who had championed his fragile life.

When his father remarried, Joseph's new stepmother denied him a place in her home. He was forced to go to work. Unsuccessful at rolling cigars in a factory due to his bulbous hands, he tried selling gloves for his father, door to door. But with his large head and face hooded to hide his grotesque features, children and adults taunted him because they were afraid of this freakish monster. Repeatedly beaten by his father for his failure to earn a living, I wonder if it wasn't the pent-up revulsion, he felt toward his own son that was trying to destroy what he could not love.

At the age of 15 Joseph escaped the humiliation from his father and entered one of England's notorious workhouse's, the last stop before utter defeat. An early and crude expression of social welfare for the destitute, the workhouse was more like a disease infested prison for the sick, insane, and every form of outcast misfit. He couldn't take it and bolted shortly after arriving only to return after another round of failure in the cruel world in which he had no place.

He spent the next three years there, working two 5-hour shifts every day, punctuated by meager meals and lots of prayer. While there he underwent a surgery, which removed mounds of flesh from his jaw. As he considered his situation, Merrick concluded that he'd have a much better chance at some kind of normal life if he was to exhibit himself in one of the popular freak shows at the time. I know—the assessment that normal life could be attained by hawking himself as a freak seems not only counterintuitive, but downright self-abusive. And yet, his decision was ingenious given the limited field of options in front of him.

Even by today's standards Merrick was what has been called a human oddity. Historians now believe that he suffered from Proteus syndrome, an extremely rare but chronic condition, unknown in his day. The skin thickens with layers of overgrowth. The bones, blood vessels, and connective tissues demonstrate this same kind of extra-layering. There are often large non-cancerous tumors on the body and a deformation of the limbs, spine, and skull. Proteus syndrome is so rare that no one, including the medical community in England, had seen such a sight before. It only appeared in American medical literature in 1976, over a hundred years after he was born.

So, in August 1884 Merrick began the only professional career he ever held, that of a side show freak. But his instincts about his fortune were right. Though he was an oddity, he discovered that people treated him well, and he received payment for revealing his deformity to a wincing crowd of gawkers who were thrilled with their own disgust. He once told the show's owner when he was asked to pass a hat for donations, "We are not beggars." Having been taught the value of an income by his mother and life's incredibly harsh lessons, Joseph saved in excess of $6,000. That was a lot of money for any common man in his day, let alone a human oddity.

Merrick wasn't the only freak. He traveled and was exhibited with the likes of Fyodor Andrianovich Jeftichew, JoJo the dog-faced boy from Russia who was afflicted with an inherited condition known as hypertrichosis—a prodigious growth of hair from all parts of his body; Krao Farini, a young girl from Laos who was dubbed the missing link; and Carl Hermann Unthar from East Prussia, the armless wonder who played the violin with his feet and who typed his autobiography late in life calling it das pediscript. These and others we discovered by the original American showman, PT Barnum, who hired them and took them to the United States, fascinating audiences there.

Merrick was happy. But the tide of public opinion turned. A kind of civility eclipsed a baser attraction to the bizarre, and so in time, the freak shows in England were shut down. Merrick wandered throughout Europe for a while but returned to England.

Once, while waiting for a train at Liverpool Station, his mask and hood fell off and the crowd panicked. Because he was suffering from bronchitis at the time, he couldn't speak and could not defend himself. During that ordeal, in a desperate moment he showed the horrified crowd a card from a physician, Dr. Treves, who had seen him when he was on display as the Elephant Man in the freak show. Treves was summoned and gave Merrick residence in his London hospital. A twist of fate seemed to once again meet Merrick as he eventually became a favorite of the Victorian Royalty; the Princess of Wales and the Queen's Consort. Even Queen Victoria herself showed him great favor.

Merrick had a strong mind and developed a keen ability to read people's glances and feigned interest in him. A conniving circus man seemed always to be lurking in the shadows, whether in the form of royalty, or a physician, or an opportunistic businessman. Unseen by the curious onlookers who were fascinated by his grotesque appearance, Merrick had grown an invisible antenna which shrewdly discerned the unspoken motives hidden inside those who gathered to gawk at him.

Longing for the love of a woman Merrick wanted to live in a home for the blind. He hoped a woman would simply respond to the sound of his voice and the tenderness of his heart. Maybe then he could be loved and give love.

Society's Elephant Man, was, as he said, "not an animal, but a man, a man!" Despite his bodily form, Joseph Merrick was a man who learned how to navigate the treacherous, dark oceans of life in ways not uncommon to those who are most grievously treated. First, there was his religious faith that his loving mother had kindled in him. To that she added a love of books, of literature, and reading. Together with barely any other counsel but that of his own soul, Merrick discerned much about the mysteries of life, himself, and others that few more favorably endowed people ever see or know. He developed a sixth sense that instructed him on the meaning of people's motives, words, and behavior.

You are about to read about Michael, a man born with life-altering deformities, who has undergone countless surgeries, struggled with self-acceptance, and found a woman who could love him just as he is. Out of his tortured trek Mike has discovered Genius that most might never see because of the sight that greets them. Can you find it?

I praise you,
for I am fearfully and wonderfully made.
Wonderful are your works; my soul knows it very well.
My frame was not hidden from you, when I was
being made in secret,
intricately woven in the depths of the earth.
Your eyes saw my unformed substance;
in your book were written,
every one of them, the days that were formed for me,
when as yet there was none of them.

Psalms 139

At the age of 70, I am a recovering fool. The biblical definition of a fool is someone who lives his life as if there is no God. I have lived a large portion of my life as if God did not exist or if He did, He was not involved with me, and certainly not moment by moment.

I am a tenth generation Mississippian. I was born at 6:15 pm on January 6, 1948. At birth I weighed 1.5 pounds and was 3 months premature. I have EEC syndrome (Ectrodactyly-Ectodermal Dysplasia-Cleft Lip/ Palate), a serious and horrible birth defect. It was a spontaneous mutation at the point of conception.

My birth brought shame on both my mother's and my father's family. The horror my existence evoked threw all of them into a fit of name-calling and accusations. Southerners in the late 40s and 50s had a Victorian belief that people who were disabled or deformed were considered "shut-ins," to live tucked away from the sight of polite society, lest anyone be offended.

My birth defect resulted in a cleft palate; harelip; abnormal hands with twisted and missing fingers; misshapen feet with web toes; flattened nose; teeth that came in rotten and had to be pulled; and no tear ducts— a condition that eventually results in blindness. The syndrome was well understood but very rare and almost always fatal. At birth the family doctor, Dr. Felts, instructed my father to buy a coffin for me, and to be prepared to buy one for my mother.

They put me in an incubator to help with my breathing since I was almost three months premature. I turned blue and refused to breathe so they took me out, put me in a crib, and waited for me to die. Taking me out of the incubator actually saved my sight. At that time the medical community did not know how to regulate oxygen levels for newborns. Many of the babies that were put into incubators suffered detached retinas and premature blindness. Six hours later, to everyone's great surprise, I had not died, so they decided to feed me.

After I was fed for the first time, which was no small accomplishment since I had a cleft palate and an open passage to my brain, I spent 90 days in the hospital, everyone hoping I'd gain weight. Success was measured in ounces and sometimes in grams.

From birth, it was more than two months before my mother was able to hold her baby boy. She spent hours a day at the hospital looking at me even though she could not pick me up. God apparently put some very committed nurses around me; Mother told me later in life that she never came to the hospital, regardless of the time of day or night, when a nurse was not holding me. There was a Catholic nurse who was very concerned that I be baptized because my survival was highly questionable. She approached my parents about it. Mom and Dad consulted with our Methodist pastor. It was decided that it was not necessary for me to be baptized then. Mother told me later that another nurse told her that the Catholic nurse baptized me herself. God put people around me that viewed life as sacred and did the very best they could to preserve it regardless of the consequences. That nurse could have lost her job for baptizing me.

After 90 days they did the first surgery to correct the cleft palate. The work was done in New Orleans. Dr. Owens was a gifted surgeon and years ahead of his time, but the man was tortured in his soul and had total disregard for pain in his patients. His goal was to make the body work no matter the cost. The cleft palate surgery was done without anesthesia. In fairness to him plastic surgery in those days was far different than it is now. The medical community believed that babies did not feel pain in any significant way. They also had a problem with anesthesia and babies: it did a good job of putting them to sleep but they were not always successful at waking them up. There was very little "cosmetic" work. Plastic surgeons primarily repaired serious birth defects, injuries, or war wounds. When I was older, I built the Doc a model of the USS Nautilus, using the motor skills in the hands that he also reconstructed. He kept it on his desk for years.

Dad observed the surgery and quickly realized that I was feeling terrific pain. He could hear me screaming half way through the hospital. He gave orders that in the future I would always have anesthesia. Dad's

217

logic was that if I died, I died, but he was not willing to see his son live in agony.

After I got out of the hospital, we made the long drive to New Orleans three times a week for a month. It was 120 miles to New Orleans one way, over a winding, hilly two-lane road. There was a railroad crossing that we went over about a mile from the doctor's office, and every time we crossed it, I would begin crying because I knew what was coming. In those years the surgeries were on my hands. They cut them apart and put them back together again. The pieces were actually held together with safety pins. As my hands healed the pins had to be pulled out, which was accomplished by holding me down and using brute force – all of which was done without pain medication. That was reserved on for in-theater surgeries.

After the ordeal, we'd turn right around and make the three-hour trip home. I remember them always being hot and miserable, especially since I had bandages on my hands. In later years they were on my arms and face.

When I was 10, they repaired the hare lip; my mouth was sewn shut for a month, except for a small opening at each corner of my mouth. Since they had not yet repaired the flattened nose, I was a mouth breather. Soda straws were inserted in each opening for two reasons: so that I could breathe and so that I could eat—well, consume a liquid diet.

This cycle went on for 14 years, at least once a year until my father died. For the record I never finished all the surgeries. I finally decided that I had had enough of it; the pain, the exhaustion—it wasn't worth the effort. Dad's death and the fact that we were broke and had no insurance gave me a much-needed escape valve—and a viable excuse to stop the agony.

Often in the first two or three years I was so uncomfortable that I could not sleep unless I was held. There were times when I would have to be held all night. Mother and her sister would cradle me propped up by pillows, with more on the floor beside them to catch me if, in their fatigue, they dropped me—there were times when that happened.

Mom and Dad built their house in 1940, a year after they married. There were three bedrooms, one bath, no air conditioning, a big front porch, and a large oak tree that we all sat under on summer nights. Granny's bedroom was built especially for her. It was a six-sided room with large windows and a side door with a ramp leading to the outside. She suffered from arthritis and was totally immobile from the neck down. She needed total 24/7 care, which we all provided—especially mom. She loved me dearly. Dad's sister Iva Nell, her husband Halman, their daughter Linda, Dad's mom, my other Grandma lived at the other end of the street. They all accepted me as their own. Much of the success that I have achieved in life came from what they taught me.

Outside of my family which had grown to accept me, I was viewed as a freak by adult society. I could tell they looked at me as someone who could not be trusted, someone who was assumed to be guilty—of something—and therefore must be watched. I remember times when I was stopped on the street by strangers and ridiculed. There were other times when people would stop what they were doing when I passed and just stares and pointed. Once I was in a drug store and was forced to empty my pockets on the counter before I could leave. Someone who looked like I did must have stolen something! For the record, I didn't— steal.

Another time, the local police department sponsored a consolidated end of the year school picnic. When we arrived and got off the bus, I was approached by an officer. He was kind, wanted my name, who was father? Then he told me gently that it wasn't my fault, but that I shouldn't be there and that I couldn't participate. I had to remain out of sight and wait on the bus until it was time to go back home. I sat on the bus for three hours while the other kids played and had a good time.

One Saturday afternoon when I was 14 my father and I were set to go fishing. That morning he'd gotten up and gone to work and I'd gone to the library. But at around 9:15, a feeling of dread came over me. Something was wrong. When I got home, Dad was there. He had an angina attack at the office, came home and called the doctor. The doctor told him to come to his office in a couple of hours. He laid down to rest until it was time to go. Ten or 15 minutes later, mother went in to check on him. He was dead and had turned blue. I will never forget the sight of him.

The loss that I felt at Dad's death was profound. My grief was so great that whenever his name was mentioned I had to leave the room. It was about three months before I could cry. I remember sitting alone in the garage with the doors closed, sobbing my heart out. He was a remarkable man and we were all blessed by God to have him as a father, husband, and provider.

He was a remarkable person. I don't remember him showing me a lot of affection, but I know that he loved me. He proved it by his actions. When I was very little, and we had just started the long ordeal of surgeries, Dad's brother (who was a doctor) offered to adopt and raise me as his own. That way the operations could be done for nothing. Dad refused and signed up for the costly operations. Where a man puts his money is generally a good measure of where his heart is.

The significance of my father giving me his name was lost on me until recently. Dency—it's a name that I never liked or used because it is odd, different, people get it wrong and often misspell it, but it is the name he went by every day of his life. Giving me his name was Dad's way of saying that I belonged to him, his way of running toward me when almost everyone in the south was running away from me in horror and revulsion.

The remainder of my teen years were generally fun. God gave me a few friends who accepted me, which wasn't easy for most people. The occasions of people stopping me in the street to laugh or make fun were becoming a thing of the past. Still, I was unable to get any part time work that involved meeting the public. But I did wind up with a couple of interesting jobs.

The first was catching the press run at the "Hattiesburg American," the local newspaper. The press was two stories high and about 100 years old. It spit out the papers in stacks of 50. You had to stick your hands down next to the horizontal rotating blades that separated the papers in order to pick up the stacks. A slight miscalculation could cause serious harm. Did someone decide I could run the risk? The boiler that was used to melt down the lead type was right next to where I worked. It was often 130 degrees when the press was running. The chief printer would keep an eye on me, and when he thought that I was about to pass out from the heat he'd stop the press. This had two positive benefits, first it gave me a chance to cool down in the merely 100-degree ambient temperature, and second, it kept me from falling into the whirling knives and messing up the press run with my mangled body.

I also became a short order cook at a hamburger joint. They would not hire me to work the front where I'd have to meet people; they would however let me cook. It was right across the street from the university so I could work between classes. It was a great job. I earned about 70 cents an hour. Gasoline in those days was about 32 cents a gallon. Life was good. I actually became a pretty good short order cook. The skills I learned have served me well, and I really enjoy cooking to this day.

When I was either 17 or 18, I was selected for a staff position at the Philmont Boy Scout Ranch. Not just any position, but a ranger, which as far as I was concerned was the best possible position. Rangers led the groups out for the first two days on the trail to get them started and to make certain that they could take care of themselves, and then the ranger would hike back for another group. I liked being in leadership and teaching others to become self-reliant.

The first day there my tent mate refused to bunk with me because I was different. The next day I was summoned to the administrator's office. He accused me of lying on the application form. For what? In the past the Scouts had allowed kids with speech impediments to serve as rangers, but some campers had complained that it lessened their Philmont Ranch experience. So, the Scouts revised the application form to identify kids with speech impediments in order to weed them out.

When I applied, I had been given the old form to fill out. I didn't lie about anything. Once more, I was offered another job out of sight. With tears rolling down my face, I refused and left. By the time it was all said and done, everyone in the office was crying. The next day when I checked out of camp no one would look me in the eye. No one said a word. They didn't know how to handle the situation any more than I did.

The reaction I got when I returned home was interesting. A few people supported my decision, but others were critical of me for not knowing my place. It was a bitter pill to swallow. I decided to keep my Eagle award because I had earned it, but in later years, perhaps nursing that wound, I never allowed my son to participate in scouting. I regret that. My response was childish. When you respond like that those who oppose you win. You and those you care about lose. I found that out the hard way.

When Dad died two significant male role models stepped in to my life. They guided me through the difficult teen years. They had been there from the beginning. But now, God used them to shape my character in significant ways, though I didn't see it at the time. I was beginning to consider that there might be something to this God stuff. But mostly I was uninterested.

Mr. Moore was my Sunday school teacher and Scout Master. In him I saw the Christian life lived out day by day for over 50 years. His example was so clear that even I knew there was something different about him. He became an anchor in my life during a period when I really needed someone to set and keep the standard for me. Mr. Moore guided me through the process of becoming an Eagle Scout with silver palms. Only three out of a hundred scouts make Eagle. He also intervened at the National Scout Jamboree, at Valley Forge when we got caught selling Mississippi moonshine to kids from other troops.

Okay, I didn't steal at the drugstore, but I did do this. Several of the guys got sent home in disgrace. I escaped because of Mr. Moore. Another time he showed up the night when I disobeyed Mom and took the car out on the highway and the engine blew up!

Mr. Moore influenced a lot of kids. There was one guy that impressed me, and I am not easily impressed. In all these years I have never forgotten Jay. Jay was a Christian, an Eagle Scout, camp counselor, and companion at Jamboree and at Philmont. But Jay was living under a death sentence. He had a serious heart defect, although you could not tell it by looking at him. It never affected his activities either, except that because of his health he had eternity already set in his heart. He knew that soon and very soon he would step over the bounds of this life into the next, just as all of us will do. Jay unnerved me because unlike almost everyone else he could see through my bullshit. Jay was the finest example of meekness that I have ever seen.

The week that Jay died, Mr. Moore spent a lot of time with him. When it was over, Jay had simply gone home. If I remember correctly, he was 19 or 20 when he died. Mr. Moore had asked me to go with him to visit Jay during his last week. I refused. The bottom line is that Jay impressed me. I was not and am not now easily impressed. I had not seen his kind before and have not seen it since. I never told him what an impact he made on me. You never know who is watching your actions and what impression you are making on them.

The second role model was my Uncle Halman. He married Dad's sister Iva-Nell. When I was very young, I didn't like him. He was big and gruff. He was a pipe fitter at the local Hercules Plant and had a limited education. But as it turned out, he was one of the kindest people I've ever known. He was a Genius at making money in real estate. I came to love him very much.

Shortly after Dad died, he showed up on our front porch. He looked at e and said, "Boy I want to talk to you. Let's go sit in the car."

I followed him out to the car, and we talked. I don't remember the exact words, but this is what I heard. "Your dad is dead. No one can replace him, but you need guidance. There is a lot that I can teach you that you need to know. When we are done you will be able to stand on your own two feet. It won't be easy. What do you say? Give me an answer right now." It took me about two seconds to make up my mind. I said. "It sounds good to me."

Over the next eight or nine years, Halman showed up almost every day after work. We would spend about an hour checking out his real estate holdings. He had about 50 rental houses among other things. All of his units had indoor plumbing, bathrooms, electric lights, running water, and sewer and they were structurally sound. Many houses didn't have these luxuries, but all of his did. He paid about 12 hundred dollars for each house and got about 30 dollars a month in rent, a 25 percent return on his money.

He bought a house with a garage apartment on a large lot. He built four townhouse apartments on the land and gave me a half-interest in it. We built the apartments together. It was my job to help collect the rent and mow the grass. One of his favorite sayings was that "figures don't lie, but liars figure." He taught me the art of critical thinking. A large portion of the skills that I use in my work were developed as a result of God using him in my life. He was a solid anchor when I really needed one.

Halman died of bone cancer in 1974. The cancer wouldn't respond to any treatment. It took him about a year and a half to die and when he did, he was in great agony. Life is strange. Had he not died, I would not have left Mississippi and my life would have been very different. I would most likely never have married nor had children; worked for 38 years at the Department of Defense, 15 years in Intel, nor ever traveled extensively in Europe and the United States. I deeded my half of the property to my aunt, Iva-Nell. He left me three thousand dollars and a lot of good experience. I used the money as a down payment on the first townhouse I bought. It was the home that I took my bride to after we were married.

Off to college. I had a great time. For the first two and a half years studying was something I did when the pool hall wasn't open. At the start of the spring semester I met Dr. Aby, a finance professor who saw beyond my deformities. He inspired me to explore the world of accounting, stocks, bonds, and banking. He was instrumental in helping me get a graduate fellowship and an MBA.

Around that time, a spiritual interest was percolating in me. I got involved with Intervarsity Christian Fellowship.

Before I finished school, I had three degrees; a B.S. in finance, an MBA in finance, and after the MBA, I went for another B.S., in accounting. When I was nearing the end of the accounting program, I started looking for a job, but no one would hire me. Based on my previous job experiences, I had anticipated this—that was the reason I got three degrees, one of them ought to land me something. I have no idea how many interviews I had. I understood that I had to be able to explain why I was unemployed. Staying in school had been the best option, because that would increase my chances of being hired. If I had only taken one degree, likely to be followed with a period of unemployment, I figured I'd lose the chance to get additional education and lose the chance a real work in my field of interest.

Once more there were two people were sent my way. The first person interviewed me for a position at Arthur Anderson and Company. At the end of our meeting he told me, "Mike, we won't hire you because you are disabled. You need to go to work for the government." He was very kind in the way he said it and took a big risk to do it. It was some of the best advice that I ever received. He contacted the chairman of the Accounting Department about our meeting. Dr. Morgan called me into his office and helped me fill out the paper work to apply for an accounting job in the Federal Civil Service. That changed my life. These two men pointed me in the right direction, just when I needed it.

Barely a month later I had a job interview in Atlanta for an entry level GS-511 Auditor Position. So, with 100 dollars in my pocket and an airline ticket paid for by my grandmother Welborn, I was off to Atlanta to interview with Bob Coffey. He took the entire office out to lunch. Because I was a complete idiot, and mostly because it was not my money, I ordered the largest steak on the menu! After lunch, Bob offered me the job. Later on, he told me the reason he hired me was because of that steak order.

What followed were three years of easy living. I traveled all over North America, and spent several months in Europe, ate well, dressed superbly, and drove very fast automobiles, very fast. It is ironic that I am a product of the sixties. Most of my friends were running to get away from the materialism represented by The Establishment. I was running like mad to get accepted and gain entry into that world. But after three years, I was lonely and bored. That feeling of emptiness and isolation prompted me to seek a transfer to our Memphis office.

When I got there, I was even lonelier. To compensate I started going home to Hattiesburg on the weekends. Two friends from high school and college who had always seen beyond my deformities, Bill and Cynthia Dever, lived halfway between Memphis and home. Bill was a Presbyterian minister. He invited me to come for supper on Friday night and lunch on Sunday. During that year, just as the surgeons had ripped and cut my hands and face apart and then rebuilt them, Bill ripped and cut my soul apart with what felt like a very dull cleaver. But his efforts resulted in me seeing the light of day, differently than I'd ever seen before. There were many long, esoteric discussions about the meaning of life. And, there were some painful, deeply hurtful discussions about why God would allow me to be born deformed. Bill challenged me with questions like this, "If you could talk to God, what would you say to him?" A lot of what Bill said to me came out in what I considered to be rather standard, theological language. It was cold and sterile. Still, I was curious. So, it was a precious and wonderful year because the God talk was underpinned by a genuine love and caring that I experienced in the gracious welcome Bill and Cynthia always gave to me. From a spiritual and theological perspective—what I felt and what I thought about God—these two saints took me apart and put me back together again, like Humpty Dumpty. I wanted more.

At the end of that year, I transferred again, this time to Washington, D.C. Before I left, I went with Bill to a seminar in Memphis. I was beginning to wake up to the fact that God had been drawing me to Himself for my whole lifetime. But that seminar was the instrument that He used to finish this phase of my transformation, my awakening. But it wasn't blue birds and angel choirs. What I heard there stabbed my heart. I remember hearing these words, "We must be able to thank God for the way that he made us." Really? "You must be f___ing kidding!" The first searing wave of pain caught me by surprise, and yet, those words would not let go of me.

That night alone in my apartment I prayed, "Ok God, if you are real, I will thank you for this mess that you created. Prove to me that you give a damn." I remember kneeling on the floor, going through the litany of thanking God for the way that He made me, naming each and every deformity, one by one—yes, I found myself actually doing this though it was contrary to every feeling I had. It was a long list. And as I was praying, hardly believing what I was saying because it seemed so ridiculous, a peace settled over me for the first time in my life. I was 28 years old.

When Bill and I parted company in Memphis, he told me to look up a guy by the name of Ron Bossom, a friend who was trying to establish a church in northern Virginia. Turns out, though Ron and his wife were following well established practices things weren't going so well. So, they decided to start a singles group. I settled into D.C. and joined up. In many ways those were the best years. None of us had anything but each other. Ron become a wonderful friend for more than four decades.

At a church picnic, I met the woman who would become my wife. I lost track of her for a while, met another lady, got engaged, and in the end had enough sense to break it off, which really pissed off a lot of people. The truth was that we were both in love with the idea of being in love, but we were not in love with each other. She later found the right guy, married, had children, and lives a good life. She got over me quickly.

A few months later I ran into Anne again, this time in the parking lot of the American Legion hall where we were meeting for church. We started dating. I knew within hours that the relationship would work. 18 months later we were married. Anne is incredibly kind and saw me like no one ever has. She's seen past the outside, actually through the outside, to the inside. Don't get me wrong, she's a straight shooter and has never had a problem calling my bluff and telling where to get off when I've needed to hear it.

I never expected to marry. I never expected to find someone that could see beyond the deformities. Both of us brought a lot of baggage to the table. I guess everyone does. We did some foolish things to each other largely due to immaturity and outright stupidity but thankfully, over the last 38 years we have matured and grown together. We now have two grown children, a son and daughter, and a grandchild on the way.

In 1995 I had a heart attack. The pain from the angina was intense, and I had three or so episodes in a 24-hour period. About two hours before the actual attack, I remember saying to Anne "take me to the hospital." The voice was mine, but the words were not; they were from somewhere else. When we got to the hospital, I had the heart attack. In the more than 20 years since, I have had six stents and a pacemaker. I have ended up in the hospital in Colorado Springs, been pulled off a plane in St. Louis, and medevacked out of Europe on two occasions due to heart issues. Still my career continued to prosper, and unlike my father, I continue to live on.

As a result of my birth defect, there are no tear ducts in my eyes. Over time the covering over the cornea dries out and eyelashes turn inward and start rubbing the cornea, which creates scarring and eventually, blindness. It is very much like looking through an increasingly dirty windshield in a car. Generally, people born with this defect go blind by the age of 20. When I was in my early 50s my right eye went. I had a cataract in the eye, and it was necessary to remove it. The trauma to the eye increased the deterioration of the cornea, and I lost the eye within a year.

In the early 2000s my left eye began a slow, 15-year decline. I had a cataract that was considered inoperable due to the degenerating cornea, the same scenario as happened in my right eye, caused by the absence of tear ducts. In late 2015, an ulcer burned through the cornea. The sight disappeared in a two-hour span, as we were on the way to Johns Hopkins for a routine appointment with my eye doctor.

Our regular eye doctor sent us immediately to the premier cornea doctor at Hopkins. We were delayed by traffic. When we got there, the A team doctor had gone for the day. We were stuck with the B team Doc. As soon as I met her, I just knew that she was the right one. She literally glued the eye back together. Unfortunately, the trauma to the eye caused the cataract to grow and the sight did not return.

I found out there was a surgical option, but it was very risky. There was a 15 percent chance that there would be total blindness—not even light perception, and a 15 percent chance that things would not improve. I would have light perception only. There was a 50 percent chance that there would be modest improvement, and a 20 percent chance that there would be significant improvement.

The experts did not want to do the surgery because they feared failure. But my B team doctor was willing to do it. They planned to use third world technology by going in around the cornea, instead of the more conventional way of going through it, to remove the cataract. The operation was scheduled for January 6, 2016—my birthday. The surgery began as planned but had to be stopped because there were too many risks.

We regrouped, and with further consultation, I was presented with alternative options to consider. But these were deemed to be even more risky. I was scheduled for another attempt at the original approach in March but couldn't proceed due to my heart issues. I got better and we went back once more in June 2016.

I've spent my whole life in and out of hospitals, doctor's offices, and surgical theaters. But In many ways, this was the most difficult procedure of all. The actual operation was relatively simple and quick. But the emotional agony was intense, and the physical pain was real too. The odds were stacked against success, and God was silent. Damn! We were going back to the well for the third time. I had some ability to perceive light but nothing else. After everything that had happened leading up to this moment, I asked myself whether I should run the risk of losing what I had. The odds were stacked against me. I guess it was blind faith, a strong impression that I should do this, that convinced me to go through with it even though I had no sense whatever about the outcome.

This time the cornea was clear, and the operation was a success. The sight came back at the exceptional level—I had become one of the 20%

for whom this works. Talk about a miracle, for the previous eight months I had been totally blind. Now my sight is at the 20/60 level.

I've since been warned that I could lose the sight again, but I take it one day at a time. I have seen sunsets, my wife, my children, and their spouses, my dog, and my friends clearly for the first time in many decades. Subsequent to the sight restoration, they discovered cancer on the underside of the eyelid. That issue is yet to be resolved.

The dark side

Yes, I've suffered. Who hasn't? I'm not trying to make light of mine, or anyone's wounds. They happened, they hurt, they are part of who I am for better, and for worse. The worse feels like a deep, wide, black river, with eddies, and swift flowing undertows that never, ever fully go away. If I don't restrain their raw power, I'm afraid they will drown me in remorse, bitterness, incessant anger, suspicion, and a profound sense of loneliness.

When a child is rejected and hurt, the wound goes deep, sometimes lasting a lifetime. If you had asked me as a child about my deformities, I might have said, "Oh, they are not so bad. I don't think about it much." That's true; I didn't think about them. That probably sounds strange after everything you've read. But it's true because I made the conscious decision not to think about them. The pain would have been too much to bear. So, I buried the excruciating events very, very deeply. And, you see, I was keen enough to realize that if I showed my anger over anything that happened, the people who did support and care for me might throw up their hands and walk away. I remember even into my early 50s that on the few occasions when I allowed myself to talk about what I'd been through I would break down in tears. It was as if I was the little boy grieving his lifetime of inexplicable physical, psychic, and emotional pain. The power of life's ordeals was, and sometimes still is, completely overwhelming.

When I was in the second grade my entire class refused to play with me during recess for a period of a few weeks. I was heartbroken. But there was one who did, her name was Lilly. Lilly and her sisters went to our school. Lilly was in my class; her sisters were in the first grade. Their father was Caucasian, and their mother was Asian. In the early 1950s people like Lilly and her sisters were called "mixed race." But, because they weren't black, they could attend the white school. Still, it was clear to me and everyone else, they were outcasts and treated as such.

No one else except Lilly played with me. One day our teacher was walking the playground and discovered what my classmates were doing to me, to us, Lilly and me. Later, when we were back in class the teacher sent me out of the room on an errand. I have no idea what happened while I was gone, but the teacher must have said something pretty serious to my classmates. Overnight they started playing with me. But Lilly was still excluded and left alone.

After the teacher had forced my classmates to play with me—I still don't know what she held over them other than a moral authority which has vanished from today's school rooms—Lilly came over to me in the school yard to resume playing. But I would have nothing to do with her. I don't have an explanation for my behavior. It wasn't racial because I didn't think in those terms. I suspect that I was afraid of losing my new status with the rest of the class and was afraid of being excluded again. I remember watching her walk away from me in tears. Not long afterward she and her family left the area. I found out that they moved to California because no one would associate with the girls. To this day it is one of my deepest regrets that I treated Lilly that way. I knew it was wrong when I did it. When they moved it was too late for me to make it right with Lilly. I vowed I would never treat anyone like that again.

Bitterness and anger are—to paraphrase the famous saying of Winston Churchill about Russia—an enigma wrapped in a conundrum. In some ways they are quite distinct and can be dealt with separately. For example, anger is a "clean" emotion that can be dealt with much more easily than bitterness, which to me is putrefied anger. But emotions are rarely that clean and distinct. Anger rarely stays just that. If permitted to fester it travels on a continuum and metastasizes into bitterness. It is difficult to tell when anger turns to bitterness. You can address anger and avoid it becoming bitter. And yet, a seemingly random, independent event can reignite that anger and bitterness about issues you thought were settled long ago. Frankly, It is a constant struggle not to give in to the dark side of the wounds I have experienced.

Honestly, the foundational question for me is "How do I reconcile anger and bitterness toward God for making me deformed, and giving me a life of pain and rejection?" I remember asking Mother why God had made me deformed and ugly. I'm certain that Mother and Dad had asked the same thing of our Preacher. "It is not an accident but rather by deliberate design. It was intentional so that in Mike's weakness God could bring glory to Himself though His power and strength, being made perfect in him." 2 Corinthians 12:8-10.

I don't care how religious you are, on the face of it, this literally correct biblical answer is an afront to everyone with even an ounce of compassion. It sounds like God gives misfortune, deformity, you name it, in order to demonstrate something about Himself that will be appreciated later on. Great! What about the hell we go through in the meantime?

Mother could not accept that God deliberately created her son deformed. So, she answered me with the only thing that made sense to her, that she could accept: "God sets things in motion but doesn't always get involved on a personal level." Mother couldn't handle the guilt and pain of being responsible for bringing a seriously handicapped child into the world, especially in light of all of the suffering she saw me experience.

But that conversation did more to shape my world view, I think, than any other in my life. I remember being hurt when I heard what she said. And I despaired afterward, feeling very lonely. So, I decided that since I was alone it was up to me to succeed on my own.

I resolved to work as hard as I could to compensate for the bad hand God had dealt me. I would rather have died than admit that there was nothing I could do about my situation. I had to excel at every social activity that I took on. So, I made Eagle Scout with silver palms; I was elected and became President of the local Boy Scout Order of the Arrow chapter; I became President of the local Methodist Youth Fellowship, President of the Accounting Fraternity in college. I won a spot on the troop that went to the National Scout Jamboree at Valley Forge in 1964; I won a spot to Philmont Scout Ranch, and later was selected for a staff position at the Philmont Scout Ranch. In high school I was spontaneously nominated by my peers as the most likely to succeed!

A lot of people aspire to these ranks and the accolades that come with them. But it was a horrible way to live because it left no time for me to rest and served no lasting purpose. The basis of my acceptance in society, and therefore my worth to others, let alone my self-worth, was only as good as my last success. I could win 99 times out of 100, but when I lost that one time it invalidated the other 99 times that I had succeeded.

I was actually "pissed" at Jesus. Why in the hell did you do this to me? Why not do it to so and so? He's an asshole anyway. He deserve this a lot more than I do. God, what did I ever do to you? This mind set was lurking just beneath the surface of my polite veneer for years, even after I became a Christian—which, in some ways, made it even more difficult for me. I was angry at Jesus because my soul was embittered by the belief that He did not care enough about me to create me whole and complete. Trust me, this was not a theoretical question because I lived with the physical reminders of my internal wound every second of my life, waking and sleeping.

No one ever mentioned my defects—unless it was someone on the street or in school making fun of me. Mom and Dad talked about the surgeries but not how I looked, my appearance. The whole subject was ignored. First, they didn't know what to say. Who could? And second, if they said anything it might have been too much—about what further medical work I'd need, about the cost of it all and not knowing where the money would come from, about their concern for the impact on me throughout my life. They couldn't talk about it because it was too much for all of us.

Consequently, I lived in a vacuum of information. I never knew what the real situation was. In any encounter I never knew what to expect or how to respond. I was always waiting for the other shoe to drop. I never trusted what I saw or what people said or didn't say. And I could only guess at their motives. The tendency to be suspicious about whether I can trust life still lingers. For example, among our circle of friends if someone holds a party and my wife and I are not included, I always feel hurt, even though no slight is intended. If we go to a restaurant and we are seated out of the way, I always wonder why. Even if the restaurant is filled to capacity and no other seats are available except the corner or the back, I secretly harbor the belief that I am being hidden away from the view of others who might be afraid or repulsed by me appearance.

Loneliness was also a big deal for me. I have no brothers or sisters. So, I was almost always alone. Even though there were some moments when I felt genuinely connected, most of the extended family tolerated me at best. I knew that Mom and Dad would die. And well into adulthood I was convinced that I would never have a family or that I would be self-supporting. Despite hearing how great He was I was sure that God didn't give a damn about me. That loneliness is gone now, but it was a long time on an arduous road to get where I am today.

I would give anything now to have an hour-long conversation with my dad today over a beer—or more likely for him, a cup of coffee. The conversation would go something like this. "Dad, it all worked out! By the Grace of God, your son escaped the cultural hell hole that we were in growing up. All the bastards were wrong. I achieved the American dream. I had a long and decent career, and a far better wife than I deserve. You have two grandchildren, a great-grandchild on the way and our family line continues. You could have put me away. But instead you stood in the breach even though I didn't understand it at the time. From you I learned the meaning of commitment, courage, and integrity. Grandpa would have been proud of us both. Well done, Dad. Thank you."

Mom lived 30 years longer than Dad, so she witnessed firsthand many of these transformations in my life that he didn't get to. I'm so glad I had her.

When I was four or five, I drowned. I was peering over the edge of a dock, got too close to the edge, fell, and went straight to the bottom. Dad, fully clothed, jumped in but could not find me. He kept diving over and over until he did. I remember hearing the commotion, I remember the water coming into my lungs and thinking "this doesn't hurt." The next thing that I remember is seeing Dad lift me from the water. I remember looking down at my body as they lay me on the dock. I remember thinking, "I don't look that bad." There was a young man there with us that started the old-style artificial respiration. The next thing that I remember is looking up at the sky from my body and coughing. Dad lost his dress wingtip leather shoes when he went in to rescue me. After I was breathing, he went back into the lake to find his shoes. While he was searching, I told my mother the things I had just seen and the people who were with us. She freaked out; it was not her finest hour to use the Battle of Britain analogy.

So back to my fundamental question, How do I reconcile my anger and bitterness toward God for making me deformed, giving me a life of pain and rejection? Here's what I've come up with. First, I've discovered through the dark side of my wound that God has never taken anything from me without giving something better in return. I haven't always been able to see this at first. Many times, it hasn't looked like what I wanted, but it is there, something I hadn't anticipated, something I never would have thought possible, right there in front of me.

Genius

God plays the long game. You and I—okay, I'll take responsibility for myself. I don't know about you, but I've seen what I'm about to describe in a lot of other people, technically, not you. Let me start again, "I" started out believing that life is pretty much cause and effect. A interacts with B and you wind up with C. Over time I got really good at calculating how life was going to work out. Except that it almost always didn't. There are so many A plus B moments when scenario C couldn't have been seen coming unless I was God. And to be clear, I'm very sure I'm not. Looking back over the span of my life, and I have a lot of decades of data to review, I now see that God has been intimately involved in every minute of it. All the formulas that I thought were the full range of information necessary to understand my life and experience have turned out to be so pitifully limited. I've discovered that there is so much more going on that I just don't have categories to account for. And let me tell you I'm quite glad to have made this discovery. Left to the limits of my formulas, I'd have been a dead duck a long time ago. Maybe living and breathing, but still a dead duck.

The wounds I've sustained as a result of the physical, psychic and emotional challenges I started off with, and which were compounded over the years, could have ruined me. But from them, out of them, in fact because of them, I have realized that God has been personally and actively present in my life. He let me find this out over time and through many amazing circumstances. It is not a mental exercise of easy or convenient theological rationalizations for me to say to you, "God is the Genius in my life who has come to me through the very instruments of my misfortunes and sufferings." And that says to me that God is The Genius, even if He is hasn't yet been discovered by you.

At the age of 70, I've concluded that my wounds are the catalyst for a permanent hands-on, day to day relationship with God. From a purely three-dimension, human perspective, the deformities were just damn bad luck, or bad genes created by happenstance. For a good part of my life that's how I would have described my situation. But I've come to believe and accept that the deformities are not accidental, but purposely designed and deliberately implemented by a kind and loving God as a gift to me to see Him and myself in an extraordinary way that He intended for me to experience. You don't have to believe this. In fact, I understand that it might baffle you to hear me say it. But after the journey I've been on, this is my absolute, rock solid sense. Trust me, no one could have talked me into this. I had to experience it for myself. Remember the crisis night I spent in Memphis asking God to give me the ability to embrace my deformities by thanking Him for them? Nuts, absolute nuts to do that. But I did, and He did.

I know that there is a God simply because I have survived and prospered. I cannot ascribe it to luck; no one is this lucky. I should have died on day one! There were too many twists and turns for the laws of statistical probability to work in my favor. Nor can I ascribe it to "self-will." I couldn't sustain that level of effort for 70 years, and if I could have, it would have so distorted my personality that no one could stand being in my company.

My experience of the deformities as "God's catalyst" has served me well. When the ulcer burned through my cornea, and my sight had been reduced to nothing more than light perception, and the first surgery had failed, and the heart issue had come up after the stent implants, I was ready to give up. When I was offered a second attempt to restore the sight, I was reluctant to make the effort and God was completely silent. I had the deep, conviction that all of this was God's plan while being absolutely clear that there was no guarantee of success. Just like the limits of my knowledge, so even the doctors could only account for a 20% probability of a successful outcome. But it happened!

One of the most amazing, and sometimes overwhelming, aspects of the Genius that flows from my wound is that I can still give and receive love. I understand full well that life is fleeting and that even the most enduring relationships are fragile. I can and do treasure the ability, or is it pure gift, to experience loving.

As someone who has experienced repeated rejection—the small, subtle versions often more devasting— I have learned to savor and treasure those who have been able to see beyond the deformities, to see me. Having been on the receiving end of love in those cases, I have learned and seen the benefits of giving love and showing kindness to people who are themselves stuck in terribly unloving situations. I know that it changes them and me in good, healing, purifying, encouraging, and very unsuspecting ways. Like you perhaps, many people I have loved, have died. So, I've known the regret of not spending more time together, not saying the things that mattered. But God has used my regret to inspire me to ponder the imponderables of life. I cannot take the value of relationships for granted.

Although this does sound strange, a Genius benefit of when you are deeply hurt and rejected is that you become suspicious and question motives in everything. You desperately evaluate every situation, trying to gain control, or at least some understanding so you will not be hurt again. You pay close attention to communication, what is said and - more importantly - what is not said. Properly channeled, you develop an excellent ability to read motives, especially when people are lying or misleading. These qualities served me well in my 38-year career as an operational auditor and project manager for the Department of Defense Inspector General.

The last 12 years I worked for the Deputy Inspector General for Intelligence. In that environment the people I evaluated did not welcome me with open arms. Deceit, slow-rolling, and often outright lies were the norm. They knew that I had a time limit to do the audit. The name of the game was to deceive me through lies, misinformation, and slow responses so I and my team would run out of time with no results. But, counterintuitively, I grew to love it. The constant tension between success and failure, professional life and death, was addictive. I got to the point where I could smell the fear when we were on to something. I'm a bit embarrassed to admit that I relished the "blood sport." But I was good at it. Professionally, it paid off; before I was done, I had won three presidential awards. Oddly enough, I never bothered to receive the awards; I would send the most junior person on the team to receive the award for us.

The opportunity to develop and exercise kindness and mercy are additional aspects of the Genius of the wound. When you have been deeply hurt, one of two things can happen. You either become so bitter that your life is destroyed, or you develop an understanding of suffering and the hell that it causes people. I have been told that I am kind and full of mercy, although I find that hard to believe. I have been a deacon at our local brick and mortar church for almost 40 years and I must admit mercy ministry is my passion. I get what other people are going through.

Oddly enough learning to be thankful is yet another Genius aspect of my wound. Thankfulness does not come easily or naturally for me. However, much to my dismay because it seems to be opposed to my natural bias, I am compelled to acknowledge the way thankfulness changes your view of everything—God, your life, and those that you influence. I am discovering that I am thankful to God, because, by all odds, I should not be here. God has sustained me through enormous difficulties despite the human odds.

Based on what I've told you, I suppose it would be easy to make the argument that I have suffered enormously and that I have not enjoyed a good quality of life. It is true that I have suffered a bit more than some. However, even in the pain and struggle, there have often been prolonged periods of pleasure and contentment. Because of the lifelong struggle I've had I am learning to savor the pleasures that others often take for granted. I know how fleeting life can be. I have learned, and sometime must relearn to "live in the moment."

God plays the long game. I know He will see me through, no matter what happens. That realization can create a sense of calm in the face of adversity and instill gratitude. It has been shown through scientific research that people who daily practice gratitude are joyful, happier, generally less stressed, more successful, and physically healthier. Quite candidly, daily practicing gratitude just by saying thank you to people changes the way they experience themselves, how they view you, and more importantly how you view yourself.

Having what someone once called an attitude of gratitude has been for me a powerful, countervailing force against covetousness, greed, and a sense of entitlement. The way you kill entitlement is with gratitude. It is not possible to be entitled and thankful at the same time. Nobody can say, "I am so grateful for my life, but the world owes me something!" The more grateful you are, the more your mind changes to recognize the blessings and the good things you have received. You realize that what you have has not come simply from your own efforts. The air, the sun, the earth, your food, the ability to think, and imagine, and feel—even if you are a God skeptic, these haven't come from you. They came from something or someone else with a lot more insight, cleverness, wisdom, power, and love than you and I have. That someone, my Genius, is God, my creator.

We all have wounds; it is a mystery why there must be so much pain, loss, and loneliness in each of our lives. It is often true that you can turn the tables on the tragedy and achieve a measure of success in life. The trouble is then you die and what you have achieved is left to idiots, is dissipated, or forgotten.

My grandmother's generation had a saying "shirt sleeves to shirt sleeves in three generations." It meant that the first generation earned the money, the second generation spent it all, and the third generation had to start over. So, what is the value of the wound? For me the answer is found in the wisdom of the Old Testament.

> *He has made everything beautiful in its time.*
> *He has also set eternity in the human heart;*
> *yet no one can fathom what God has done*
> *from beginning to end.*
>
> Ecclesiastes chapter 3:11

Although I have overcome much and have achieved a modicum of success, much to my disgust none of it will last. The "valuable" Genius in my wound is that it is God's real-world catalyst to build a daily relationship with Him. It forces me to view issues from a spiritual perspective as much as I often hate to. I encourage you to discover and release the hidden Genius of your wound. He is right there.

Reflection

Mike has lived a remarkable life. When he was a small child, he remembered his father's friend saying: "It would have been better if he had been born dead." He stumbled forward seeking help and seizing opportunity. As in the story of Joseph Merrick, both help and opportunity came to Mike in time. His good strong mind, operating within his feeble, frail body, began to build a plan... develop a motivation... and through the sufferings he endured he has discovered his Genius—God, Himself.

Mike can read you, your voice, body language, and your response to his wicked, sometimes dehumanizing humor (that only he can land by the way) without you knowing you are being read. It's a shockingly accurate radar, like a living, breathing lie detector. But, it's even more complex than that. Out of his unstated, but evident, self-compassion, Mike has cultivated a care for others, making allowances for the common human weaknesses he sees that have touched him many, many times. He is welcoming and forgiving. After all, he saw the wounds of others in himself when he shunned poor little Lilly.

Mike has the uncanny ability to find those who cannot fend for themselves, either mentally or physically. Those who stumble and break all the rules of the house are still within his care because he has the capacity to weigh their wounds, read their lives and behavior, and act with strategic grace and mercy. He has an internal compass fixed on the due north of justice that defies what you and I often experience at the hands of others because he hears and sees and acts with an innate understanding of the brokenness in himself and in all people.

Go ahead. Try to fool him. See where that gets you – and where that takes him. He has several Geniuses. The first is thankfulness. He loves his wife who loves him. The second is mercy for those who were born with little or no mercy. His most powerful Genius is his antenna that sees, tracks, and measures the motives of those around him. This Genius got him a job, three presidential level awards for his auditing work in the government, a wife, a family, a way to view life, and a way, like Joseph Merrick, to see past his own distorted frame, and the distorted character that lives in others.

I've watched this barely one-eyed man in my bar when he thought I wasn't looking or noticing him. Many times, another soul has stumbled into Mike with bizarre, confusing, and disjointed sentences. A sign of wound and brokenness that probably needed a PhD counselor, a seer, or a perceptive minister to address. I could see Mike's antenna appear, like an ant saying hello to a fellow ant, rubbing each other's antenna. With his sixth sense Mike was feeling his way to the core of who the person is. To my surprise many have sought out this strange story of a man who has bestowed mercy, welcome, and safety, just because he reads them, their true self, so well.

Did you know that Joseph Merrick, The Elephant Man, died passionately longing to be normal, doing what he wanted to do, what you and I take for granted? On the Sunday before it happened in 1890, instead of the usual morning worship service, he attended two, as if he was in special need of a divine encounter. A few days later, he was found lying in bed, deceased. Throughout his years at Dr. Treve's hospital Merrick had gone to sleep each night reclining in his chair, his massive head supported so that he could breathe without obstructing his airway. But this night, he made a conscious decision to risk it all, quite likely knowing this would be his end. He lay down, like any other man, to take his rest. When he was found the next morning, Joseph's neck had been broken, the twisted structure of his frame could not sustain the weight of his head. He was 27 years old.

Being normal, while carry life-threatening wounds in our bodies and souls, and living by Genius rarely works easily. As we have seen, for many life is a crucible. Both Joseph Merrick and Mike Welborn, always wanted to be normal. But their unwanted gift of being able to read others developed very early on and was not able to be turned off.

Limited in so many ways, Joseph Merrick, was a man of letters. He was known to love nature and would often press flowers into the folds of the missives he wrote before sending them off. And just as often he signed his letters with what became his calling card, a kind of self-declaration of who he knew he was in the site of others, and with whom he shared the same desires for wholeness. These lines, first penned by the father of English hymnody, Isaac Watts in 1706, are perhaps the insight of every Genius who

has bravely shown us who they are.

Tis true my form is something odd
But blaming me is blaming God;
Could I create myself anew
I would not fail in pleasing you.

If I could reach from pole to pole
or grasp the ocean with a span,
I would be measured by the soul;
the mind's the standard of the man.

False Greatness, Isaac Watts

Chapter 16: Afterword

It's time to stop writing. This adventure has been full of laughter, heart-stopping, life-altering moments, and many, many tears. Every story told here, like every life, is precious. No two of them are the same, but all speak about the human dilemma that confronts us—how to live with meaning and purpose, deriving good out of bad. But before I leave you, I want to recount one more story. Not long ago I made a new friend, a woman I'll call Terry. She is an attorney who is helping the Yazidi people of northern Iraq process war crimes committed against them. The atrocities stem from the conflict and barbarism that erupted as ISIS swept the Middle East, bent on exterminating all non-Islamic people, practices, and culture. The ultimatum offered to their captives is "Join or die."

The Yazidis are considered by many to be ethnic Kurds. But while they participate in Kurdish culture and speak the language, they are a distinct, though small, religious sect that considers itself direct descendants of Adam. Elements of Judaism, Christianity, and the ancient religion of Mesopotamia are all part of their monotheistic religion. Nearly all competing religions in the region, along with some Western scholars, have disparaged the Yazidis by wrongly branding them as devil worshippers. This makes them a convenient target in a region beset with vigilantes whose acts of inhumanity are cloaked in a guise of religious purity.

In 2007 a violent wave of persecution against the Yazidis began in Iraq. In 2014 ISIS captured Sinjar District, a majority-Yazidi district on the country's northwestern border with Syria. More than 200,000 people, including 50,000 Yazidis, fled to Sinjar Mountain. Those who could not escape were captured, killed, or sold into slavery. Those who made it to the mountain faced starvation and dehydration. Women and girls were taken as ISIS "brides," otherwise known as sex slaves. Estimates say that at least 5,000 were killed, although the number is thought to be much higher. Seven thousand were kidnapped. Over 85% of the remaining Yazidi population has been displaced.

I met Terry at a swing dance at my blues bar, which is my parish. Terry's a thin beauty who needs no makeup to turn a head. As we talked, I told her about various aspects of my work, including helping people in Rwanda after the genocide of the 1990s. Then, she began to tell me how she routinely travels to Baghdad, often in armored caravans protected by military escorts. She has to wear body armor and a helmet. One time her guards warned, "If you hear glass shattering, drop to the floor." She's received firearms training and learned how to maneuver a vehicle fast enough to escape through smoke and bullets. I was struck by the incongruity of her appearance and the description of the settings where she pours herself out to help others. While I was taking all this in, I heard Terry mention that her grandfather had served in the Pacific during World War II. He returned a badly damaged man with serious posttraumatic stress disorder. While he was always kind to her, she said, she never saw him outside of a veteran's hospital.

As she was speaking and for long afterward, I imagined Terry as a little girl holding her father's hand following a visit with her grandfather, asking "Daddy, what happened to Grandad?" I have the intuition that a simple, yet profound narrative began to take up residence in a little girl's heart and mind. And then it hit me like a ton of bricks—Terry is the Genius in her grandfather's wound!

Even though I am convinced that there is a Genius superpower triggered for release from the most awful wounds, sometimes that Genius cannot be fully expressed in our lives alone. If I'm right, Terry and her grandfather graphically illustrate this point. He was so utterly devasted by the effects of war that the best that could be accomplished was that his wounds were tended. He spent the rest of days on earth in an institution.

Meanwhile, his son carried his father's wound, and the Genius—like the DNA responsible for male pattern baldness—skipped a generation. When Terry witnessed the violence of war on television and in news reports, something was triggered in her. It's hard to believe this has nothing to do with her grandfather's legacy. So now, two generations later, the wounds of a warrior have released a Genius that flows out of his petite, body-armor-wearing granddaughter. This diminutive beauty, who earned multiple law degrees, has been transported to one of the most uncertain war zones on the planet. She's driven to help women and children who've suffered indescribable trauma, people who could only be helped ... by her superpower, a Genius unleashed by the wounds of her grandfather. He too was called to intercede on behalf of others in another time and place. This is the irrepressible power of the Genius, a glimpse of divinity in flesh and blood.

Most people run from danger. Those driven by a Genius superpower run toward it. Even those not yet aware of what is happening are energized by an instinct that calls them to champion others who have been bruised by life. Like trees that spring out of the side of a rock face, people who have been wounded often defy the emotional and psychological physics of their situation to accomplish great things for others. This may be the closest and most tangible expression of how we have been made in the image and likeness of God. This is God's character.

You have read the story of the Genius in our wounds. So, what is the "take away" from this book? In many ways the answer is complex and quite candidly still unfolding. To put this in context let's do a quick recap.

How this journey started

After 30 years in the ministry, I've concluded that the church in America is stagnant. For the most part we do little more than swap members from one failing congregation to another. I also discovered that 80% of the general public doesn't go to church. Some of these are former members who have fallen away, but most don't have any kind of religious affiliation and never have. I've decided that whatever good the church has to offer—and believe me, there's lots of it—the most effective way forward is for its ministers to venture outside of their church buildings and its institutional strictures to once again enter the untamed, chaotic realm of the wild. Otherwise it is of no real good to anyone, least of all those in the church who claim it for themselves. This realization launched my residency program, in which I coach other ministers who serve congregations all over the country.

Recently I visited Ed, a pastor in Virginia. He told me that before he came south, he'd pastored what eventually became a failed church in Pennsylvania. No matter what he did to help the struggling congregation renew its vision, the steady decline continued until the doors finally closed. As frustrating as this was for my friend there was a silver lining behind this otherwise dark cloud.

Knowing that his ministry was not only to the folks who attended and held membership in the frail congregation, Ed regularly spent time at the local rescue mission, a place filled with the broken, beaten, and battered. This was their last stop after losing everything. Here, with every façade of functional life and success stripped away, Ed found himself deeply drawn to the men and women whose gaping wounds could not be overlooked. Here, Ed came to life because the people who'd lost—or were about to lose—everything were that much closer to what really matters. Here, Ed experienced an amazing connection with those whom Jesus called "the least of these"—not only because of his desire to offer hope to the hopeless, but also because he could risk admitting his own limitations and human failures. The recognition of his own brokenness, unrealized dreams, and stillborn efforts to experience transformation made Ed authentic: someone who could be listened to, someone who could be trusted.

As we talked about his time in Pennsylvania, Ed was animated about his relationships with what I call his congregation in the wild. But as he spoke about his new ministry in Virginia he began to weep. "None of the people in the wild are coming into my church, and none of the church folk dare go near the wild." His heart was breaking with compassion over the need he saw all around him and lamenting the Sunday morning crowd that remained in self-imposed exile, walled off from the wild.

What gripped me most of all was the power of Ed's Genius, the acknowledgment of his own brokenness and need that put him in touch with that same thing in others. He uses this sensitivity like a giant machete to hack his way through the thick overgrowth of franchised Christianity, which has separated the church from the very world Christ called his first followers to enter. Ed's wound propels him to listen to, live with, and love those who are most broken. And Ed is just one example. Stepping into the wild has put my residents in touch with the wild that lives within them.

Can the church change?

This book is not about sniffing out theological weaknesses or inconsistencies. Life is not and never can be neatly tied up in systems of thought that answer every dilemma. If you read this book with a critical eye, I ask you to let the power of your own life wounds speak about our common need for grace, for mercy, for care, for being heard, and for being held while we are in the process of being healed.

As the Western church has ossified inside its protective structures and theologies, it's become a closed society obsessed with theological precision and regulation. It has drawn a sharp distinction between us and them; it holds ministers captive inside a sacred institution, feeding the sheep within but leaving the those outside to starve, searching for meaning, purpose, direction, and guidance.

Jesus spent time among people that the religious elite considered off-limits—tax collectors, prostitutes, fishermen with no formal education. Jesus listened to them, spent time with them, and inspired them with hope, dignity, grace, and mercy. These, and not the religious elite, were the ones who received His words of truth and life, whose lives were changed, and who changed the world. They became His ministers, His followers, His emissaries of blessing. Where is that church? Where is the connection between wounds and the word of life today? Seriously, where is it?

I drove past a church on a busy six-lane road in Florida. The sign out front read: God still moves, come in and see. Really? Come to the Sunday morning worship service at 11:00 o'clock once a week and see how God is at work in the world? Are you kidding me? That's like watching a NatGeo program on Antarctica and saying you've been to the South Pole. No, it's time to get out into the wild.

Gone are the days when the church could pretend that simply articulating orthodox spiritual precepts would be a beacon to draw those who were lost and searching. Among those in the wild, respect for every institution, especially the Church, has evaporated. Now more than ever it is the individual witness, the story of each person's life, that makes the difference to someone who is searching. They have almost certainly disqualified the Church—the denominational institutions they associate with official bigotry— as an agent of truth.

One night at my bar I sat next to a woman; she was a single mom—actually a single grandma. As we talked, she discovered who I was. "So, you're Pastor Al!" Apparently, she'd heard something about me from her friends there and was now connecting the dots. She looked away reflectively for a moment, then back at me. "I don't believe any of that stuff." It wasn't important for me to know what she thought "that stuff" is. I wasn't put off. I wanted to know who she was, what she was about. I nodded and said, "OK." We sat in silence as she seemed to introspect for the better part of a half hour. Suddenly, she stood up and put her coat on. Before turning to go, she bent down, kissed me on the cheek, and whispered, "… but I wish I did."

When the church seems to demonstrate superiority by claiming mastery over the details of human experience, then we have become a hollow shell that serves no one, not even ourselves. Even Protestantism's central emphasis (dare I say its "sacred cow") of preaching is a one-way communication that reinforces the role of spiritual answer man. The focus on preaching to the exclusion of visceral connection with people makes the message an anemic expression of faith, despite the minister's biblical knowledge, spiritual wisdom, and public speaking ability. It does not save broken people. Those who hope for another Great Awakening inspired by prayer and powerful pulpiteers ignore the mission to which we have been called—in the wild.

How did we get into this situation? There are many reasons. One that I have experienced is the "pastor scholar" model of ministry so heavily weighted with academic rigor and reason as to nearly quash the influence of God's spirit on a young man or woman who feels called to serve the world. Think about the first class of ministers who were taught by the master Himself. None had graduate degrees; none were holed up in ivory tower seminaries; none held rank or social status. No indeed! The first "graduating class" of ministers were among the most socially disrespected people of their time. They were hounded by civil and religious authorities alike; they were jailed, beaten, and hunted like common criminals.

The first, and arguably most effective ministers were groomed by Jesus Himself, who, as you might recall, routinely sent them out into the wild with little more than the clothes on their backs. Their mission? To bring a message that God lives among us, God desires us to enjoy Him, and God invites us to be born anew into a new relationship with Him so that we can experience life on a more substantial plane than we ever thought possible—in a way, to discover the Genius in our wound.

Of course, the professionalization of the church's clergy has created opportunity for ministers. Graduate degrees are very common and have brought the dignity of academia to the profession. Most ministers have received education in a wide array of social and psychological sciences, the history of religions, and the world's greatest wisdom. Equipped with this knowledge, ministers can see what's going on in the world with an amazing capacity to address it for good. But the "professionalizing" of ministry by the church's assembly line (its hierarchy, dogma, and seminaries) leaves many clergy wondering what happened to the power of the spirit that first moved them to serve God. How have they become so isolated?

Eighteenth-century England was a nation on the verge of social collapse. Poverty and moral decay were rampant. In those days the Church of England was known more for its rigid control than its ability to transform lives. But one of its priests, John Wesley, would not sit idly by. Like Jesus, Wesley's energy, passion, and dedication to serve people in the wild put him constantly at odds with the religious elite. Unwilling to be bound by ecclesiastical order, he told his bishop, "I look upon all the world as my parish." (Translation: "I am called to the wild.") His unorthodox ministry earned him censure and persecution. Despite these obstacles, Wesley's persistence inspired a spiritual revival throughout England that historians credit for saving the nation.

A way forward

Thanks be to God; this story of rebellion and renewal has been repeated from time to time throughout the history of the church. But can it happen again?

What's the solution, the resolution for this disconnect between the professional life of the spokesperson for God and the personal life of the wounded, broken soul that longs for relief? I think it has three components.

First, clergy belong in the wild. It's where we're called to be. The intersection of minister and people in in a quality "non-selling" encounter is essential to knowing them and introducing them to a life of greater hope and fulfillment than they may now know. Further, the minister in the wild must learn to be a pastor in the wild who first cares for souls before he ever evangelizes them.

Second, ministers must come to terms with their humanity by opening themselves to the power of the message they proclaim: God created you. God loves you. God has redeemed and restored you. God is at work in you and through you. That is just as true for ministers as it is for everyone else. But the imaginary robes of righteousness the church institution has placed on its clergy have made it more difficult for ministers to admit their need because there is an unspoken conspiracy that keeps them in bondage. That conspiracy is the expectation that only those who have reached and who maintain moral and spiritual purity are worthy of the office of ordained clergy. The institution, its hierarchy, its members, and we, the clergy, have foolishly participated in this soul-shattering myth.

For those who believe that I am condoning sin among God's ministers, listen carefully: All I am saying is that clergy are men and women who experience the very same wounds that you do. If the Good News is true, God has not blessed us on the basis of any merit we possess, but simply because that's what He chooses to do. The only thing a minister (or anyone else) has to commend himself or herself to you, me, or to God is the gift of amazing grace given by Jesus Christ.

My fellow clergy, my fellow believers, I beg you to accept this. The point of spiritual redemption and salvation is not individual perfection. It is releasing the Genius character of God's own being through us to touch one another, bringing the world a little bit closer to the wholeness, beauty, and goodness we all yearn for.

Since better than 80% of the general public has no religious affiliation, the church writ large—its members, hierarchy, and mission—must be rekindled. The church must, in all humility, nakedly shed its own self-righteousness. We too must go into the wild, just as the Good Shepherd left the 99 to find the one who was lost. How we go into the wild will change the way the church fulfills its ministry of evangelism.

People in the wild don't care whether something is theologically true. They care about whether it works. So ... get ready for this ... here it comes ... those in the wild need to see ministers speak from the depths of their wounds. This is truth that changes lives. When the minister in the wild is aware of his or her own affliction and need for grace, this becomes a Genius superpower—compelling, insightful, wise, hopeful, and prophetic.

The Catholic theologian Henri Nouwen captured many of these dynamics in his 1980 book The Wounded Healer, a term first coined by the psychologist Carl Jung. But long before Jung, the Greek mythological character Chiron was the archetype of the wounded healer. In his search for his own cure he learned how to bring healing to others. For Christians it is Jesus Himself who embodies this reality, for "by his stripes we are healed." (Isaiah 53:5)

The transition from wounded victim to wounded healer can make a profound difference in the lives of those who experience it. The journey changes the way you view God, the way you view the world, the way you view other people, and most profoundly the way you understand the meaning of your own life. If we can maintain brave, even heroic, engagement with our wounds, we can discover untold wisdom and perception about our life and purpose and change the meaning of our suffering and pain. I'm convinced this journey, through our wound to discover its Genius, is the key of life.

Third, the Church must revive its pastoral ministry by encouraging its shepherds to nurture the flock that lives outside of the sanctuary, as well as those who are within. No real sheep-herding shepherd is ignorant of the wild. They know how to avoid foxholes and predators' lairs. They know the terrain their flock must traverse. They are armed with knowledge, weathered by experience, and a crook that can beat off attackers and pull sheep to safety from their inevitable slips and falls.

Is there room for Genius?

Historically, geniuses and church culture have mixed about as well as oil and water. Few organizations have a place for disruptive innovators.

Inside church culture—influential, tall-steeple churches, seminaries, denominational offices, and organizational structures—a genius, like your garden-variety Old Testament prophet, is an unwanted shock wave. Come to think of it, wasn't that the problem the religious folks had with Jesus?

Jordan B. Peterson, professor of psychology at the University of Toronto, in a recent online video talks about the decision people make to take tiny steps forward in life. He calls it "the path of humility." To illustrate the point Peterson pointed to the phenomenon of people who visit St. Joseph Oratory on Montreal's Mount Royal. It is Canada's largest cathedral and boasts the second-largest church dome in the world. But what caught Peterson's attention is the history of people with all kinds of illnesses who have made their pilgrimage to St. Joseph's. Whether on crutches or wheelchairs, millions have struggled up the huge stairway that leads to the cathedral door, some on their knees, one step at a time, praying for a desired change. That incremental movement from the bottom to the top is emblematic of what he calls our "proper aim toward the city of God on the hill."

According to Peterson the millions of wounded, broken and scarred pilgrims who climb the cathedral's stairs are a picture of all people who heroically act out the great purpose and direction of their lives, aimed toward the place where we find wholeness, meaning, and integrity—in God. St. Joseph's is only one of the many shrines that beckon us toward what every human heart longs to touch, the Genius buried in our wounds.

Have you taken that journey? If you haven't, I hope you will.

Small Group or Personal Study Questions

The purpose of the following questions is to invite you into a thoughtful process of introspection about your wound and its Genius. These can be used individually or in a small group setting. Hopefully this exercise will serve as a springboard to more self-discovery.

How to use these questions

I suggest that you read all the questions, so you know what's there. Then pick one that captures your attention and begin there. There is no need to address every question here. And, It's likely you'll begin to ask even more questions that will light the path you take to discover your Genius.

I welcome your feedback and hearing about your discoveries. You can reach me at evangelizetoday@gmail.com. Blessings, Al Dayhoff

This book asserts that there is a direct connection between wounds and Genius. Where are you on the journey of discovery about that connection in your life? Have you seen it in others?

1. What is your wound? How does it behave? Is there any connection with the behaviors described in Chapter 3. Do you see other behaviors that seem to be characteristic of your wound?

2. Is God in the wound? Is God the author of suffering?

3. Despite how your wound originated, do you derive any meaning from it? What is it?

4. How do you think God might be connected to your wound?

5. Are there any benefits derived from suffering? If so, what have they been for you, or someone who has told you of their experience?

6. Does God equip us to cope with or manage the effects of our wounds? How?

7. What would you say are the positive ways you have responded to your wound?

8. What would you say have been the destructive responses which have made the wound more influential in your life than it was at first?

9. Do we, or should we embrace the suffering and pain that flows from our wounds?

10. Have you experienced any benefit from having gratitude despite suffering? What was it?

11. How has the practice of gratitude changed your life?

12. Have you observed in yourself or others a kind of victim identity which has come from a wound?

13. Has that created an attitude of entitlement or special consideration that affects how you live?

14. How has your wound affected your relationships?

15. How has your wound affected your ability to give and receive love?

16. Can we fix the wound, or is it ever with us?

17. Have you ever considered that you have a Genius? If not, have others experienced Genius in you. If so, is there any correlation with the characteristics noted in Chapter 4?

18. How does your Genius compare with or differ from the gifts and fruit of the spirit found in the Bible?

- Galatians 5:22-23 The fruit of the Spirit is love, joy, peace, forbearance, kindness, goodness, faithfulness, gentleness and self-control

- Isaiah 11:2-3 the spirit of wisdom and understanding, the spirit of counsel and might, the spirit of knowledge and the fear of the Lord.

- 1 Corinthians 12:7-11 To each is given the manifestation of the Spirit for the common good. To one is given through the Spirit the utterance of wisdom, and to another the utterance of knowledge according to the same Spirit, to another faith by the same Spirit, to another gifts of healing by the one Spirit, to another the working of miracles, to another prophecy, to another the discernment of spirits, to another various kinds of tongues, to another the interpretation of tongues. All these are activated by one and the same Spirit, who allots to each one individually just as the Spirit chooses.

About the Cover Artist

Deborah Dayhoff is an artist, teacher, potter, and wife of the author. She graduated from the Corcoran College of Art and Design in 2011 earning a master's degree in Art Education. Art is an integral part of Deb's family, identity, and faith journey. Other interests include loving family and grandchildren, camping on the beach, and ministering to people with disability.

Everyone walks through life experiencing joy and sorrow, peace and turmoil. Sometimes the harsh, jarring events damage us leaving us forever changed. Whether we are conscious of it or not walls of protection are erected behind which we can hide. But in time the walls, like our wounded souls, become weathered and worn. All our efforts to protect ourselves from being more deeply wounded seem to crumble. Even though the effects of life's wounds remain, there's something else there—something which has incubated deep within—something that becomes more intent on breaking out than our inclination for self-preservation. It's a kind of "genius" that refuses to remain in darkness.

I wanted to capture this moment when "genius" shines out like a blinding ray of light, bright and clear. The past that created this burst of light now dims in the birth of something utterly new.

Hope in the journey,
Life from death.
Light in darkness.
This is genius.

About the Editor

Michael DeArruda is a native of Massachusetts and was raised in the Roman Catholic Church. He did his undergraduate work in Education and Russian Language and Culture at Oral Roberts University in Tulsa, OK and Bridgewater State University in Massachusetts, earning a BS. Ed. In 1984 he was awarded the Master of Divinity degree from Princeton Theological Seminary and ordained to the Ministry in the Presbyterian  Church. Mike has served as a pastor to congregations in seven states.

For three years he coordinated pastoral care for internationally based missionaries. In 2014 he became the Stated Clerk of the ECO Presbytery of Florida. He's traveled extensively to five continents.

Today Mike directs DeArrudaWeddings.com which provides relationship coaching, marriage preparation and wedding ceremonies. Over the past ten years he's served more than 600 couples from every part of the country and some from Canada, Mexico, and Europe. For the past two years Mike has introduced this unique approach to marriage ministry to seminarians in Moscow, Russia. Mike and his wife Amy live outside Tampa, Florida with Murphy, their rescued Westie-Cairn terrier.

About the Author

Allan Dayhoff received a Doctor of Ministry degree from Covenant Seminary in St. Louis, MO. Pastoring for over thirty years, he has become known as something of a spiritual anthropologist. His groundbreaking book, "God and Tattoos" received critical attention.

Each year Al receives numerous invitations to tattoo conventions throughout the US and abroad. He writes, "More the 40% of Americans are writing on themselves. I want to know why.

Genius is an account of Al's continuing venture to understand human experience, this time through the lens of the wound.

He makes his home with his wife Deb in the metro DC area where he pastors Blue Church and acts as executive director of Evangelize Today Ministries, a member church in the Presbyterian Church in America (PCA).

Want to hear more?

- Workshop: The Naked Truth About Evangelism
- Conference: How Does Faith Get Shared in this Time and Space?
- Residency Cohort: Ministers who want to study with Al Dayhoff, full or part-time.
- Books: Church in a Blues Bar, Tattoos: Telling The Secrets of The Soul, and The Genius in Your Wound. Coming soon Can We Re-find Lewis and Clark: Breaking out of the Echo Chamber
- Consulting Services available.
- Contact Al at evangelizetoday@gmail.com for information.